T0354734

UNVEILING SCRIPTURE

MELVYN LAWSON

WESTBOW
PRESS®
A DIVISION OF THOMAS NELSON
& ZONDERVAN

WestBow Press books may be ordered through booksellers or by contacting:

WestBow Press
A Division of Thomas Nelson & Zondervan
1663 Liberty Drive
Bloomington, IN 47403
www.westbowpress.com
844-714-3454

ISBN: 978-1-6642-6027-6 (sc)
ISBN: 978-1-6642-6029-0 (hc)
ISBN: 978-1-6642-6028-3 (e)

Library of Congress Control Number: 2022904165

Print information available on the last page.

WestBow Press rev. date: 03/21/2022

DEDICATION

To Merete my wonderful wife—a woman of God. Thank you for your support and patience whilst this book was being written.

To Lisanna my daughter—a hidden treasure—and James her husband—a gifted worship leader. I trust you will both find nuggets that guide your future.

To David, my brother—who is forever drawing out diamonds from the Word of God – an inspiration to all who love the word of God!

Thanks to Yvonne for proof reading.

Last but not least, to Jeannie and Colin for all their input to our church over the years—prophet and intercessor—a powerful combination! Colin, a man with royal blood here on earth and now promoted in the summer of 2021 to eternal glory in the presence of the King of kings.

FOREWORD

The secret of the kingdom of God has been given to you.

—Mark 4:11

When we encounter the word 'secret', we naturally think of something hidden and mysterious—something being kept from us. That is not so in scripture. There we find a group of related words around the theme of 'hidden', 'secret', and 'mystery'. Such things are revealed by God to those who seek after them.

This book is such a 'seeking after' what God has revealed. There are many words and phrases in scripture which we become accustomed to and, in our studies, slip past, thinking that we already know what these things mean. Or sometimes, perhaps often, we find them 'too hard to understand' and, again, move on without much further thought. This book asks us to stop and think—to seek after God's teaching in these more difficult themes of scripture.

One of the strengths of this work is that it helps us make connections from the Gospels and the Epistles back to the Old Testament. It asks us to consider what Jesus meant for us to understand about the 'secret' or 'hiddenness' of the kingdom of God. Then there is the teaching laid down by the apostle Paul: what did he mean by 'mystery'? And what is revealed in Revelation?

Wrestling with that draws us close to Christ and God's plan for salvation and redemption. To pursue understanding of these themes in scripture is a deeply spiritual encounter with God and how he relates to us through Jesus and the Holy Spirit. It also points us forward to things yet to be revealed as the kingdom of God extends into the world. The mystery of Christ and the kingdom is yet to be fully revealed—can we grasp something of that hope which waits for us and for creation?

This book is useful for personal scripture study and reflection as well as for generating discussion and prayer in a group setting. It is accessible to all and worthy of study.

Rev. Richard Darroch
Epiphany 2021

PREFACE

In 2011 I attended a conference at Sheffield in England. The conference turned out to be one that left a big impression upon me for two reasons. During a time of prayer with a number of other attendees, one of those praying turned to me and said, "You are to write a book."

You can imagine my reaction. It was like a bolt out of the blue taking me by complete surprise. Writing a book was something I had never, ever considered; therefore, it was the last thing on my mind. Like all prophetic words, I never dismissed the comment but kept it at the back of my mind. Over the following two years, I had this same word spoken over me by other individuals who were strangers.

It was one thing to have these confirmations, but it was a totally different thing to know what I was to write. For some reason most of the people who had given this word to me assumed it would be an autobiography, but that was the one thing I knew it would not be.

One thing I know about prophetic words: they are promises to be pursued and prayed into, for God's timing is not dictated to by our human calendar. As I continued to pray, slowly I was drawn to what is now the content of this book. What initially caught my attention was how Jesus caught the attention of ordinary people so that we keep coming upon this sentence: 'They were astonished at his doctrine.'

The mysteries which we read of in the New Testament I also felt impressed upon to cover. I began with the verse 'Let a man so account of us, as of the ministers of Christ, and stewards of the mysteries of God' (1 Corinthians 4:1). It is a basic tenet of belief that the church is responsible to make known to all followers of Jesus.

This book is written so that each chapter can stand alone, with plenty of scripture passages supplied for study purposes, although it is not an exhaustive study on each subject. There is some overlap of content among various chapters due to the nature of the topics. Some chapters are longer than others, due to the amount of material available and to provide a better overview. A number of appendices have been added to give background information or to expand on particular areas.

The depths of scripture can never be fathomed. My hope is the material here provides impetus for the reader to seek to know the Author of scripture, the Holy Spirit, who is the Spirit of truth.

What was the second reason for the conference leaving such an impression upon me? Discovering God has a sense of humour! A particular speaker shared his experiences of holding gospel crusades in a country antagonistic to the gospel. In one incident, members of an extremist group turned up at his meeting. As the speaker described how the police had left him to decide if he should ask for their help or not, I turned to my wife and uttered something like 'I do not think I would ever like to go there.' It was the wrong thing to say, for within eighteen months, I made the first of three mission trips to that country. Be warned what words you utter!

February 2021

CONTENTS

INTRODUCTION

Setting the Stage

The Bible is a compendium of sixty-six books written over a period of several thousand years. It was written in different continents, and it was written by more than forty authors. When people talk about the Bible, you will find it also being called the Holy Scripture or the Word of God. The Bible comprises the Old Testament and the New Testament.

The Old Testament is also known as the Hebrew Scriptures. It is made up of three parts: the Law, the Prophets, and the Writings. The psalms are included in the Writings. The Law comprises the five books of Moses, known as the Pentateuch, and is given pre-eminence by Jewish rabbis over the rest of the Old Testament.

For Christians, the Old Testament and New Testament are not two separate books but one complete work. However, a period of four hundred years separates the writing of the last Old Testament book, called Malachi, and the gospels in the New Testament.[1] One of the most fascinating observations about the design of the bible is given by Missler where he states, 'It is an integrated message system' and continues, 'This message system is from outside our dimensions of space and time. It is literally of extraterrestrial origin.'[2]

---

[1] See appendix 1.
[2] Chuck Missler, *Learn the Bible in 24 Hours* (Nashville: Thomas Nelson, 2002), 1.

The New Testament opens with four different accounts of the life and teaching of the Lord Jesus Christ. These are the gospels of Matthew, Mark, Luke, and John. Matthew provides the genealogy of Jesus, which shows he is the rightful heir to the throne of David by linking him to David and Abraham: 'the book of the generation of Jesus Christ, the son of David, the son of Abraham' (Matthew 1:1).

John provides a genealogy to establish Christ's deity by letting us know Christ existed before the creation of heaven and earth. Therefore, John writes, 'In the beginning was the Word, and the Word was with God, and the Word was God' (John 1:1). Then John goes further to let us know that Christ has stepped out of eternity into time. He speaks of the incarnation: 'And the Word was made flesh, and dwelt among us, (and we beheld his glory, the glory as of the only begotten of the Father,) full of grace and truth' (John 1:14).

With this revelation of the credentials of Jesus, it is no surprise to find throughout the Gospels how the people were constantly astonished when they heard Jesus speak. Therefore, this book will look at each of these occurrences to glean something of the subject taught and the impact that captivated those who were privileged to listen to the Son of God.

What is important to understand is the gospel writers unveil to us what was foretold by the prophets in the Old Testament. Matthew in his gospel presents 'the Royal Son of David' prophesied by Jeremiah. 'I will raise unto David a righteous Branch, and a King shall reign and prosper, and shall execute judgement and justice in the earth' (Jeremiah 23:5). When the angel appears to Mary, he announces that she would bear a child and tells her to call the name of the child Jesus. The angel then reveals that this will be no ordinary child, but the long-awaited Messiah who will sit on David's throne: 'He shall be great, and shall be called the Son of the Highest: and the Lord God shall give unto him the throne of his father David' (Luke 1:32).

Mark, on the other hand, concentrates on the servanthood of the Lord. Zechariah is the prophet who states, 'Behold, I will bring forth my servant the BRANCH' (Zechariah 3:8). No importance is given to the genealogy of a servant, so it is not found in Mark.

Luke the physician writes about the Son of Man, also prophesied by Zechariah: 'Behold the man whose name is The BRANCH; and he shall grow up out of his place, and he shall build the temple of the Lord' (Zechariah 6:12). It is the portrayal of the man Christ Jesus, who is 'in all points tempted like as we are, yet without sin' (Hebrews 4:15). The final reference is from Isaiah and covers John's gospel, which presents Jesus as the Son of God, 'the branch of the Lord' (Isaiah 4:2). An excellent work for studying these four attributes of the Gospels is that of Bickersteth and Pain.[3]

Jesus comes and ministers to the Jewish people. He confirms this when he states, 'I am not sent but unto the lost sheep of the house of Israel' (Matthew 15:24).

Everywhere Jesus taught, his doctrine captivated the people, and scripture repeatedly tells us people were astonished. From scripture we know Jesus spoke with power and authority. When Jesus preaches peace, peace is released into lives; when Jesus preaches healing, healing is released into lives. The substance Jesus preaches becomes the substance released. The people listening to Jesus came from a background of religious observance, conforming to the Law of Moses. Yet when Jesus speaks, a dynamic is released and his words become alive to them. Jesus, who is the Word, releases the living words of the living God.

According to *Vine's Expository Dictionary of the New Testament*, 'astonishment' comes from the Greek word ekplesso *ek*, 'out of', and *plesso*, 'to strike' (literally 'to strike out', to be exceedingly struck in mind, to be astonished). Notice that individuals never left Jesus's presence without a lasting impact upon their lives.

When Jesus is revealed to the people at the River Jordan, John the Baptist says, 'Behold the Lamb of God which taketh away the sin of the world' (John 1:29). Now John himself had a supernatural birth. His father, Zacharias, a priest at the Temple in Jerusalem, was told his son 'shall be great in the sight of the Lord, and shall drink neither wine nor strong drink; and he shall be filled with the Holy Ghost, even from his

---

[3] John Bickersteth and Timothy Pain, *The Four Faces of God,* (Cranbrook: Ashburnham Thanksgiving Trust, 2009)

mother's womb' (Luke 1:15). John is a priest in his own right. Therefore John, in introducing to the Jewish people their Messiah, does this in his capacity as a priest. The duty of a priest when the people came to the Temple to offer a sacrifice was to examine the sacrifice to make sure it was perfect, that it had no blemishes, before it could be offered up on the altar. At the River Jordan, John fulfils this role in the ears of all those present by declaring Jesus to be God's perfect sacrifice for sin.

John represents the Levitical priesthood, but there is One standing before him who represents a better priesthood. The lesser priesthood giving way to a greater priesthood which is after that of Melchisedec (Hebrews 5:6). As the writer to the Hebrews elaborates, 'If therefore perfection were by the Levitical priesthood, (for under it the people received the law,) what further need was there that another priest should arise after the order of Melchisedec, and not be called after the order of Aaron?' (Hebrews 7:11).

The Levitical priesthood offered sacrifices continually, but the blood of animals could not remove sin permanently. The Melchisedec priesthood is far superior, for the sacrifice is the Son of God and the blood shed is God's blood, therefore requiring only one sacrifice for sin. God's blood is eternal blood! It was the Melchisedec priesthood that blessed the Levitical priesthood while still in the loins of Abraham. Abraham is the father of the Jewish people; consequently the priesthood that blessed the Levitical priesthood was not a Jewish but a Gentile priesthood.

With that introduction, nothing could ever be the same. Therefore, when Jesus starts to preach, we read,

> And it came to pass, when Jesus had ended these sayings, the people were astonished at his doctrine. (Matthew 7:28)

> When the multitude heard this, they were astonished at his doctrine. (Matthew 22:33)

They were astonished at his doctrine: for he taught them as one that had authority. (Mark 1:22)

And they were all amazed, insomuch that they questioned among themselves, saying, What thing is this? what new doctrine is this? (Mark 1:27)

And he taught them many things by parables, and said unto them in his doctrine. (Mark 4:2)

The scribes and chief priests heard it, and sought how they might destroy him: for they feared him: because all the people were astonished at his doctrine. (Mark 11:18)

And they were astonished at his doctrine: for his word was with power. (Luke 4:32)

Jesus answered them, and said, My doctrine is not mine, but his that sent me. (John 7:16)

If any man will do his will, he shall know of the doctrine, whether it be of God, or whether I speak of myself. (John 7:17)

The high priest then asked Jesus of his disciples, and of his doctrine. (John 18:19)

After the resurrection and the ascension of the Lord Jesus Christ, the church comes into being in Acts 2. As the church grows, a man called Saul of Tarsus, a vehement persecutor of early believers, has an encounter with God on the road to Damascus. Saul's name is changed to Paul, and he is greatly used to take the gospel to other parts of the Roman Empire. In the book of Acts, we read of his missionary journeys. We know him today as the apostle Paul, the writer of many of the epistles found in the New Testament. To this man was granted revelations by God, which we will also cover in this book.

The apostle Paul writes to the church at Corinth, 'Let a man so account of us, as of the ministers of Christ, and stewards of the mysteries of God' (1 Corinthians 4:1). In another place, Paul tells the Corinthians, 'We speak the wisdom of God in a mystery, even the hidden wisdom, which God ordained before the world unto our glory' (1 Corinthians 2:7). In both of these verses mystery has been translated from the Greek word mysterion, meaning mystery or secret. These mysteries, previously hidden, have now been made known to us by God giving revelation of his counsels. [4]

In the Old Testament, Daniel is the prophet who has revelations of a similar nature. In interpreting Nebuchadnezzar's dream, he states, 'As for thee, O king, thy thoughts came into thy mind upon thy bed, what should come to pass hereafter: and he that revealeth secrets maketh known to thee what shall come to pass' (Daniel 2:29). In this instance the word secrets comes from the Aramaic word raz and is consistently translated throughout Daniel as secrets. Nebuchadnezzar saw in his dream a great image. Daniel describes this image as having a head of gold, breast and arms of silver, belly and thighs of brass, legs of iron, and feet of a mixture of iron and clay. It is a revelation of the kingdoms to come after Nebuchadnezzar is no more.

God revealed to Nebuchadnezzar the things his heart had pondered. Scripture states God reveals secrets. The secrets, in this instance, turned out to be the empires that would follow Babylon. The dream listed the empires that Israel would be associated with before the Lord comes to set up his own kingdom. The unfolding of these secrets takes place in the earthly realm.

Paul, on the other hand, talks about mysteries, for they are revelations of a higher nature and encompass the spiritual realm. The important thing about the mysteries Paul writes in his epistles is not that they cannot be understood; rather, mysteries can be understood, and we should know all about them.

Therefore, the apostle Paul gives a charge to the Corinthian church and tells them that they are now stewards of these revelations he has

---

[4] Strong's Greek Lexicon, https://blueletterbible.org/lexicon/g3466/kjv

told them about. In effect, Paul is saying, 'Like a good steward who is given something valuable, make sure you take care of it.' These truths are to be taught to the people of God, and we are to ensure these truths are passed down through the generations.

What are the mysteries mentioned in scripture?

Larkin lists eleven mysteries: eight attributed to the apostle Paul, two to the apostle John, and one to Jesus Christ himself. They are:

Mystery of Godliness

Mystery of the Divine Indwelling

Mystery of the One Union of Jews and Gentiles in the One Body called the Church

Mystery of the Seven Stars and Seven Candlesticks

Mystery of the Kingdom of Heaven

Mystery of the Translation of the Living Saints

Mystery of Israel's Blindness

Mystery of Iniquity

Mystery of Babylon the Great

Mystery of the Church as the Bride of Christ

Mystery of the Restoration of All Things or Mystery of His Will

Amid all the things the Holy Spirit revealed to Paul, he is still very careful when he writes his letters to continue in Jesus's footsteps and stress the importance of doctrine. The revelations from heaven received by Paul did not replace the words and teachings of Jesus. Paul's revelations added to those teachings. This was a major foundation stone that Paul did not turn from. When he writes to Timothy, he makes it clear that all scripture is given by inspiration of God and is profitable firstly for doctrine (2 Timothy 3:16). Paul also gives Timothy the charge to preach no other doctrine than that which he has received (1 Timothy 1:3). Timothy is not to teach anything contrary to sound doctrine (1 Timothy 1:10) and is reminded that it is good doctrine he has been taught (1 Timothy 4:6).

It is good doctrine because it contains that which is true about God. Returning to the four gospels and to the words Jesus spoke, the apostle Paul tells Timothy that the words are 'wholesome words, even the words of our Lord Jesus Christ, and to the doctrine which is according to godliness' (1 Timothy 6:3).

Whereas we read that Jesus's ministry was to the lost sheep of the house of Israel, Paul tells us his calling: 'For I speak to you Gentiles, inasmuch as I am the apostle of the Gentiles' (Romans 11:13).

Therefore, it is helpful to understand these mysteries in the same way we understand doctrine. In this context, they are central to the beliefs and teachings of the Christian church.

In the gospels, we read that Jesus taught doctrine. Within this doctrine, Jesus reveals the Father's heart and the character of God—a glimpse of what God was like. Paul draws our attention to the importance of the words of the Lord Jesus Christ, for he is the final authority in all matters of doctrine. When Jesus is equated with godliness that reminds us of the mystery of godliness. God became flesh. Paul urges Timothy to be godly and states, 'Godliness with contentment is great gain' (I Timothy 6:6).

We have the words of Jesus, and we have the revelations given to the apostle Paul, which he calls mysteries. It is the unveiling of eternal truth.

PART I

INCIDENTS IN WHICH PEOPLE WERE ASTONISHED AT JESUS'S DOCTRINE

CHAPTER 1

MYSTERY OF THE KINGDOM

And it came to pass, when Jesus had ended these
sayings, the people were astonished at his doctrine.

Matthew 7:28

I n Matthew's gospel, there are two occasions when we are informed
about people being astonished at Jesus's doctrine. The first account is
found as Jesus concludes his Sermon on the Mount (Matthew 7:28).
In the second account, the multitude are astonished at Jesus's doctrine
as he takes to task the Sadducees for not believing the Word of God
(Matthew 22:33).

We know from scripture that the Jewish people have been awaiting
the return of their Messiah to establish his throne in Jerusalem. At Jesus's
birth, Mary is told Jesus will be given 'the throne of his father David'
(Luke 1:32). In the Sermon on the Mount, Jesus lays out the details of
this kingdom. In many ways we can liken it to a constitution. There are a
number of things to pay particular attention to. There is no mention of the
death, burial, or resurrection that we find Paul writing about to the church
at Corinth. Neither is there any reference to Paul's writing in Ephesians
about being saved by grace. It is also interesting to note that, although
Jesus had called four disciples, the twelve apostles are not commissioned

till a later time. Furthermore, in Matthew's gospel, three times we come across 'the kingdom of heaven is at hand' (Matthew 3:2, 4:17, 10:7).

The kingdom of heaven and the kingdom of God invite some scrutiny, for they are not the same. It is certainly true that during the time of John the Baptist's and Jesus's ministries, these kingdoms are seen together. The kingdom of heaven points to the earthly kingdom spoken of by the prophets. Daniel for instance, as he finishes the interpretation of the dream to Nebuchadnezzar, gives details of the messianic promise of God's kingdom: 'And in the days of these kings shall the God of heaven set up a kingdom, which shall never be destroyed: and the kingdom shall not be left to other people, but it shall break in pieces and consume all these kingdoms, and it shall stand for ever' (Daniel 2:44). Daniel concludes by assuring Nebuchadnezzar that he has been given a true interpretation, and every detail of the dream will surely come to pass (Daniel 2:45).

Amos gives a similar message of God's promise: 'And I will plant them upon their land, and they shall no more be pulled up out of their land which I have given them, saith the LORD thy God' (Amos 9:15).

Therefore, we are not surprised to find the disciples asking Jesus when this kingdom will be set up. The question is asked after Jesus's resurrection and during his teaching of the disciples before his ascension: 'When they therefore were come together, they asked of him, saying, Lord, wilt thou at this time restore again the kingdom of Israel?' (Acts 1:6).

The kingdom of heaven is a physical kingdom that will be established when the Lord Jesus Christ returns to earth in all his glory at the Second Advent. It is only when Jesus, the Prince of Peace, comes to sit on the throne of David that this earth will experience peace.

The kingdom of God, on the other hand, is a kingdom of righteousness. The apostle Paul defined it for us: 'For the kingdom of God is not meat and drink; but righteousness, and peace, and joy in the Holy Ghost' (Romans 14:17). Looking at this verse carefully, we find the order which God adheres to: righteousness and then peace. This is also found in the Old Testament: 'And the work of righteousness shall be peace; and the effect of righteousness quietness and assurance forever' (Isaiah 32:17).

Let us take this a step further and look at an Old Testament character who is surrounded in mystery: Melchisedec. The Bible states, 'For this Melchisedec, king of Salem, priest of the most high God, who met Abraham returning from the slaughter of the kings, and blessed him. To whom also Abraham gave a tenth part of all; first being by interpretation King of righteousness, and after that also King of Salem, which is, King of peace' (Hebrews 7:1-2). The interpretation of his name stands out. Once more, we see that righteousness comes before peace. Salem is Jerusalem, and it is where the prophet refers to when he writes, 'The glory of this latter house shall be greater than of the former, saith the LORD of hosts: and in this place will I give peace, saith the LORD of hosts' (Haggai 2:9).

Therefore, before the kingdom of heaven can come and peace be brought to earth, the kingdom of God has to come first. The kingdom of God came when Jesus arrived on the earth, for he is the righteousness of God.

We can also grasp the significance of this order and distinguish between the two kingdoms by looking at the first thing we read in scripture: 'In the beginning God created the heaven and the earth' (Genesis 1:1). The bible opens with God and he creates the heaven and the earth. God the Creator, who is righteous, establishes his righteousness first, which then allows the physical kingdom to be set up. Righteousness must always come before peace can be brought in.

Jesus has come to fulfil the Law and the Prophets. The Sermon on the Mount points towards the beginning of a transition that is now underway with the final outcome being the realisation and manifestation of the covenants given to Israel.

Ludwigson makes an astute observation that few theologians give much consideration to. After Jesus's resurrection, everything is in place for the kingdom of heaven to be set up. So in a very real sense, the kingdom is at hand. However, with the rejection of Jesus as Messiah, the kingdom that was near at hand is pushed out by over two thousand years.[5]

Disobedience caused Israel to wander in the wilderness forty years. God states, 'Forty years long was I grieved with this generation, and said, It is a people that do err in their heart, and they have not known my ways' (Psalm 95:10). Disobedience resulted in captivity in Babylon for seventy years. In the ensuing years, Israel was subjugated by different empires. The rejection of Jesus, the Messiah, is at the root of two thousand years of Israel being scattered across the nations.

We find in the Psalms a most remarkable statement: 'Keep back thy servant also from presumptuous sins; let them not have dominion over me: then shall I be upright, and I shall be innocent from the great transgression' (Psalm 19:13). What is the great transgression? Surely it is the rejection of Jesus. 'But they cried out, Away with him, away with him, crucify him. Pilate saith unto them, Shall I crucify your king? The chief priests answered, We have no king but Caesar' (John 19:15).

When we turn to the book of Acts, we discover a second opportunity extended to Israel to acknowledge their great transgression. In Solomon's porch, people gather around Peter after they see the lame man who had sat at the gate known as Beautiful leaping and shouting and praising God. Peter tells the people the miracle they have just witnessed was done through faith in the name of the Jesus. Peter reminds them, 'The God of Abraham, and of Isaac, and of Jacob, the God of our fathers, hath glorified his Son Jesus; whom ye delivered up, and denied him in the presence of Pilate, when he was determined to let him go' (Acts 3:13). He goes on to say, 'And now, brethren, I wot that through ignorance ye did it, as did also your rulers' (Acts 3:17). Whoa! What an opportunity to rectify their great transgression and receive forgiveness.

However, the Sanhedrin, the religious hierarchy of Israel, never repented of their offence. The consequence to the nation of Israel has been two thousand years of wandering among the nations, unable to

---

[5] R. Ludwigson, *A Survey of Bible Prophecy* (Zondervan, twelfth printing, 1981). For further discussion, see appendix 2.

obey the Law of Moses. They have no Temple and no place to present the people before God.

However, scripture gives hope and lets us know a day is coming when they will be confronted with their great transgression and will repent: 'And I will pour upon the house of David, and upon the inhabitants of Jerusalem, the spirit of grace and of supplication: and they shall look upon me whom they have pierced, and they shall mourn for him, as one mourneth for his only son, and shall be in bitterness for him, as one that is in bitterness for his first born' (Zechariah 12:10). This will take place when Jesus comes back to earth to reign as King of kings and Lord of lords! In the meantime, we read, 'I will go and return to my place, till they acknowledge their offence, and seek my face' (Hosea 5:15). That day is still to come.

Larkin also highlights 'the rejection of the Godhead'.[6]

In the days of Samuel, they rejected God the Father:

> And the LORD said unto Samuel, Hearken unto the voice of the people in all that they say unto thee: for they have not rejected thee, but they have rejected me, that I should not reign over them. (1 Samuel 8:7)

In the days of Christ, they rejected God the Son:

> And they cried out all at once, saying, Away with this man, and release unto us Barabbas. (Luke 23:18)

In the days of Stephen, they rejected God the Holy Spirit:

> Ye stiff necked and uncircumcised in heart and ears, ye do always resist the Holy Ghost: as your fathers did, so do ye. Which of the prophets have not your fathers persecuted? and they have slain them which shewed

---

C. Larkin, *Dispensational Truth,* (Santa Fe: Sun Publishing, 1998), 171.

before of the coming of the Just One; of whom ye have
been now the betrayers and murderers. (Acts 7:51-52).

The offence, the great transgression, will be acknowledged at the
Second Coming of Jesus.

So what else was so special about the Sermon on the Mount? What
did Jesus say that caused the people to be astonished at his doctrine?
Literally, the people were overwhelmed and stunned. They came to hear
a teacher who exceeded their wildest expectations in everything that he
taught and did.

From scripture we know that Jesus taught only that which he had
heard from his Father (John 15:15). The sermon begins with different
categories of people and the blessings they will receive. There is
nothing controversial until Jesus brings up the scribes and Pharisees, a
prominent sect in Jesus's day. 'Except your righteousness shall exceed
the righteousness of the scribes and Pharisees, ye shall in no case enter
the kingdom of heaven' (Matthew 5:20). The scribes and Pharisees were
the Jewish religious leaders given the responsibility of teaching the Law
of Moses and the writings of the prophets. They were the custodians of
all the scripture given by God to Israel. If their righteousness was found
to be insufficient, where did that leave the multitude?

To give an idea of the shock people would have felt from Jesus's
teaching, consider Paul's testimony before his conversion, 'Concerning
zeal, persecuting the church; touching the righteousness which is in the
law, blameless' (Philippians 3:6). In effect, Jesus is saying that you must
exceed Paul's righteousness. That is very tough when you are looking at
your leaders to help you understand scripture.

In Luke's gospel, there is another glimpse of how a Pharisee thought:
'I fast twice a week, I give tithes of all that I possess' (Luke 18:12). The
book of Malachi states, 'Will a man rob God? Yet ye have robbed me. But
ye say, Wherein have we robbed thee? In tithes and offerings' (Malachi
3:8). A Pharisee would be well aware of the accusations God has made
against his forefathers about robbing God in tithes and offerings. He
sees himself being righteous, for he does not want to rob God. He
gives tithes, and it is done publicly for everyone to see. The people for

all intents and purposes hold this Pharisee in high esteem, for he is complying with what is required of him according to their own writings.

So what was different about Jesus? The outstanding thing to notice is Jesus preached from the Hebrew Scriptures, verifying their authenticity. In itself that is not surprising. To ensure that everyone knows what those scriptures are, Jesus spells it out: 'From the blood of Abel unto the blood of Zacharias' (Luke 11:51). The blood of Abel is found in the early part of the book of Genesis; Cain's murder of his brother Abel is the first murder recorded in scripture.

In 2 Chronicles we read of Zachariah's murder:

> And the Spirit of God came upon Zechariah the son of Jehoiada the priest, which stood above the people, and said unto them, Thus saith God, Why transgress ye the commandments of the LORD, that ye cannot prosper? Because ye have forsaken the LORD, he hath also forsaken you. And they conspired against him, and stoned him with stones at the commandment of the king in the court of the house of the LORD. (24:20-21)

The first book in the Hebrew Scriptures is Genesis, and the last book is 2 Chronicles. Jesus's statement includes the Law, the Prophets, and the Writings. That is the entirety of the Old Testament.

In the Gospels, the religious council is the Sanhedrin. There were two major groups in the Sanhedrin: Pharisees and Sadducees. The Pharisees were known for upholding rabbinical traditions. The Sadducees were aristocratic priests who tended to get on well with Rome. The charge against the teachings of the Sanhedrin was that they substituted commandments of men for doctrine. Jesus warned his disciples to be aware of this (Matthew 16:12).

In Mark's gospel, we find a further confrontation when some Pharisees and scribes witness the disciples eating bread before washing their hands. The tradition of the elders held that hands should be washed often. The questioning of the Pharisees provokes a sharp response from Jesus. He points out that such traditions are not true worship; the

Pharisees were deceiving themselves, and their traditions were in vain (Mark 7:7).

Throughout Jesus's ministry, there are glimpses of the sharpness of this division between himself and the Jewish religious establishment. The Sadducees, for example, taught that there is no resurrection. Jesus sternly rebukes them: 'Do ye not therefore err, because ye know not the scriptures, neither the power of God?' (Mark 12:24).

We are also aware from scripture how the ordinary men and women noticed that Jesus was not like their leaders, for there were power and authority in his words and ministry which they had never heard nor seen before (Matthew 7:29). On one occasion when the Pharisees and chief priests sent officers to apprehend Jesus, the officers returned empty-handed. Their testimony must have had a chilling effect when they said they had never heard a man speak like Jesus (John 7:46).

It was these groups of religious leaders who eventually called for the death of Jesus. It is something to note that when a people are turning away from God, it usually begins with those who are custodians being unfaithful. Jeremiah came up against a similar group of priests and prophets in his day. Scripture tells us that they found Jeremiah worthy of death and refused to believe his words: 'Then spake the priests and the prophets unto the princes and to all the people, saying, This man is worthy to die; for he hath prophesied against this city, as ye have heard with your ears' (Jeremiah 26:11).

In addition to the teachings found in the Old Testament, the Pharisees held to oral traditions as part of their standard teachings. All of their activities were public so as to receive the praise of men. These included fasting, prayer, giving to the poor, and religious rites. Unlike the Sadducees, who did not believe in angels, the Pharisees believed in good and evil angels. They held an expectation of a Messiah, who would come and rule over Israel, and they also had a hope for resurrection from the dead. Paul uses this argument when he is brought before the Sanhedrin in the book of Acts. However, the Pharisees' belief in a resurrection was not straightforward. They believed this resurrection would take place 'after a preliminary experience, either of reward or of penalty in hell, they would be recalled to life by him (God), and be requited each according to his individual deeds'. In other words, their good works would determine their salvation, for within Judaism, a person is righteous if they comply with the Law.

The stage was set for the continual clash between Jesus and the Pharisees and Sadducees, and they remained bitter enemies of Jesus throughout his ministry.

We have a great contrast in Jesus's ministry. He speaks only what he hears from his Father. He expounds the Hebrew Scriptures. Jesus maintains these scriptures are the Word of God. On the other hand, the teachers of the Law elevate their traditions above the Hebrew Scriptures. Furthermore, within the ranks of those teachers are some who do not believe in the resurrection of the dead, contrary to biblical teaching that God is the God of the living and not the God of the dead. This is a fundamental biblical teaching, found not only in the Old Testament but also in the New Testament!

The impact on the crowd that heard Jesus on the mount no doubt was electrifying and would have left an enduring impression on them. They had never heard anyone speak with such power and authority, nor challenge the integrity of their religious leaders with such force. Therefore, we read they were astonished at Jesus's doctrine.

We are left with no doubt that the traditions taught in Jesus's day nullified the effectiveness of the teaching of the Law and the Prophets. Jesus, on the other hand, captivated his audience with his teaching. He expounded scripture with authority.

This is the second thing to note: Jesus zooms in to analyse how the heart responds to the Law. In Matthew chapter 5 Jesus states three times, 'Ye have heard that it was said by them in old time' (Matthew 5:21, 27, 33) and twice 'Ye have heard that it hath been said' (Matthew 5:38, 43) then brings a completely new perspective and begins to expound his teaching by prefacing it with the words 'but I say unto you' (Matthew 5:22, 28, 32). When, for instance, the Pharisees state the commandment not to commit adultery, Jesus takes it a step further and says if a man looks on a woman with lust in his heart, then he has committed adultery already with her.

Jesus talks about the commandment to love one's neighbour, and tells the crowd to love their enemies and bless those who would curse them. He told them to pray for those who hate and to do good unto them, even when they manipulate and persecute oneself for their own purposes. Jesus highlights the importance of right motives. There is the letter of the Law, and there is the heart's response to the Law. The Pharisees are strong on outward appearances and the letter of the Law, but Jesus brings them back to scripture and tells them that God looks at the heart.

When Samuel was sent to the house of Jesse to anoint one of his sons as king, God told him not to look at the outward appearance. 'But the LORD said unto Samuel, Look not on his countenance, or on the height of his stature; because I have refused him: for the LORD seeth not as man seeth; for man looketh on the outward appearance, but the LORD looketh on the heart' (1 Samuel 16:7).

Some of the strongest teachings given by the prophet Jeremiah during the time of great apostasy in Judah was that the heart is deceitful above all things, and the Lord searches the heart and tries the reins of every man 'according to his ways, and according to the fruit of his doings' (Jeremiah 17:10). The message to Judah is extremely stark: 'The sin of Judah is written with a pen of iron, and with the point of a diamond: it is graven upon the table of their heart' (Jeremiah 17:1). This hardness of heart brought the response that God would no longer hear their prayers.

The writer to the Hebrews tells us not to be carried away by different or 'strange doctrines' (Hebrews 13:9). In other words, we are not to be deceived or come under their spell because these doctrines tingle our ears or capture our imaginations. This was what took place in the nation of Israel and then in Judah as they turned from God, subsequently sacrificing their children on the altar of Baal and introducing male prostitution in addition to female prostitution as part of worship. Jeremiah calls it 'a vision of their own heart, and not out of the mouth of the LORD' (Jeremiah 23:16). Jeremiah also takes the prophets to task and asks 'How long shall this be in the heart of the prophets that prophesy lies? yea, they are prophets of the deceit of their own heart' (Jeremiah 23: 26).

Exceeding the righteousness of the Pharisees requires not just keeping the Law but having a correct heart attitude for God to bless. Giving of tithes is required, but Jesus lifts us up to a higher level. It is the giving of tithes with a heart attitude that is in alignment with God that allows blessings to flow, not just a religious duty.

As Jesus speaks to the people on the mount, the confrontation is set out for all to see. Jesus declares the truth of scripture and the importance of a heart right with God. Opposed to him is a religious system upholding oral traditions and looking for the approval of man instead of the approval of God. By displacing the Word of God, the elites of the Sanhedrin became enemies of God, eventually leading the Jewish people into two thousand years of exile before returning to their own land on 15 May 1948.

When John baptises in the River Jordan, we find an intriguing conversation taking place between John and the Pharisees, Sadducees, priests, and Levites who had been sent from Jerusalem to 'suss out John'. They were well aware that it was not unusual for prophets to do things that appeared strange in order to put over a message. And John's deliberations at the River Jordan had come to their attention in Jerusalem. So they come in force, representing the broad opinions of the Sanhedrin, to find out what John is teaching and the meaning of water baptism, for it is not in the Old Testament. Purification rites were in the Old Testament—are John's actions loosely connected with purification? If so, how?

One outstanding thing to reflect on regarding this encounter: the Pharisees believed in a coming Messiah. However, they fail to recognise their Messiah when he shows up. Remember, John was also a priest in the linage of Aaron, and the responsibility of a priest was to examine the sacrifice to ensure there were no blemishes before it was sacrificed. John in his capacity as a priest declares to the people, 'Behold the Lamb of God, which taketh away the sin of the world' (John 1:29).

Now the reason for this failure to recognise their own Messiah may have been due to many things, but at its heart was the fact that these

11

religious leaders had allowed ideas to grip their minds that we can term 'a mixture': truth mixed with error. Their hearts were far removed from their God because they had replaced the Law of Moses with their own traditions. This is seen in John's stinging rebuke, 'O generation of vipers, who hath warned you to flee from the wrath to come?' (Matthew 3:7).

We know from scripture that they did not accept the witness of John. Jesus states, 'For John came unto you in the way of righteousness, and ye believed him not: but the publicans and the harlots believed him: and ye, when ye had seen it, repented not afterward, that ye might believe him' (Matthew 21:32). They had their traditions, and they were also self-righteous. They had become fixated on who should show up and how they should show up. They cited scripture passages that they considered cornerstones of their expectations. Yet they stumbled when John said 'I am the voice of one crying in the wilderness' (John 1:23). Their hearts were not right with God. They missed the hour of God's visitation. The truth was hidden from them, and they became the enemies of God. Listening to Jesus, we find the words of John the Baptist made little impression upon them. They remained in the same condition of unbelief.

The Sermon on the Mount includes Jesus talking about giving. What we immediately see is how unorthodox this is. In scripture, alms are provided for the poor. Jesus expects the people to give alms. The equivalent of alms today is charity giving. Notice carefully that if there is the expectation of giving alms, then the giving of tithes is taken for granted by Jesus. Alms are in addition to giving tithes. A tithe is ten per cent of a person's income. Jesus's teaching is to give alms in secret. God, the heavenly Father, will reward the giver openly.

Jesus also talks about prayer. Notice again, Jesus expects people to pray. As with alms, he directs his listeners to pray in secret. God will openly reward the one who prays. Jesus teaches the people how to pray, in what we know as the Lord's Prayer. It is an outline culminating in the request for God's will to be done on earth as it is in heaven.

The Lord's Prayer is the catalyst for Jesus to speak on the importance of forgiving people for the wrongs done to you. Jesus uses the phrase 'if ye forgive' (Matthew 6:14). So there is the awareness that this is not going to be the attitude or response everyone will undertake. It is framed in such a way that the seriousness of the warning should not be ignored. Forgive and your heavenly Father will forgive you; do not forgive and your heavenly Father will not forgive you.

In our society, there are people who suffer immense hurt. Sandy Davis Kirk asks how to forgive the unforgivable.[7] If you are in that position, I recommend picking up her book, in which stories of redemption and the processes God uses to bring complete healing are detailed.

Jesus also takes for granted that his audience fasts. Jesus again directs his audience not to let others know, and God will openly reward the one who fasts.

Jesus draws attention to the distinction between that which is temporal and that which is eternal, that which passes in a moment and that which lasts for eternity. We see this when Jesus expounds the comparison of true riches that are laid up for eternity versus treasure that can deteriorate, rust, or be stolen and lost forever. Jesus again touches on that which is a core teaching throughout the Bible: the condition of the heart. If God is your treasure, your heart is going to be in the right place, for your body will be full of light. If your body is not full of light, Jesus asks how great the darkness is that is in you. The light or the darkness—who do you serve?

It is instructive to see how Jesus brings everything back to that which sustains life: food, drink, and clothing. Jesus understands that people require these things but puts them into perspective for us. He gives the examples of 'the fowls of the air' (Matthew 6:26) and 'the lilies of the field' (Matthew 6:28). 'Your Father knows what things you have need of' (Matthew 6:8).

Jesus compares his audience to the Gentiles (Gentiles are non-Jews). He says these material things are what the Gentiles seek, but the important thing is to seek first the kingdom of God and his righteousness. Those material things will be added.

---

[7] Sandy Davis Kirk, *The Pierced Generation: Healing Hearts and Igniting Revival* (Chambersburg, PA: eGenCo. LLC 2013), 29.

This is the first time the kingdom of God is mentioned in scripture, and it is associated with righteousness. It goes beyond the mere natural necessities of life and speaks of a spiritual kingdom.

When Jesus returned from being tempted in the wilderness, Mark tells us the message that he preached was the kingdom of God (Mark 1:15). As mentioned earlier, Paul in his letter to Romans says the kingdom of God 'is not meat and drink; but righteousness, and peace, and joy in the Holy Ghost' (Romans 14:17). This takes us back to the condition of the heart. A right relationship with God is required for righteousness to be established in a person's life. And righteousness needs to be established in a nation for God's kingdom to come.

Jesus warns his audience to be aware of false prophets. The warning is given in this context: there is a broad way that leads to destruction, and there is a narrow way that leads to life. Few find this narrow way.

Jesus lets the people know it is not sufficient to believe a person because of the words that person speaks. Jesus goes further and says some of these people will stand before God and say, 'Have we not prophesied in thy name, cast out devils in thy name, and done many wonderful works in thy name?' And God will turn around and say, 'I never knew you. Depart from me, you that work iniquity.' A tree that brings forth good fruit is the standard by which a person is to be judged, not their words.

Jesus concludes this sermon by comparing two men who each built a house. One man built his on sand, and the other man on rocks. One had no stable foundation; the other had a solid foundation. Jesus exhorts his hearers to be wise and do all that he has taught them, and they will be like the wise builder. In other words, when the storms of life come, they will not be moved. They will remain steadfast and hold to the truth.

The people are astonished, for they have grown up in an environment where there has been no reason not to trust their religious leaders. They have observed their religious leaders conform to all the outward appearances and requirements of the Law. Yet Jesus attacks those leaders for not being faithful to scripture, for adding to the canon of scripture, and for allowing commandments and traditions of men to become prominent, making the Word of God ineffectual.

The audience is also astonished when Jesus takes the Law and says, 'You have read', and then goes on to state, 'But now I say unto you' (Matthew 5:34). In this way, he goes beyond the letter of the Law and introduces a higher standard of righteousness. The motives of the heart are brought into full view for all to see. Because he introduces the kingdom of God and the kingdom of heaven, the people are made aware that the righteousness of God must come first, before the physical kingdom of heaven that they look for can be established on earth.

Human nature gravitates towards embellishing the Word of God in one form or another. There is the compulsion to do something over and above what scripture teaches. When we hold on to our traditions and build up moats around scripture, we put ourselves in a place from which, when God moves, we fail to recognise it as the Holy Spirit. We find ourselves in opposition to God. Let us be like Jesus, who stood on the Word of God and taught directly from scripture. Let us watch to see how the Holy Spirit quickens the Word in people's hearts.

We can only imagine all the thoughts going through people's minds as they began their homeward journey after listening to Jesus. They had to come to terms with Jesus's teaching, as did those Pharisees and Sadducees who were on the mount that day.

CHAPTER 2

THE RESURRECTION

And when the multitude heard this, they
were astonished at his doctrine.

Matthew 22:33

A core teaching of the Bible, found throughout the Old Testament and New Testament, is the bodily resurrection of all the dead to stand before God. That makes a story in Matthew's gospel of particular relevance to us today, when Jesus comes face to face with those who do not believe there is life after death.

In Matthew's gospel, we read that people were astonished at Jesus's doctrine, a response that was elicited through a confrontation Jesus had with a sect known as the Sadducees. The Sadducees were a religious group that came to prominence around 200 BC, during the Second Temple period, which began with the construction of the Temple in Jerusalem in 516 BC and lasted until the Temple's destruction in AD 70. They approached Jesus to ask a question about the resurrection of the body, in an attempt to trap him, for they did not believe in the resurrection.

The Sadducees had reached this conclusion because they did not take the Holy Scripture literally. They also did not believe in angels or anything supernatural. Their level of religion was basically to set moral standards and the parameters that people were to live their daily lives by. It was a form of religion with no supernatural power attached to it, so their question was a philosophical attempt to discredit Jesus. They brought up the Law of Moses and asked Jesus a question that pertained to raising up children on behalf of a brother who has died and left no family. Their hypothetical case concerned seven brothers who, one after another, take the same woman as wife and then die. None of the brothers have children by her. In such a case, whose wife will the woman be at the resurrection (Luke 20:28–33)?

It is insightful to note how Jesus deals with such questions. He is very dismissive of the Sadducees and tells them bluntly of their condition: they do not know scripture, nor do they know the power of God. In this confrontation, Jesus continues with a stinging rebuke and tells them they are greatly in error. Jesus's reply to these religious authorities is direct and to the point. It reveals their true condition: they are charlatans, teaching the people their own opinions and not the truth of scripture.

Before examining Jesus's rebuke to the Sadducees, let us look at what scripture teaches about the resurrection.

The resurrection permeates the Old Testament like a thread weaving in and out. As it does so, there is progressive revelation. The earliest revelations of this truth are found in the book of Job, who boldly declares, 'I know my redeemer liveth, and he shall stand at the latter day upon the earth' (Job 19:25). Job goes on to declare his complete confidence that God will raise him from the dead so that he will stand in a body of flesh and see God face to face (Job 19:26). He has no problem believing that God can bring forth a body that has decayed in the ground and restore it to its former glory. Job's statement is full of revelation: God is his saviour, a time is coming when God will stand on the earth, and in that day Job's earthly body is going to be resurrected from the grave. He will see God face to face.

Daniel provides further insight when he defines death as sleep. Always bear in mind that the Bible defines death as sleep in many places. We also find Jesus himself define death as sleep in the story of

Jairus daughter (Mark 5:39). Daniel elaborates by telling us that many of them that sleep in the dust, are going to be awakened, some will inherit eternal life while others are going to awaken to shame and eternal contempt (Daniel 12:2). In other words, Daniel tells us that yes, there is a resurrection, but not all people who are resurrected are going to end up in the same place.

Daniel then defines the two alternatives for people going into eternity; some will partake in 'the resurrection of life' and some to 'eternal contempt'. John the disciple reflects these two categories in his gospel: those who have done good 'resurrection of life' and those who have done evil 'the resurrection of damnation' (John 5:29).

The prophet Isaiah re-emphasises this doctrine of the resurrection of all men and women and makes it explicit when he writes, 'Thy dead men shall live, together with my dead body shall they arise; the earth shall cast out the dead' (Isaiah 26:19).

There is also another remarkable verse found in the book of Hosea, in which God prophesies judgement on both the grave and death: 'I will ransom them from the power of the grave; I will redeem them from death: O death, I will be thy plagues; O grave, I will be thy destruction' (Hosea 13:14).

We can therefore summarise the revelation regarding a resurrection of the body up till the time of Jesus as follows:

- There is a redeemer. God is the redeemer. (Job 19:25–27).
- Our dead bodies are going to be resurrected, and we will see God face to face (Isaiah 26:19; Job 19:26).
- The time when this will take place is defined as 'at the latter day on the earth' or 'last day' (Job 19:25).
- This will result in either a person being raised to 'everlasting life' or resurrected to 'shame and everlasting contempt' (Daniel 12:2). The context is when the Jewish Messiah comes.

What was Jesus's position on the resurrection of a person's body?

Jesus's teaching on the resurrection is found in John's gospel. It is a reiteration of what has been given above. Jesus tells us about a future time when his voice will be heard by all those in the grave (John 5:28). When they hear his voice, the graves are going to be opened. Everyone will be resurrected to stand before God and have pronounced upon them their eternal fate.

As this teaching is still very much in a Jewish context, those who have done well by keeping the Law of Moses experience the resurrection of life, and those who have been evil are condemned to the resurrection of damnation (John 5:29). Notice that Jesus emphasises one of two scenarios will be the outcome when the dead are raised to stand before God: either they are raised *unto the resurrection of life* or they are raised *unto the resurrection of damnation*, and it all depends on whether a person has done good or evil in their lifetime.

This concept of good and evil is found throughout the Old Testament. Often 'good' and 'evil' are stated in terms of 'righteous' and 'wicked'. In Judaism, a person is righteous if they do right. A righteous person is one who keeps the Law of Moses. It is important not to confuse this characterization or equate it with the New Testament concept that all have sinned. We must always remember a transition takes place between the Old and New Testaments. The Law and the Prophets were the standard until the time described in the gospel of John. Jesus comes to fulfil the Law.

One further observation about this passage: when Jesus states 'a future time is coming', he is letting everyone know there is a judgement that will take place.

Returning to Jesus's rebuke to the Sadducees, he reaffirms the teaching of the Old Testament on the resurrection, but he does more than that. Jesus pulls back the veil to give his Jewish audience an insight as to what a resurrected body will look like to those who take part in the resurrection of life. They 'are as the angels of God in heaven' (Matthew 22:30). Notice how specific this is: the resurrected are as the angels of God in heaven, not as the fallen angels who followed Lucifer. Throughout scripture we find the words 'as' and 'like' used in figures of speech known as *similes*.

When we consider the teaching of Job, Daniel, and Isaiah with regard to what takes place at the resurrection of the body, what is brought into sharp focus is the two alternatives everyone faces. One is everlasting life, the other everlasting damnation. One is to be like the angels of God in heaven, and by implication the other is to be like the fallen angels who will be judged.

Today there are many people who follow in the footsteps of the Sadducees and do not believe in life after death. Look at Jesus's response to those Sadducees who were the forerunners of this heresy. He brings up Abraham, Isaac, and Jacob, declaring that they are alive, for God is not the God of the dead but the God of the living. Again and again, the Bible makes clear that death is not the end, and reinforces this doctrine by describing death as sleep, awaiting a resurrection.

As the crowd listens to this theological debate unfold, they are astonished at Jesus's doctrine (Matthew 22:30–33).

The various commentators provide a number of observations about this passage. Matthew Henry states that Jesus 'carried the great truths of the resurrection and a future state, further than they had yet been revealed'. His observation about the Sadducees and others of the same persuasion is 'How wretched are those who look for nothing better beyond the grave!'[8]

Barnes comments, 'It is absurd to say that God rules over those who are "extinct or annihilated," but he is the God only of those who have an existence.'[9]

Luke the physician reiterates the truth spoken by Jesus, reminding his audience that man is an eternal being and the grave is only a stepping stone into another realm, for God is not the God of the dead (Luke 20:38).

Perhaps the most profound comments come from Matthew Poole, who goes straight to the heart of this matter. People do not get excited about carrying out religious duties, but they do get excited when the Word of God is quickened in their spirits and becomes alive in them. No longer are they going through the motions of laborious religious

---

[8] Matthew Henry, *Commentary,* https://biblehub.com/commentaries/mhc/matthew/22.htm
[9] Albert Barnes, *Barnes' Notes on the Whole Bible,* https://biblehub.com/commentaries/barnes/matthew/22.htm

works. There is a revelation of the plans that God has for them, not only in this life, but in eternity. Death is not the end. Poole words it this way: 'Our Saviour ... asserted the doctrine of angels; here he asserts both the doctrine of the immortality of the soul, and also of the resurrection of the body.'[10]

Poole goes on to tell us why the people were astonished at Jesus doctrine: 'Poor people, they had been used to hear discourses from the Pharisees, about the traditions of the elders, rites and ceremonies, washing hands before meat, and the necessity of washing pots and cups; and the Sadducees, declaiming against doctrines of angels and spirits, and the resurrection; they were astonished to hear one instructing them in things concerning their souls, the resurrection and life eternal, and confuting their teachers from books of Scripture.'[11]

Despite the teaching of the Sadducees, many still believed in a resurrection in the days of Jesus. Martha articulates this teaching when speaking with Jesus. Martha affirms her belief in a resurrection in the last days and that her brother Lazarus will be raised at that time (John 11:24). Martha is given a great revelation when Jesus reveals to her that he is the resurrection (John 11:25).

We need to pause here, for something absolutely astounding has just taken place. A revelation of the greatest magnitude has just been unveiled, and it is not given to any Pharisee nor Sadducee nor priest— not to any of those who held the privilege of being the custodians of the Hebrew Scriptures. This literally means that these custodians are totally unprepared for the events about to unfold before their eyes when Jesus is raised from the dead, for they do not believe Jesus is their Messiah. It is an event their wildest imaginings never contemplate nor predict. The veil of the Temple is about to be torn in two so that the people can stand and gaze into the Most Holy Place and not be struck dead.

Scripture does not provide any light on how the Sanhedrin explained to the masses how they could gaze into the Holiest of Holies and remain alive. By continuing to refuse to believe Jesus was their Messiah, they

---

[10] Matthew Poole, *Commentary*, https:/biblehub.com/commentaries/poole/matthew/22.htm.
[11] Ibid.

faced having to make up a theology to save face with the people. However, before ink can be put to paper, another event explodes on the scene. Jesus comes out of the tomb, as he said he would, and along with him other graves are opened up. Scripture details how many of the saints who had died—defined again as sleep—arose and walked through the city of Jerusalem, appearing to many people (Matthew 27:52, 53). Talk about a wild scene!

Before looking further at the revelation given to Martha by Jesus, let us look at an important event in the life and ministry of Jesus. On the Mount of Transfiguration, Jesus's appearance was changed. The glory of God was manifested in him, and all his white clothes shone brightly (Luke 9:29). Moses and Elijah appeared and talked with Jesus (Mark 9:4). From scripture, we know Elijah had been caught up in a chariot to heaven without dying. On the other hand, Moses died and God buried him. This may help us understand why scripture tells us that Satan contended with Michael the archangel over the body of Moses (Jude 1:9)—for here on the Mount of Transfiguration, God resurrects Moses before the last days.

A question arises. If Moses can be resurrected ahead of the general resurrection of all people, can others be resurrected ahead of time too?

Turning to the story of the raising of Lazarus from the dead, both Martha and Mary tell Jesus that if he had been with them, their brother would not have died. Jesus comforts them by saying that their brother will be resurrected. It is in this context that Jesus reveals to Martha, 'I am the resurrection, and the life' (John 11:25). The implication of Jesus's statement is that if Martha believes in Jesus and what Jesus is telling her, there is no need to wait till the last days (John 6:39).

Martha does not grasp the revelation Jesus gives her. Jesus tells Martha her brother will rise again. Martha's response is that she knows her brother will rise again in the resurrection at the last day. Martha is giving us the standard Jewish understanding of her time.

Jesus follows up by asking Martha, Do you believe this? (John 11:26). Martha's answer bears scrutiny, for she avoids answering the question. Instead, Martha acknowledges Jesus as Messiah and acknowledges his deity. She calls him the Christ, the Son of God, and the one that scripture speaks of as coming into this world (John 11:27). Martha hears Jesus speak, but she does not grasp the significance of what she is being told. She is missing the revelation.

This is significant because there are times when we have our own expectations about how certain scripture passages will unfold, just like the Pharisees who questioned John the Baptist. When fresh insight and revelation comes along, we may fail to grasp their significance. In this story, Jesus reminds Martha of his words, telling her to believe what he had already spoken. If she does that, then with her very own eyes she will see the glory of God (John 11:40).

What happened when Jesus rose from the dead?

When Jesus rose from the dead, those who had been held in Paradise, both men and women, awaiting this day—no doubt with great expectation—rose with him. This was prophesied in the Psalms: 'Thou hast ascended on high, thou hast led captivity captive: thou hast received gifts for men; yea, for the rebellious also, that the LORD God might dwell among them' (Psalm 68:18). It was confirmed years later by the apostle Paul when he wrote to the church at Ephesus, unveiling the events that took place when Jesus came out of the tomb (Ephesians 4:8).

It is important to point out that not all people came out of their graves at this time. Those in the same category as the rich man of Luke 16 remained in hell, awaiting the final judgement at the end of days.

Let us update where we now stand with regard to the resurrection:

- There is a redeemer. God is the redeemer (Job 19:25–27).
- Jesus (God manifest in the flesh) provides his credentials by stating, 'I am the resurrection' (John 11:25).
- Jesus demonstrates this truth by rising from the dead, bringing all the Old Testament saints with him (Matthew 27:52). He leads the captives out of captivity (Psalm 68:18).
- Many of these Old Testament saints walk through the streets of Jerusalem. It is a wild scene! (Matthew 27:53).
- Those not resurrected with Jesus will be resurrected at a future time and will see God face to face. That will cover all the unrighteous from the time of Adam (Isaiah 26:19; Job 19:26).

- The time when this will take place is defined as 'at the latter day on the earth' (Job 19:25) or the 'last day' (repeated in John 11:24).
- This will result in either a person being raised to 'everlasting life' or resurrected to 'shame and everlasting contempt' (Daniel 12:2). The context is when the Jewish Messiah comes. Jesus confirms Daniel's words: 'resurrection of life' and 'resurrection of damnation' (John 5:29).

In Matthew's gospel, Jesus rebukes the Sadducees concerning their denial of scriptural revelation about the resurrection—a peculiarly Jewish teaching, especially the resurrection of the body. The reaction of the Greeks to this message is seen in the response Paul receives when he visits Athens. The Epicureans and Stoics called him a 'babbler' because he preaches on the resurrection of the dead (Acts 17:18). Jesus tells his audience that their bodies are eternal and will be resurrected. As Spurgeon states, 'The very flesh in which you now walk the earth is as eternal as the soul, and shall exist for ever. That is the peculiar doctrine of Christianity.'[12]

The Sadducees, although having scripture in front of them, did not believe what was written in it. It is interesting to note that the Old Testament contains three stories of people being raised from the dead: the widow of Zarephath's son (1 Kings 17), the Shunamite's son (2 Kings 4), and a Moabite's dead body thrown into Elisha's tomb, where it touched Elisha's bones (2 Kings 13). That is, three witnesses in the Old Testament testify about people being raised from the dead and record that testimony for posterity. Scripture says that when two or three witnesses provide their testimonies, then their words are settled (2 Corinthians 13:1).

The doctrine that some will be resurrected before the last days was vehemently attacked by the Sadducees. In particular, they persecuted the early church, which preached Jesus and the resurrection from the dead (Acts 4:2). Notice carefully that the disciples preached a resurrection

---

[12] Charles H. Spurgeon, *Text Commentaries*, https://blueletterbible.org/commentaries/spurgeon_charles.

from the dead, not a resurrection *of* the dead. This is the teaching of Jesus when he talks about those who will be found worthy to enter into glory through being resurrected from the dead (Luke 20:35). Those who rose with Jesus rose *from* the dead.

It is important to understand and distinguish these two fundamental positions. At the Great White Throne Judgement, death and hell shall give up their dead, and all who are therein will stand before God. The Bible informs us there is no escape for them from this face-to-face encounter with God. This is the resurrection of the dead.

In Jesus's encounter with the Sadducees, he tells them in no uncertain terms that there is a resurrection from the dead, and that those who attain this resurrection and enter into glory do not marry, nor are they given in marriage (Luke 20:35). After the resurrection of Jesus, we find the Sadducees continuing to hold to their same theological position. This is amazing when we consider that the period of time leading up to the crucifixion through Acts 4 was such an extraordinary point in history.

It starts with Jesus raising Lazarus from his grave after he has been dead for four days. Notice the reaction of some of the people who witness this miracle. They cannot wait to tell the Pharisees they have witnessed a dead man being raised from the dead. They share everything that they heard and saw Jesus do (John 11:46).

This causes such consternation that Caiaphas, the high priest, makes an astounding statement. He proposes that it would be a good time for a man to die for the Jewish people, lest the nation be no more (John 11:50). Of course, Caiaphas is not thinking of the promises of God to provide a redeemer, nor of the truth of the words he speaks that echo God's salvation plan: the Lamb of God who will lay down his life as a sacrifice for sin and for all humanity. Caiaphas's motives were clearly selfish. He has trouble believing God's words that the nation of Israel will continue to exist in one form or another into eternity.

At the crucifixion of Jesus, noon darkness covers the sky. This was an exceptional phenomenon. It was a very unusual event. In the midst of it, the centurion confesses that Jesus was truly the Son of God.

Upon the death of Jesus, the veil of the Temple is torn. The people stand and gaze into the Holy of Holies, yet nobody drops dead. There are no consequences.

When Pilate is asked to post guards at Jesus's tomb, it is due to the high priest and the Sanhedrin recognising Jesus's own words: 'For as Jonas was three days and three nights in the whale's belly; so shall the Son of man be three days and three nights in the heart of the earth' (Matthew 12:40). They took the words of Jesus very seriously about coming out of the grave after three days. (Matthew 27:63). They fully understood what Jesus was saying when he ministered in Galilee and in Jerusalem. Yet they remain obstinate: they refuse to recognise Jesus's credentials as the Son of God. Instead, they pay guards to keep quiet about the stone in front of Jesus's tomb being rolled away by an angel. Those responsible for ensuring that the Law of Moses was taught to the people found themselves paying to conceal truth.

It is unthinkable for the whole religious hierarchy not to be aware of the events that took place after Jesus rose from the dead. Nor would they be ignorant of people's eyewitness accounts of graves being opened and of encounters experienced when the living recognised people who had been dead (Matthew 27:52). These saints entered Jerusalem and appeared too many people! Jesus rose from the dead and all the saints of God from the Old Testament who had been in Paradise rose with him. This proves the claims he spoke to Martha were true.

To add to this came news of different people testifying to seeing the resurrected Christ. For the space of forty days Jesus makes himself known to people with infallible proofs. It culminates with five hundred people, gathered together in one place, seeing Jesus. In the letter to the Corinthians, Paul notes most of those people are still alive, although some have 'fallen asleep'—that is, some have died (1 Corinthians 15:6).

It is easy to imagine the uproar in Jerusalem, especially among the Sanhedrin, as this news spreads around the city day after day. Finally, at the end of forty days, Jesus is taken up into heaven in the presence of his followers. Angels declare to them that Jesus will return in similar fashion as they have seen him go.

Scripture tells us that the testimony of Jesus is the spirit of prophecy (Revelation 19:10). That is why we read that Jesus's resurrection was demonstrated by 'infallible proofs' (Acts 1:3). It verified the Old Testament prophecies that the Messiah had truly come and fulfilled the scripture passages concerning his life and death. And if that were not enough, then comes the day of Pentecost, the outpouring of the Holy Spirit. Jews from all around the Roman Empire hear their own languages being spoken. Peter, with boldness, preaches on the crucifixion and resurrection of Jesus.

Yet none of these things moved the Sadducees from believing no one rises from the dead!

In the book of Acts, we read of a man called Saul of Tarsus, his conversion, and his name being changed to Paul. He is a man well known in the religious circles at Jerusalem. Paul gives us his credentials: he came from the tribe of Benjamin and was circumcised according to the Law of Moses. He was a Pharisee. He saw the church as a sect, propagating teachings that he thought were in conflict with the Hebrew Scriptures. This led him to physically oppose and persecute the early church (Philippians 3:5, 6). After his conversion, Paul declares Jesus is indeed the Son of God. Jesus demonstrated his credentials and power by being raised from the dead by the Spirit of holiness (Romans 1:4).

Spurgeon makes the following statement: 'I was led to look back to apostolic times, and to consider where in the preaching of the present day differed from the preaching of the apostles. But the main difference I observed was in the subjects of their preaching. Surprised I was when I discovered that the very staple of the preaching of the apostles was the resurrection of the dead.'[13]

In the early church, when they looked to replace Judas, the one who betrayed Jesus, Matthias was chosen. Notice the reason for his appointment: he witnessed the resurrection of Jesus along with the other disciples (Acts 1:22).

---

[13] Spurgeon, *Text Commentaries*, https://blueletterbible.org/commentaries/spurgeon_charles.

When we turn to Jesus's disciples and in particular look back to the day of Jesus's resurrection, scripture states they were ignorant of the passage that revealed Jesus had to be raised from the dead (John 20:9). It is a most remarkable statement made about those closest to Jesus, who heard his teachings and were eyewitnesses to numerous miracles. After Jesus was raised from the dead, Mary Magdalene saw the Lord. But the response of the disciples was to not believe her. They refused to believe Jesus was alive, and they refused to believe her report that she had seen him (Mark 16:11).

When Jesus appeared to two unnamed disciples on the road to Emmaus, the response from the other disciples was very similar— they did not believe what was being told to them (Mark 16:12). Luke summarises their response succinctly, comparing it to old wives' tales (Luke 24:11).

The two men on the road to Emmaus, although not realising they were walking with Jesus, talk about their disappointment and how they were convinced Jesus was the Messiah, the one who would redeem Israel (Luke 24:21). Jesus spoke about these things to his disciples. He tells his disciples how he must go to Jerusalem, how those in religious authority will be behind having him arrested and put to death, and how on the third day he will rise again. (Matthew 16:21). Peter's immediate response is to vehemently contradict Jesus. We can easily imagine Peter crying out, 'No, no, no, I will not allow it' (Matthew 16:22). But Jesus rebukes Peter, telling him, in effect, 'Your heart is in the wrong place. You are continuing to think on the natural level, but it is not the way of the Spirit' (Mark 8:33).

On the Mount of Transfiguration, Jesus has accompanying him Peter, James, and John. They hear Jesus speak of his death with Moses and Elijah, and they also hear the voice of God. Luke records the disciples being told three times while on the mount that Jesus will be put to death (Luke 9:22, 31, 44).

Notice the conversation as they come down the mountain: Jesus forbids them to mention to anyone what they have seen and experienced. He instructs them not to speak of it till after the Son of Man has come up out of the grave. Then they will be free to share it with others. Looking back at this event, it gives us a chuckle to see the disciples reasoning among themselves about what Jesus meant when he spoke of 'rising from the dead' (Mark 9:9, 10).

In the gospel of Mark, it is recorded that Jesus told the disciples of the things that would befall him. Using his designation as the Son of Man, Jesus shares how he will be delivered into the hands of men and how those men will kill him. He tells the disciples of his coming resurrection after three days.

The disciples never grasp this momentous unveiling, which marks the greatest day in the history of mankind. Their experience on the mount, caught up in the glory of God, must have been on par with that of Moses when he was on the mountain. Yet the disciples come down the mountain afraid to ask Jesus to enlighten them about the words they have just heard (Mark 9:31, 32).

Luke records that the disciples never understood what Jesus was telling them. He adds that it was concealed from them, made impossible to decipher (Luke 9:45). When the disciples are told about the scourging Jesus will suffer, his death, and his resurrection, scripture repeats that they did not understand any of these things, for the truth was concealed from them (Luke 18:34).

When scripture reveals details of the Saviour, it is through prophecy. Some of these prophecies provide graphic pictures of the sufferings the Messiah will bear in his body. There are types given, like the Passover lamb. The Lord even appears in the Old Testament as the Angel of the Lord. Nowhere do you find clearly the death, burial, and resurrection of Jesus after three days. A type is given by Christ when he brings up Jonah being three days and three nights in the belly of a whale. So the disciples still require light to shine on their understanding.

Peter, in his epistle, makes mention of what took place on the Mount of Transfiguration and states he was an eyewitness of Christ's majesty. He stresses that what he has seen is not a fable. He urges his readers not to believe those who would scoff; he has seen the power and coming of the Lord Jesus Christ. The Father himself gave Jesus glory and honour, stating that this was his beloved Son in whom he was well pleased. The appearance of Christ was changed. The disciples saw him in his glorious body. Peter states that this is the glory people will see when Christ returns (2 Peter 1:16–18).

After the resurrection, it is sobering to read that Jesus upbraids the disciples for being so slow to believe what the prophets had spoken concerning the things he would suffer (Luke 24:26). Jesus reminds the disciples that he spoke to them about his death and all that was written in the Law of Moses, the Prophets, and the Psalms. Then Jesus did something remarkable. He removed the dullness and lack of perception surrounding their minds, enabling them to comprehend the Word of God (Luke 24:25). What a moment that must have been!

Before the crucifixion, Jesus also unveiled scripture to his disciples about events coming on the earth before his return at the Second Advent. A rapture takes place:

> Then shall two be in the field, the one shall be taken, and the other left. Two women shall be grinding at the mill, the one shall be taken, and the other left. (Matthew 24:40-41)

> And he shall send his angels with a great sound of a trumpet, and they shall gather together his elect from the four winds, from one end of heaven to the other. (Matthew 24:31)

This information is given to Jewish believers before the church comes into existence. The question we want to ask is how this fits in with the apostle Paul's revelation about a rapture, described to the Corinthians and to the Thessalonians. I will discuss this in the chapter 'Mystery of the Translation of the Living Saints'.

To summarise, Jewish teaching was unique in that many Jews believed in a resurrection—not just resurrection of the soul and spirit, but resurrection of the body also. In Jesus's day, there was a group called the Sadducees who did not believe in any kind of resurrection. Jesus rebuked them for not knowing and believing scripture. Jesus also revealed that the time of the resurrection had been brought forward, stating, 'I am the resurrection' (John 11:25). To demonstrate this, Jesus rose from the dead, and the Old Testament saints held in Paradise rose with him.

Jesus reiterated, in his time on earth, the teaching of the Old Testament about the bodily resurrection of all people some to eternal life and others to eternal damnation. Furthermore, scripture makes a clear distinction between those two events. Different words are used: 'resurrected *from* the dead' and 'resurrection *of* the dead'. Importantly, as we will discover in the chapter covering the Mystery of the Translation of the Living Saints, these events do not take place at the same time.

CHAPTER 3

POWER AND AUTHORITY OF JESUS

And they were astonished at his doctrine: for he taught them as one that had authority, and not as the scribes.

Mark 1:22

And they were all amazed, insomuch that they questioned among themselves, saying, what thing is this? What new doctrine is this? For with authority commandeth he even the unclean spirits, and they do obey him.

Mark 1:27

After the forty-day temptation in the wilderness, scripture tells us Jesus returned to Galilee full of the Holy Spirit and with power— so much so that his fame spread from Galilee to the region round about (Luke 4:14). As Jesus made his way to Capernaum, he called the first of his disciples to come and follow him: Simon, whose name would be changed to Peter, and Andrew his brother, along with two other brothers, James and John. They immediately left their fishing nets to follow Jesus. It must have been a remarkable encounter.

These four disciples, along with others whom Jesus would call later, began what we would call a three-and-a-half-year internship with the

Lord that would eventually be manifested in an impact that changed the world. They were privileged to have been chosen to receive teachings from Jesus and see first-hand the working out of the authority that rested upon him.

At the River Jordan, John baptised Jesus in the water and saw the heavens open and the Holy Spirit, in the form of a dove, come down and rest upon Jesus (Mark 1:10). Therefore, when Jesus entered the synagogue at Capernaum, a confrontation was inevitable with any demonic presence. Sure enough, once Jesus begins to speak, it is not long till there is an interruption. Scripture does not elaborate on what Jesus was teaching—his presence was enough to make it unbearable for the unclean spirit. In Mark's gospel, we are told there was a man with an unclean spirit (Mark 1:23). Strong' Greek Lexicon gives the meaning of unclean from the Greek word 'akathartos' as unclean in a moral sense, unclean in thought and life. [14]

Jesus lived in Capernaum; it was the town in which he had his base (Matthew 4:13). So we are not surprised to find him teaching in the synagogue there. Here he casts out an unclean spirit in his first encounter of power. It is extremely significant, for in another part of scripture, Jesus states, 'But if I cast out devils by the Spirit of God, then the kingdom of God is come unto you' (Matthew 12:28). This was never said when blind eyes were opened nor deaf ears unstopped nor even when the dead were raised. When the kingdom of God, which is a righteous kingdom, comes, its signature is the casting out of devils.

Capernaum was a place where people witnessed many miracles. The centurion recognised Jesus's authority and came with a request for healing for his servant, who was being horrendously tormented with a degenerative disease that caused paralysis, weakness, and uncontrolled body movements (Matthew 8:6). Jesus was overwhelmed by the faith of this centurion. 'Verily I say unto you, I have not found so great faith, no, not in Israel' (Matthew 8:10). In another instance we are informed about a nobleman who lived at Capernaum and heard that Jesus had returned to Galilee from Judea. Having a son who was near the point of

---

[14] Strong's Greek Lexicon, https://blueletterbible.org/lexicon/g169/kjv

death, he sought out Jesus to come to his house and heal his son (John 4:46, 47). This nobleman and his son would have been well known in such a small community.

Now let us look at what happened in the synagogue at Capernaum. A number of things stand out which we should be aware of. Firstly, all unclean spirits in scripture are evil and are not interested in human well-being; every one of them ultimately seeks human destruction. Secondly, the unclean spirit already knows that Jesus is the Holy One of God. Furthermore, it recognises him as 'Jesus of Nazareth' (Mark 1:24). Twelve times in the four gospels we read of this title being given to Jesus. It must have been commonly known, for it is the title Pilate has written to be put on the cross when Jesus is crucified.

This lets us know that unclean spirits are miles ahead of individuals when it comes to identifying Jesus as the Son of God. People can argue among themselves about whether Jesus is God or a good person, or even if he actually existed. We know how even Broadway shows speculate about Jesus. Compare this to the realm of the demonic. They know who Jesus is, they know he has authority over them, they know he holds their immediate destiny in his hands, and they are fully aware he is God manifested in the flesh. That is a very comprehensive list.

Furthermore, demonic spirits also recognise a person carrying an anointing of the Holy Spirit in their life, even if no one else does. This is important. A Jewish leader who had seven sons observed Paul casting out a devil. The sons sought to emulate Paul and got a hold of a man who had an unclean spirit. The unclean spirit spoke acknowledging that it knew Jesus and it knew Paul, but it did not know this leader or his sons (Acts 19:14, 15). The man with the unclean spirit had supernatural strength, and the imposters ran away with their clothes in tatters.

In Capernaum, while people are caught up and astonished at Jesus's doctrine, the unclean spirit recognises Jesus's power and authority and asks if Jesus has 'come to destroy us' (Mark 1:24). Right in front of the priests and the people in their synagogue, the spirit confesses, 'Let us alone; what have we to do with thee, thou Jesus of Nazareth? art thou come to destroy us? I know thee who thou art, the Holy One of God' (Mark 1:24). The statement must have stunned the priests. It is not difficult to imagine the priests talking among themselves after this event questioning did we really hear right, did this unclean spirit really say Jesus is the Holy One of God? They were confronted with an extraordinary event and to process its ramifications was just beginning.

Pay attention to what takes place next: 'And when the unclean spirit had torn him, and cried with a loud voice, he came out of him' (Mark 1:26). The man experienced sharp pain as the devil was cast out. As Jesus left the synagogue the priests are silent.

The events recorded by Mark would be fresh in the minds of those at Capernaum when we come to the next discussion recorded by John. Let us look at the reaction this provokes in the synagogue. The immediate response of the people is one of exuberance and excitement for it takes place after Jesus has fed the multitude. It is a typical reaction of people seeing something powerful which they would love to be able to do themselves. The people clamour around Jesus, all wanting to know how they can do the same miracles, how they can be used by God (John 6:28). Jesus in his answer unveils his deity and states the prerequisite for being able to move in the supernatural. This first step is to believe that Jesus is sent by God and is who he claims to be—the Son of God (John 6:29). Eternal consequences flow from our response to this revelation.

In the encounter described by John the people ask for a sign that they might believe on Jesus. This is normal for a Jew, for scripture tells us that the Jewish people are a people who look for signs (1 Corinthians 1:22). They are looking for something to identify who sent Jesus. Remember, for the previous four hundred years, no prophet has been in their midst. Jesus comes along, and unclean spirits declare him the Holy One of God.

As is the case in many encounters in the New Testament, people want to know if Jesus is greater than Moses. Yet when they get a positive confirmation, their response is one of unbelief. In Capernaum, the people bring up Moses and boast how, through him, God fed their fathers with manna in the wilderness. Jesus's reply to them is very direct. He makes it clear that it was not Moses who gave them the bread that came down from heaven. Jesus gives them a revelation by stating his Father gives them the true bread from heaven—himself (John 6:32). Jesus tells the people that when they come to him, they will never hunger again, neither will they thirst (John 6:35). However, many found his words incomprehensible, and it is recorded that the people began to murmur. They found his words 'too much to stomach' (John 6:41).

The conversation among the people soon degenerated into an argument. Notice how quickly the confession of the unclean spirit that many had previously witnessed is forgotten. This squabbling was a very fleshly reaction to the supernatural power of God being released into a man who was bound. It is a lesson that forever stands the test of time. The supernatural cannot be understood by the natural. Sadly, the crowd asks if this is not the son of Joseph, who is called Jesus (John 6:42). A great division arises as the people strive among themselves, and many who had been following Jesus turn away from him and are no more to be found walking with him (John 6:66). It reminds me of another occasion when Jesus turned to his disciples and asked them if they would also leave him.

We can gloss over the reaction to Jesus in the synagogue at Capernaum. However, we can infer that the Hebrew Scriptures were being read on a regular basis, as evidenced by the people bringing up what happened in the wilderness. Yet the carnality of the flesh exploded to the fore, demonstrating that it is not enough to know the words of scripture only. Those words need to be quickened by the Holy Spirit to produce the life of God in us.

When we pay attention to Jesus's words, we realize they are not the easiest of words to comprehend. To me, they look designed to separate the hearers into two groups: those who are carnally minded and caught up with the things of the world, and those who love God and scripture and have a heart for the things of God. For this latter group, I believe there would have been a resonance in their spirits—a knowing that the words they heard were true. This division between the people would last throughout Jesus's time on earth. Glimpses are given of this undercurrent when, instead of approaching Jesus to ask him a question directly, the tax collectors pick Peter to interrogate about whether Jesus is paying his tax (Matthew 17:24).

Capernaum was highly favoured and blessed with Jesus's presence and ministry. The inhabitants scorned their privilege, and forever the epilogue over Capernaum is 'And thou, Capernaum, which art exalted unto heaven, shall be brought down to hell: for if the mighty works, which have been done in thee, had been done in Sodom, it would have remained until this day' (Matthew 11:23).

Returning to what happened to the man with the unclean spirit, we find the spirit inflicts sharp pain on him as it leaves his body. One can imagine the grip of this spirit literally being torn from him. The spirit screams loudly as it leaves the man. In the presence of the holiness of God, the screaming of the unclean spirit is not surprising (Mark 1:26).

I recall an early experience I had while at church one day. In the middle of the service, the pastor was preaching from the pulpit to a church full of people. Suddenly in the back, congregants began screaming. They fell to their hands and knees and began foaming at the mouth.

So people with unclean spirits may convulse. They may writhe and scream and foam at the mouth. Don't let that intimidate you. They can be delivered and set free through the name of Jesus. Francis MacNutt states, 'We see the same extravagant phenomena today when we pray for the oppressed.'[15]

In other passages, scripture talks about the man who brought his child to the disciples because the child was 'sore vexed' and often fell 'into the fire' (Matthew 17:15). When the disciples could not help, the man brought the child to Jesus. Jesus rebuked the evil spirit, and immediately the spirit left the child. From that hour the child was made completely whole (Matthew 17:18). Notice the sequence that took place: first deliverance, then healing.

There is another case where people brought to Jesus a man who was unable to speak. Scripture states he had a devil (Matthew 9:32, 33). Jesus cast this devil out, and the man who had been dumb began to speak. On this occasion, the crowd marvelled, stating they had never seen such things in Israel (Matthew 9:33). Again, notice the sequence: first deliverance, then healing.

---

[15] Francis MacNutt, *Deliverance from Evil Spirits* (Grand Rapids: Chosen Books, 2009), 45.

Mary Magdalene was a lady who had seven devils cast out of her (Mark 16:9). This brings up a question: how can a person have so many devils? The most incredible instance of this was the man of Gadarenes. He was living among the tombs, excommunicated from society. He was a wild man, and nobody could control him. When he saw Jesus, the spirits in him were terrified and began screaming. The man fell down at the feet of Jesus. The spirits recognised Jesus, just like the one in Capernaum, and declared he was the Son of God. They begged not to be tormented—a plea they had ignored when they were the tormentors (Luke 8:28). People had said the man had a devil, but when questioned by Jesus, the spirits disclosed that their name was legion. So this man had a multiplicity of devils that he needed deliverance from (Luke 8:30). Once again, notice how the demons knew who Jesus was. This man had been bound in chains and fetters, yet he had been able to burst these chains and set himself free (Luke 8:29). He displayed supernatural strength. He lived in caves and was full of scars from cutting himself (Mark 5:5). This is self-mutilation.

How can we comprehend this phenomenon of so many unclean spirits being in one person's body?

In the Old Testament, King Ahaziah sends a messenger to enquire of Baalzebub, the god of Ekron, a deity worshipped by the Philistines (2 Kings 1:2).[16] In the New Testament, Satan has the same title: Beelzebub, lord of dung or of filth, lord of the house.[17] The Pharisees held this evil deity to be the supreme leader in the demonic realm, and they gave it the title of prince of devils (Matthew 12:24).

If these unclean spirits are the size of flies, then we can understand why they called themselves legion. Unclean spirits can come in various forms and sizes. From this we deduce that these unclean spirits are not angels. In scripture we are told about different categories of heavenly beings, such as cherubim, seraphim, and angels. Some have wings and

---

[16] Strong's Hebrew Lexicon, https://blueletterbible.org/lexicon/h1176/kjv Baalzebub: lord of the fly. *Baal* means 'lord or master', and *zebub* means 'of flies', hence also translated Lord of flies

[17] Strong's Greek Lexicon, https://blueletterbible.org/lexicon/g954/kjv

others have no wings. Then there are different ranks of angels. When an angel appears to a person, it often looks like a man. Some people entertain angels and are completely oblivious to it.

Unclean spirits do not appear as angels. Scripture does not go into any great detail about the origin of unclean spirits. One possibility put forward is that they are the spirits of the giants and the hybrids that were the offspring of the giants, which we read about in Genesis 6.[18]

So what do we know about unclean spirits? In the book of Romans, Paul makes a very enlightening statement: that we can understand the invisible realm by looking at the natural realm. In particular, we should look at what has been created from the beginning of the world (Romans 1:20). That is one of the reasons you may hear someone say, 'as in the natural, so in the spirit.'

How can we apply this to unclean spirits? The book of Leviticus lists clean and unclean birds and clean and unclean animals. When Jesus was baptised at the River Jordan, scripture informs us that the Holy Spirit, in the form of a dove, came down from heaven and rested on Jesus (Luke 3:22). A dove is classified as a clean bird.

In the parable of the sower, the sower sows the Word of God (seed). We read that the 'fowls of the air came and devoured it up' (Mark 4:4). They are unclean birds.[19] When the disciples were alone with Jesus, they asked him about this parable. Jesus's reply is worth noting. The mystery of the kingdom of God was to be revealed to the disciples, not the multitude. When the Word is sown, it is Satan who comes to snatch it away before it can take root in a person's heart (Mark 4:15). So the fowls of the air are identified with Satan. Scripture is letting us know that the unclean spirits can be compared to birds and flies in the natural realm. This may explain the passage in Ecclesiastes that states: 'Curse not the king, no not in thy thought; and curse not the rich in thy bedchamber: for a bird of the air shall carry the voice, and that which hath wings shall tell the matter' (10:20). The king of Syria, when coming against Israel,

---

[18] See appendix 3.
[19] Strong's Greek Lexicon, https://blueletterbible.org/lexicon/g2719/kjv *devour*: to waste, to squander.

was thwarted at every turn. He demanded to know who the spy was. A servant told him there was no spy, but Elisha the prophet heard all the words the king spoke in his bedchamber and relayed the information to the king of Israel (2 Kings 6:12).

In the book of Revelation, we read of the fall of Babylon the great. 'Babylon the great is fallen, is fallen' is the refrain. Scripture unveils what it has become: a dwelling place of devils, a place for every type of unclean, foul spirit, and an enclosure for every unclean and hateful bird (Revelation 18:2). A foul spirit is the unclean spirit we have already come across. Here again the habitation of devils is pictured as an unclean, hateful bird.

A similar picture is given in Isaiah 34 at the Second Advent. The description leaves us in no doubt: this is not an environment in which natural birds can survive. 'And the streams therof shall be turned into pitch, and the dust therof into brimstone, and the land therof shall become burning pitch. It shall not be quenched night nor day; the smoke therof shall go up for ever: from generation to generation it shall lie waste; none shall pass through it for ever and ever' (Isaiah 34:9-10). In a book called *The Divinity Code*, the authors provide a whole list of scripture passages relating birds to the spiritual realm and detailing what these birds represent.[20]

We may ask how people end up with unclean spirits. The obvious possibility is that such people become involved in areas that God in his Word describes as no-go areas. Francis MacNutt expands on the different kinds of evil spirits, some of which are mentioned above.[21] The first kind does not come as a surprise to Christians: spirits of the occult. In the Old Testament, Israel degenerated into such an apostate state that they literally traded in the worship of Jehovah to offer up the lives of their sons and daughters on the altars of false gods. They offered their children to devils (Psalm 106:37). In Leviticus and Deuteronomy, these devils represent a deity that the heathen worship. Another kind of

---

[20] Adam F. Thompson & Adrian Beale, *The Divinity Code* (Shippensburg: Destiny Image, 2011), 249-250.

[21] MacNutt, *Deliverance from Evil Spirits* (Grand Rapids: Chosen Books, 2009), 90-96.

spirit, the spirits of sin, can range from lust to murder and every other human vice. These spirits will try to express themselves in the natural realm through a person.

Some areas of the operation of the demonic are not so obvious. For example, there is watching the wrong type of film. Gerry Markowicz writes about his experience: 'After watching a satanic film called 'The Exorcist' I had been haunted by an evil spirit appearing at night telling me to commit suicide and surrounding me by day in a circle of fear.'[22] Demons also take advantage when bad things happen to people, such as trauma or unexpected death. People who never get over these events may find it is due to a spirit of trauma or similar spirit oppressing them. MacNutt mentions this as a third category of evil spirit.

An interesting example is found in James Maloney's *Dancing Hand of God*.[23] He details how God revealed to him that a spirit of rejection had entered him while he was in his mother's womb, because he was an unwanted child. His mother had had an affair while her husband was in prison. Maloney also describes how he was delivered from this demon of rejection. Derek Prince states that in his experience, when operating in the realm of deliverance from evil spirits, the greatest root problem is in the area of rejection.[24]

A fourth category listed by MacNutt is ancestral or familiar spirits. These can come down through the human generational line. They reflect certain types of sins that can be passed down for ten generations. Sexual sins come into this category.

The Bible makes it clear that what we speak with our tongues has consequences in our lives. That is why we are urged to speak life, health, and strength over ourselves. When we speak negatively over ourselves, we are in fact speaking death. Imagine a person who keeps declaring, 'My father died at fifty from cancer. I expect to get cancer.' These words are an invitation to the demonic realm. Literally, this person is giving

---

[22] Gerry Markowicz, *Raising the Dead* (Victoria: Fresh Fire Ministries, 1996), 57.

[23] James Maloney, *Dancing Hand of God* vol. I (Answering the Cry, 2008) and vol. II (Bloomington: WestBow Press, 2011).

[24] Derek Prince, *derekprince.com/radio-series/3, Basics of Deliverance.*

that realm the opportunity to come and afflict them with cancer, fulfilling what the person is declaring over themselves. The Bible lets us know that life and death are in the power of the tongue.

Subritzky points out something that is never emphasised in teaching today: Jesus never sent out his disciples to preach the gospel without telling them to cast out demons.[25] This implies that everywhere we go when preaching the gospel, we are going to come across people needing some kind of deliverance. As we see in scripture, healing only follows after deliverance takes place. The instructions to the disciples is cast out demons and heal the sick.

The level, power, and number of unclean spirits we encounter may also depend on geographical location, as in the case with the man of the Gadarenes. It certainly depends on what people open their lives up to. There is no level playing field. The devil will take advantage of bad things that happen to people. Subritzky notes, 'Demons are spirit beings without bodies.'[26] The term *disembodied spirits* is widely used in Christian literature to describe those evil spirits.

Can a Christian have a demon? Firstly, we need to define what is meant by 'have'. Can a Christian be possessed by a devil? The answer is no. If we word the question a little bit differently, to ask whether a Christian can be attacked by a spirit of infirmity, we may take a different view.

We each have a spirit. When we are born again, our spirits comes alive, and we have fellowship with God, for God is a Spirit. It is the Spirit of God that confirms to us that we belong to him and that we have been brought into his family (Romans 8:16). However, we also each have a soul and a body that are influenced by this world. The soul includes the mind, emotions, and will. Both soul and body can be afflicted by illnesses and diseases.

Thus, we can also ask, 'Can a Christian fall into sin?' The answer of course is yes. But if the soul or body suffers due to a demon or a falling into sin, that does not involve the spirit.

---

[25] Bill Subritzky, *Demons Defeated* (Sovereign World, 1990), 63.
[26] Ibid., 59.

Derek Prince asks the question 'Can a Christian be demonised?'[27] He shares his own personal experience to answer the question.

Randy Clark, Global Awakening, also asks the question, Can a Christian be demonised? Looking at the story found in Mark 5 leads him to believe this can be possible.[28] However, he does make it clear he does not believe a Christian can be totally demonised or possessed according to the usual understanding of that term, for we are the possession of Christ. Therefore, we cannot become the possession of the enemy, if we are born again. Furthermore, if a Christian is full of the Holy Spirit then he cannot have a demon, but, qualifies this by saying, a Christian can be demonised or influenced by evil spirits if not full of the Holy Spirit. Like MacNutt, Clark points out some of the demonic affliction comes through generational sins.[29]

The scriptures also gives a warning to those who have received the Lord Jesus Christ into their lives (Colossians 2:6) not to turn again to the rudiments of the world that you have been delivered from such as vain deceit, philosophy, and traditions of men otherwise you will come under bondage (Colossians 2:8).

The Bible covers the various areas where men align with the demonic realm. For instance, in Egypt, the Pharaoh had his own wise men and his own sorcerers, and these magicians performed enchantments (Exodus 7:11). Wise men, or *chakamin*, are men who use magic to counsel a ruler. Magicians, or *chartammin*, use ritualistic magic in worship. Jannes and Jambres fall into this category, and we read that they fought against truth. They were men whose minds were corrupt and unprincipled when it came to faith (2 Timothy 3:8).

In Deuteronomy, the Lord warned the Israelites not to become involved with one who is an observer of times—*anan*, a diviner who uses signs or omens—or a charmer—*chab-chebar*, one who use charms and amulets in practicing magic. Also included on the list of those to avoid is an enchanter or hypnotist: someone who casts spells on people

---

[27] https://youtube.com/watch?v=NIKznEbETQ

[28] Randy Clark, *The Biblical Guidebook to Deliverance* (Lake Mary: Charisma House), 49.

[29] Ibid., 50-52.

to bring them under their power. Neither were the Israelites to seek out a wizard or *yiddehonie*, literally a 'knowing one', who practices magic from arcane knowledge found in books, nor necromancer, who enquires of the dead, nor a diviner, a *qosemin*, who tells the future through communion with unclean spirits (Deuteronomy 18:10, 11, 14).

Scripture further warns about people who have familiar spirits or *owb*—that is, demons that come when called (Leviticus 20:27). Astrologers or *ashshaphim,* who predict the future from planets and stars, are to be avoided (Daniel 1:20). Likewise a similar category, called stargazers or *hozim bakkokabim,* who predict the future from looking at the constellations, are forbidden (Isaiah 47:13).

In the New Testament, we read of an encounter Paul had. A girl had a spirit of divination. She followed Paul, declaring he was a servant of the Most High God (Acts 16:16). She was possessed by a spirit of python.[30] Paul took authority over this spirit and used the name of Jesus to command the spirit to come out of her. Within one hour this girl was totally delivered and free from its power (Acts 16:18).

At this point it is good to remind ourselves of why Jesus came: 'For this purpose the Son of God was manifested, that he might destroy the works of the devil' (1 John 3:8). Jesus was full of the Holy Spirit. So there is a demarcation line that is sharp and could not be made any clearer: The Holy Spirit is come to set people free and to give life.

Paul, writing to the Galatians, lists the evidence that they should see from this transaction, which encompasses all the traits found in Christ: the love of God, the joy of our salvation, and the peace of God residing within us. Therefore, there is no need to be anxious about anything. We can afford to be long-suffering and full of compassion, allowing our faith in Christ to be manifested to others (Galatians 5:22, 23). The Holy Spirit is the source and the giver of all good gifts.

Contrast this with a demon, which wants to hold a person in bondage, torment their mind, and afflict their body and soul. Demonic spirits want to suck the very life out of their victims. Deliverance comes

---

[30] Strong's Concordance, https://biblehub.com/greek/4436.htm, a spirit of python: the serpent or dragon that dwelt in the region of Pytho.

through repenting, declaring that you will no longer partner with evil spirits, and making declarations of life over yourself. When the apostle Paul writes to Timothy, he gives Timothy instructions on how to minister to a person who is caught in the devil's trap, so that the person can free themselves (2 Timothy 2:26). There is hope.

Jesus walked with authority. Jesus spoke with authority. The presence of God that he carried produced a reaction from every unclean spirit that came into contact with him. All the unclean spirits and their counterparts, without exception, recognised who Jesus was: the Son of God, the Holy One of God. Jesus's mission was to destroy the works of darkness and set people free from the oppression these unclean spirits wrought in people's lives.

Sadly, at Capernaum, after the initial enthusiasm passed, instead of paying attention to the truth of the unclean spirit being proclaimed in their ears, the people focused their eyes on their familiarity with the man Jesus. They dismissed the revelation given of his true identity and forever lived in that blindness, missing the day of their visitation.

Every individual and every church could not be given a more profound example of how easy it is to miss a time of visitation by the Holy Spirit.

CHAPTER 4

PARABLE OF THE SOWER

And he taught them many things by parables,
and said unto them in his doctrine.

Mark 4:2

The next incident in Mark's gospel happens when Jesus sits on a boat and teaches the people on the shore of the Sea of Galilee. This teaching includes the parable of the sower. When the disciples ask Jesus about this parable, he tells them, 'Unto you it is given to know the mystery of the kingdom of God: but unto them that are without, all these things are done in parables: That seeing they may see, and not perceive; and hearing they may hear, and not understand; lest at any time they should be converted, and their sins should be forgiven them' (Mark 4:11-12).

These are very strong words spoken by Jesus, so they deserve particular attention, especially when we find this parable recorded in three of the gospels, the other two being Matthew and Luke. Each gospel quotes a passage from the prophet Isaiah in one way or another: 'Make the heart of this people fat, and make their ears heavy, and shut their eyes; lest they see with their eyes, and hear with their ears, and understand with their heart, and convert, and be healed' (Isaiah 6:10).

This condition of not perceiving the Word of God hearkens back to Jesus's teaching from the Sermon on the Mount: hearts must be open and receptive to the Word of God for revelation to be received.

This passage from Isaiah is such a strong warning that it is repeated once more at the end of the book of Acts: 'For the heart of this people is waxed gross, and their ears are dull of hearing, and their eyes have they closed; lest they should see with their eyes, and hear with their ears, and understand with their heart, and should be converted, and I should heal them' (Acts 28:27). Paul also makes reference to this condition that has befallen the Jewish people: 'According as it is written, God hath given them the spirit of slumber, eyes that they should not see, and ears that they should not hear' (Romans 11:8). This has a particular application to the nation of Israel, prompting the apostle Paul to talk about the mystery of blindness that has happened to them.

In John's gospel, we read of a similar situation shortly before the crucifixion. John makes the observation that the abundance of miracles that people saw Jesus perform did not produce faith. People did not believe in him (John 12:37). This prompted John to write a somewhat unusual critique: the people's eyes were blinded so they could not see, and their hearts were made hard so they could not respond to the preaching of Jesus, and therefore could not be converted and healed (John 12:40). The principle of seed, time, and harvest operates with the consequence that people reap what they sow. The people were presented with their Messiah, but did not believe Jesus was the one that the prophets had pointed towards.

Contrary to what is sometimes said, Jesus did not teach in parables to help elucidate truth. The parables were not given to help a person's understanding. The situation, in fact was exactly the opposite: if a person did not have their heart right with the Saviour, the parables obscured the truth. The Pharisees accuse Jesus of casting out devils (Matthew 12:24). Then Jesus goes out from the house to the Sea of Galilee, where he speaks in parables to the multitude who have gathered to hear him (Matthew 13:1–3).

In other words, once Jesus has been rejected as the Messiah, the truth of his kingdom is provided in a format that can only be understood if the listener's heart is open to his words. This is seen when the disciples come to Jesus and ask him to explain the parables. Jesus's reply bears some scrutiny. It is easy to imagine the scene. Jesus turns to them and questions their ignorance. He tells them that if they do not know the foundational parable describing how the sower sows the Word of God, then how were they going to know all parables? (Mark 4:13). If the disciples are stumped, then the crowd is no better off. They have heard great words and walk away with their ears tingling, but they are left relying on their own ability to interpret the parable—and that is not going to happen.

At this point it is good to look at what is written in the gospels of Matthew and Luke. One talks of the mysteries of the kingdom of heaven, and the other of the mysteries of the kingdom of God.

> Because it is given unto you to know the mysteries of the kingdom of heaven, but to them it is not given. (Matthew 13:11)

> Unto you it is given to know the mysteries of the kingdom of God: but to others in parables; that seeing they might see, and hearing they might not understand. (Luke 8:10)

At first glance it appears the two kingdoms are one and the same, until we take a closer look. In Matthew's account, the seed of the kingdom of heaven is defined as 'When any one heareth the word of the kingdom, and understandeth it not, then cometh the wicked one, and catcheth away that which was sown in his heart. This is he which received seed by the way side' (Matthew 13:19). It is the physical kingdom represented by Jesus sitting on the throne of David at Jerusalem.

Luke, on the other hand, defines the seed this way: 'Now the parable is this: The seed is the word of God' (Luke 8:11). This seed is given to produce a new birth. 'Being born again, not of corruptible seed, but of incorruptible, by the word of God, which liveth and abideth for ever' (1 Peter 1:23).

In Matthew's account of the parable of the sower, Jesus goes on to state, 'For verily I say unto you, That many prophets and righteous men have desired to see those things which ye see, and have not seen them; and to hear those things which ye hear, and have not heard them' (Matthew 13:17). Why are the mysteries being revealed to the disciples?

Notice that the disciples are curious about this as well, and one asks Jesus, 'Lord, how is it that thou wilt manifest thyself unto us, and not unto the world? Jesus answered and said unto him, If a man love me, he will keep my words: and my Father will love him, and we will come unto him, and make our abode with him' (John 14:22–23). The basis for revelation and knowledge is all down to the relationship the disciples have with Jesus. As the old hymn says, what God has done for others, he will do for you, for he is no respecter of persons. Peter, when at Cornelius's house, has one of those moments when this truth hits him in a profound way (Acts 10:34).

There are a number of other things we know about the people of Jesus's day and the words spoken by Jesus about their condition. One such comment is 'when the people were gathered thick together, he began to say, This is an evil generation' (Luke 11:29).

During the ministry of John the Baptist, it is said that the people of Jerusalem, Judea, and the region around about came out to hear the preaching of John (Matthew 3:6). Among the people is a group of Pharisees and Sadducees. John's words to them are a stinging rebuke: 'O generation of vipers, who hath warned you to flee from the wrath to come?' (Matthew 3:7). These same religious people heard the message of John when he declared he was a voice in the wilderness, preparing the way of the Lord, and preaching messages of repentance and baptism. When Jesus comes to be baptised, John the Baptist points to Jesus and declares, 'Behold the Lamb of God' (John 1:29).

With regard to the Pharisees and Sadducees, we know their reaction to John's preaching. Jesus asks them a straightforward question: 'The baptism of John, whence was it? from heaven, or of men? And they reasoned with themselves, saying, If we shall say, From heaven; he will say unto us, Why did ye not then believe him? But if we shall say, Of men; we fear the people; for all hold John as a prophet' (Matthew

21:25-26). They never believed the word of John and would not believe Jesus was the Son of God, causing them to transgress their laws as their hatred for Jesus consumed them.

The people gladly listened to Jesus. Mark records, 'In those days the multitude being very great, and having nothing to eat, Jesus called his disciples unto him, and saith unto them, I have compassion on the multitude, because they have now been with me three days, and have nothing to eat' (Mark 8:1-2). This is the time when four thousand are fed from seven loaves of bread and a few fish. It is an amazing miracle.

Immediately after this miracle, we read about another incident with the Pharisees, who come to Jesus to tempt him. They are looking for a sign—but not just any kind of sign. They want one from heaven (Mark 8:11). What has just taken place with the multitude being fed is a powerful miracle and demonstration of Jesus's credentials. At the very minimum, it is a reminder of God feeding Israel in the wilderness. Yet the Pharisees show up, asking for a sign as if nothing has happened.

Notice the context: they are tempting him. It was the wrong way to approach the Saviour back then and is the wrong way to approach him today. It is only a smokescreen camouflaging their attempt to trap Jesus.

What kind of sign are they looking for? Jesus has fed the multitude, cast out devils, healed the sick, opened blind eyes, unstopped deaf ears, cleansed lepers, and raised the dead. The winds and the waves obey him. These are a fairly wide spread of signs. The Pharisees and Sadducees have abundant testimony that never a man spoke with such power and authority.

Scripture goes on to say, 'This is an evil generation: they seek a sign' (Luke 11:29). Jesus obliges them and gives them a sign to look for—but it is not what they are seeking, nor will it do them any good. Jesus tells the crowd the sign he will give them and brings up the prophet Jonah: 'For as Jonas was three days and three nights in the whale's belly; so shall the Son of man be three days and three nights in the heart of the earth' (Matthew 12:40). It is the sign of his death and resurrection!

When we go back to when Jesus was taken into the Temple at Jerusalem. Simeon spoke words over him: 'And Simeon blessed them, and said unto Mary his mother, Behold, this child is set for the fall and rising again of many in Israel; and for a sign which shall be spoken against' (Luke 2:34).

By picking Jonah, Jesus messed up lots of people's theology. Who believes Jonah was dead and in hell for three days and three nights? Who believes Jonah's own report, 'out of the belly of hell cried I' (Jonah 2:2) and 'thou hast brought up my life from corruption' (Jonah 2:6)? Talking about Jesus, scripture states, 'thou wilt not leave my soul in hell neither wilt thou suffer thine Holy One to see corruption' (Acts 2:27).

Something else is overlooked. The crowd keeps referring to Jesus as the prophet from Nazareth of Galilee (Matthew 21:11). This designation provoked a lot of controversy, and it splits the opinion of the crowd. Some people believe Jesus is the prophet spoken of by Moses. Some ask, 'Is this the Christ?' Still others question Jesus identity; 'shall Christ come out of Galilee' (John 7:41). Some point out the Messiah will be of the seed of David and be born in Bethlehem. Another group is very emphatic that according to scripture, no prophet came from Galilee (John 7:52). These people would have made good poker players, for their answers are intimidation and bluff.

In this story we learn something very significant: scripture records what people say even if what they say is not true. Jesus picks Jonah as a sign. Jesus is a prophet from Galilee, and he picks a prophet from a place called Gathhepher: 'He restored the coast of Israel from the entering of Hamath unto the sea of the plain, according to the word of the LORD God of Israel, which he spake by the hand of his servant Jonah, the son of Amittai, the prophet, which was of Gathhepher' (2 Kings 14:25). Gathhepher happens to be in Galilee. Jonah too is a prophet from Galilee!

The importance of the words we speak can never be stressed enough. What is in our hearts is what comes out of our mouths (Matthew 12:34). Notice the solemn warning: 'That every idle word that men shall speak, they shall give account thereof in the day of judgement' (Matthew 12:36). This lets us know that everyone is going to appear before God. Oh, the futility of being rebellious like Nimrod! (See chapter 17) The futility of becoming involved in any practice that stands in opposition to the work of the Saviour! Even the demons recognised Jesus's authority: 'What have we to do with thee, Jesus, thou Son of God? art thou come hither to torment us before the time?' (Matthew 8:29). Eternity is endless, whereas time is but a moment! Choose wisely.

Again, notice carefully: 'For by thy words thou shalt be justified, and by thy words thou shalt be condemned' (Matthew 12:37). When the unpardonable sin is committed, it is done by speaking words. 'And the scribes which came down from Jerusalem said, He hath Beelzebub, and by the prince of the devils casteth he out devils' (Mark 3:22). Scripture states, 'Death and life are in the power of the tongue' (Proverbs 18:21). These scribes spoke death not only over themselves, but over everyone who believed them.

Jesus reminds the crowd how the people of Nineveh humbled themselves and repented at the preaching of Jonah. Then Jesus tells them there is one standing in front of them who is greater than Jonah. He was telling them they had seen things the people of Nineveh never saw. Yet the people of Nineveh repented and the crowd before Jesus is untouched and disbelieving. They are an evil generation; they talk the talk, but their hearts and attitudes are far from God.

How did the people end up in this condition? Responsibility rests with the custodians of the Word of God. By the time John the Baptist shows up, we can see from his encounters with the Pharisees and Sadducees that they have replaced the Word of God with the commandments of men and the promotion of human traditions.

This is the same group of Pharisees, along with the scribes, whom Jesus accused of stopping people entering the kingdom of heaven (Matthew 23:13). Jesus labelled them hypocrites who do not enter in, and who are a stumbling block for others to enter in. They came and looked at John, but they did not repent (Matthew 21:32). They projected a moral, upright image as opposed to those whom they called 'sinners'. Jesus's words to them were sharp: 'Woe unto you, scribes and Pharisees, hypocrites! for ye are like unto whited sepulchres, which indeed appear beautiful outward, but are within full of dead men's bones, and of all uncleanness' (Matthew 23:27). Whited sepulchres only disguise the rottenness that lies within.

The counterpart to the Pharisees in the Jewish hierarchy was a sect known as the Sadducees. Their mantle was passed through the generations and can be detected by what they stood for. They did not believe in the virgin birth. They did not believe in the resurrection. They did not believe in angels. They did not believe in the supernatural. They did not believe Jesus Christ was the Son of God. They did not believe the Word of God. They had nothing of value to give to the people. What the Bible says about them is 'Let them alone: they be blind leaders of the blind. And if the blind lead the blind, both shall fall into the ditch' (Matthew 15:14).

What we learn from this story is the importance of a right heart-attitude. In Jesus's day, outward appearance, self-righteousness, and works before men were prevalent. People believed in projecting their persona at the cost of allowing the Word of God to change their character and produce the life of God. They were accused of rejecting 'the commandment of God' so that they could maintain their traditions (Mark 7:9).

This came at a high cost. Scripture provides a strong warning about rejecting God's Word. Hosea put it succinctly when he wrote, 'because thou hast rejected knowledge, I will also reject thee' (4:6). The result was failure to hear the truth and the doctrine that Jesus taught in parables. They heard truth being spoken, but due to their hardening of their hearts, they 'shall fall into mischief' (Proverbs 28:14). They were unable to grasp the significance of Jesus's teaching and missed the day of visitation prophesied in their very own scripture.

CHAPTER 5

JESUS CLEANSES THE TEMPLE

And the scribes and chief priests heard it, and sought
how they might destroy him: for they feared him, because
all the people were astonished at his doctrine.

Mark 11:18

Jesus cleared the Temple of money changers, those who bought and sold, and those who carried vessels through the Temple. Jesus indicted those with responsibility to run the Temple and oversee sacrifices: 'Is it not written, My house shall be called of all nations the house of prayer? but ye have made it a den of thieves' (Mark 11:17). The purpose of the Temple—to be a place where people could come to pray and worship God—had degenerated into a place for private businesses to make money out of worshippers. It was one occasion when a righteous anger arose in Christ.

The right function of the Temple was displayed when Jesus ministered to the people after he had cleared the place of its corrupt practices. Matthew's gospel says the blind and lame came to Jesus, and he healed them. Look at the reaction: 'And when the chief priests and scribes saw the wonderful things that he did, and the children crying in the temple, and saying, Hosanna to the son of David; they were sore displeased' (Matthew 21:15). This was one of the greatest moments in the history of the Temple since it was built in the days of Ezra, but the Pharisees and Sadducees could not rejoice in seeing men and women receiving healing and being made whole. They saw the demonstration of God's power in their midst and the rejoicing that it brought in the hearts of the people. Everyone in the Temple saw and experienced exceptional ministry. Countless people received their miracles that day. The contrast could not be greater between the people experiencing miracles in their bodies, with the result that they worshiped God, and the custodians of scripture, the scribes and chief priests, afraid of Jesus and upset at the people's reaction.

This is the second time that Jesus clears the Temple. It takes place after the triumphant entry into Jerusalem, before the crucifixion, when Jesus comes riding on the colt of an ass. He comes as the King of the Jews, as the Jewish Messiah, and declares, 'It is written, My house shall be called the house of prayer' (Matthew 21:13). When Jesus clears the Temple, it is done in his kingly capacity. When Solomon, the son of David, is crowned, we read, 'The king also said unto them, Take with you the servants of your lord, and cause Solomon my son to ride upon mine own mule, and bring him down to Gihon. And let Zadok the priest and Nathan the prophet anoint him there king over Israel: and blow ye with the trumpet, and say, God save King Solomon' (1 Kings 1:33- 34). Jesus, the greater son of David, comes into Jerusalem riding upon an ass, and the people cry hosanna.

In contrast, the first time Jesus clears out the Temple, which is recorded by John, Jesus comes in his priestly capacity, makes a whip (which is not done in a moment), and overturns tables. The Temple is not a place for business, but a place for prayer (John 2:16). In the parallel account in Mark's gospel, Jesus says, 'My house shall be a house of prayer' (Mark 11:17).

On various occasions during the life of Jesus, people attempted to make Jesus king. On all occasions, Jesus did not respond. However, when Jesus arrives at Jerusalem, he allows himself to be called King. This is in order to fulfil scripture: 'Rejoice greatly, O daughter of Zion; shout, O daughter of Jerusalem: behold, thy King cometh unto thee: he is just, and having salvation; lowly, and riding upon an ass, and upon a colt the foal of an ass' (Zechariah 9:9). As the psalmist wrote many years earlier, 'Blessed be he that cometh in the name of the LORD' (Psalm 118:26).

The Pharisees approach Jesus to rebuke the people. Jesus answers them, 'I tell you that, if these should hold their peace, the stones would immediately cry out' (Luke 19:40). In the Hebrew calendar these events happened on 10 Nisan AD 32. The equivalent date on the Christian calendar is 6 April AD 32.

The scribes and chief priests in the Temple, who heard the words of Jesus, are confronted with a situation that is out of their depth. It is out of their depth because they are not being faithful stewards of the Word of God. They have plenty of examples in scripture that stand as warnings when the priesthood becomes unfaithful. They are not ignorant of what happened to Eli and his sons. They know what happened to Miriam when she came against Moses. They know Elijah's confrontation with the false prophets of Baal and the outcome on Mount Carmel. They have before them the writings of Jeremiah the prophet. They know what happened during that time in Judah's history and how the priesthood opposed Jeremiah and turned away from God.

They now find themselves confronted with the one who claims to be the owner of the Temple and states 'My house shall be called the house of prayer' (Matthew 21:13). Jesus reminds them what is already written, 'mine house shall be called an house of prayer for all people' (Isaiah 56:7). The triumphant entrance into Jerusalem is also reflected in the worship Jesus received 'Out of the mouth of babes and sucklings hast thou ordained strength' (Psalm 8:2). People are rejoicing in the Temple, giving worship to God, and the scribes and chief priests seek how they might get rid of Jesus because they feared him (Mark 11:18).

The scribes and chief priests fear Jesus. What a tragic situation. It is a strange paradox: miracles take place before their eyes, and they want to put to death the one being used to bring miracles to the people. Jesus exposes their wickedness; there is no place for them to hide. Instead of repenting, they let the wickedness that is alive in their hearts putrefy.

A similar situation arose when Jesus was invited to Simon the Pharisee's house (Luke 7:49). The Bible tells us a woman who was a sinner came and washed Jesus's feet with her tears, dried them with her hair, kissed them, and anointed them with ointment. Jesus, perceiving Simon's thoughts stated that when one was forgiven much, they loved much. Turning to the woman, Jesus told her that her sins were forgiven (Luke 7:48). Simon, along with all those in his house, questioned within themselves who this person was who was forgiving this woman her sins (Luke 7:49).

In another instance, after the healing of a blind man at Bethesda pool, the Jews sought to kill Jesus. They accused him of making himself equal with God by stating God was his Father (John 5:18).

Mark tells us that the 'scribes and chief priests feared him' (Mark 11:18). They wanted to destroy Jesus because the people were 'astonished at his doctrine' (Mark 11:18). Luke reiterates that the people were astonished at his doctrine and says why: 'for his word was with power' (Luke 4:32).

John, who was the beloved disciple, provides further insight. Firstly, Jesus tells the people that his doctrine is not his, but the doctrine of the one who sent him (John 7:16). Immediately Jesus goes on to say, 'If any man will do his will, he shall know of the doctrine, whether it be of God, or whether I speak of myself' (John 7:17).

It is a very sobering scripture passage for the custodians responsible for instructing the people in the Law and the Prophets, in the difference between the profane and the holy. They are the same group that finally has its way and calls on Pontius Pilate to crucify Jesus.

We read that the early church 'continued stedfastly in the apostles' doctrine and fellowship, and in breaking of bread, and in prayers' (Acts 2:42). But we also read about Paul's journey to Cyprus, which contains an amazing passage about a man who was 'astonished at the doctrine of the Lord' (Acts 13:12). This was Sergius Paulus, the deputy of the country. In his court was a man named Barjesus. Barjesus was a sorcerer and apparently very well known for his enchantments. This man withstood Paul and attempted to turn Sergius Paulus away from hearing the Word of God.

Paul never minced his words when he responded to Barjesus. Paul spelled out his wickedness: Barjesus was a child of the devil and an enemy of all righteousness. To seal it all, Paul told Barjesus he would be blind and not see the sun for a season, which indeed occurred. After reading about this confrontation, we are not surprised that Sergius Paulus was astonished and became a convert to Christianity.

True biblical doctrine is not something that is abstract. True biblical doctrine contains words that are quickened by the Holy Spirit, spoken with authority, and accompanied by power and demonstration. Doctrine is powerful. Jesus was crucified because of his doctrine.

The first mention of doctrine is found in Deuteronomy 32:2. This sets for us its purpose throughout the Bible. Doctrine is likened to rain: as drops of rain falling on the tender herbs and as showers falling upon the grass. Rain is required to give life and sustenance to the earth just as true doctrine gives sustenance to the spirit. Without rain nothing grows, and without true doctrine we will never know the truth. If we never know the truth, then there is no hope of being set free from sin.

Notice the dual functionality: drops of rain for that which is tender, and showers for the tougher grass. For the woman taken in adultery who was brought to Jesus, this doctrine was like raindrops (John 8:3). It was tender, with no condemnation. She walked away a changed person. The crowd walked away in shame. As scripture so eloquently states, 'A bruised reed shall he not break' (Matthew 12:20).

Another woman in a similar lifestyle had an encounter with Jesus at a well in Samaria (John 4:7). The disciples were off to find provisions for human need at a local village. They returned and saw Jesus speaking to this woman. The woman turned out to be a great evangelist. She returned to her village, the same one the disciples had just visited, and told the villagers all about a man who had told her everything she had ever done, Jesus the Messiah. The disciples returned with food for the body, natural bread, but this woman brought spiritual food to the people and introduced them to Jesus. To this woman, the doctrine was gentle drops of rain on herbs.

One day Jesus found a man who had been born blind (John 9:1). After Jesus healed him, the authorities grilled the formerly blind man about what had taken place. They sent for his parents to verify that this was their son. They were angry that Jesus had done such a miracle on the Sabbath day. After much questioning, the man asked them if they would not become Jesus's disciples as well (John 9:27). This made them angry, and they cast the man out of the synagogue. Jesus found this man and spoke into his life. Jesus spoke the gentle drops of rain.

However, doctrine is not just raindrops. It also comes in showers. If ever there was a time that the showers fell, it was on the day of Pentecost, the outpouring of the Spirit of God. The purpose of Pentecost was to allow the disciples to have a supernatural walk with God and witness for Jesus in signs and wonders. This event was so awe-inspiring that the writer of Acts can only explain the coming of the Holy Spirit as a 'likeness' or 'appearance' 'as of tongues', for it was beyond description.

The old hymn by Daniel W. Whittle puts it nicely:

> There shall be showers of blessing:
> This is the promise of love;
> There shall be seasons refreshing,
> Sent from the Saviour above.
>
> Showers of blessing,
> Showers of blessing we need:
> Mercy-drops round us are falling,
> But for the showers we plead.
>
> There shall be showers of blessing,
> Precious reviving again;
> Over the hills and the valleys,
> Sound of abundance of rain.
>
> There shall be showers of blessing;
> Send them upon us, O Lord;
> Grant to us now a refreshing,
> Come, and now honour thy word.

There shall be showers of blessing;
Oh, that today they might fall,
Now as to God we're confessing,
Now as on Jesus we call!

There shall be showers of blessing,
If we but trust and obey;
There shall be seasons refreshing,
If we let God have his way.

In Mark's gospel, Jesus speaks to the people and shares his doctrine with them (Mark 4:2). Jesus's doctrine centres on the sower and the seed sown. This metaphor is given in three of the four gospels. The seed is the Word of God. Even as the rain and the snow come down from heaven to water the earth, God's Word goes forth. It accomplishes its purposes and does not return void (Isaiah 55:10–11).

Jesus's doctrine takes us back to Genesis 2, in which the Lord God, Jehovah, sets in motion the operation or government of God. It is this aspect of God, the Lord God, who sets in motion how the world operates—as distinct from the Godhead of Father, Son, and Holy Spirit, which the Bible opens with: 'In the beginning God' (Genesis 1:1).

When Jesus says that when we see him, we have seen the Father, he is giving us insight into the goodness of God. It is the goodness of God that leads people to repentance. The life of Jesus reflects his Father. When the disciples wanted to call down fire from heaven, Jesus rebuked them, for it did not reflect on the true nature of God, who is good.

It is the Lord God who set up a governmental system for people to be blessed. When this system is abused and people plant their own seed, it has severe consequences.

The seed God plants contains everything that we need to produce the life of God in us. The seed is planted, and after due time the harvest is reaped. Jesus's doctrine is the sowing of the Word of God, the seed. The harvest can be judgement, for you reap what you sow. Scripture says to sow righteousness to reap mercy (Hosea 10:12). Sin has consequences: you can sow your seed in vain (Leviticus 26:16).

The importance of sowing and reaping is to make you aware of the impact on your life, even on the life of your nation. It is not God, per se, issuing judgement. It is an individual reaping what has been sown. It is the system of the government of God.

How do you break this cycle? By pleading the blood of God that was shed for you on Mount Calvary by the Lord Jesus Christ. His blood cleanses from all sin. It purges, and we are clothed with the righteousness of Jesus, which allows us to come and stand in the presence of a holy God.

The early church spoke the words it had heard Jesus speak. The disciples did the miracles that they had seen Jesus do, and they lived lives they had seen Jesus live. The doctrine that people were astonished at when they had encounters with Jesus was the doctrine the early church proclaimed to a lost world. It is said that within one hundred years of the gospel, all of the gods of the old world were vanquished.

People were astonished at Jesus's doctrine because the words he spoke were life. People were hearing the living words of the living God, and its impact divided the nation of Israel. From the beginning of Jesus's ministry, there were those who wanted to stone him.

In the book of Job, we have the statement 'My doctrine is pure, and I am clean in thine eyes' (Job 11:4). The psalmist writes that God's words are 'pure words; they are like silver tried in a furnace of earth seven times' (Psalm 12:6). Daniel tells us what happened when the furnace was heated seven times: it consumed the guards who threw in the three Hebrew slaves (Daniel 3:19). The dross was consumed.

So the people were astonished at Jesus doctrine, his doctrine is pure for he spoke pure words, he declares it with power and the Bible says 'the common people heard him gladly' (Mark 12:37). His doctrine, like fire, penetrated their hearts. Furthermore, this doctrine is good doctrine (Proverbs 4:2). It is the right theological truth which should not be forsaken. It is the theological truth that Paul encouraged Timothy in. When we follow and apply Jesus's doctrine to our lives, we also can come to the place where we declare, 'I am clean.'

What was the doctrine that Jesus taught?

The outstanding doctrine was the revelation that God appeared in the flesh. This is called the 'mystery of godliness' in scripture. It is the virgin birth of Jesus Christ. 'And without controversy great is the mystery of godliness: God was manifest in the flesh' (1 Timothy 3:16). John opens his gospel by telling us that 'In the beginning was the Word, and the Word was with God, and the Word was God' (John 1:1). Then he provides this wonderful revelation: 'the Word was made flesh, and dwelt among us' (John 1:14). Jesus entered this world as a baby. It is called 'the Incarnation'. God became flesh. The Word was made flesh. Jesus inhabited a body of flesh. Peter calls the body a tabernacle (2 Peter 1:13–14). Paul calls 'this earthly house' a tabernacle (2 Corinthians 5:1).

At the start of Jesus's ministry, his calling was confirmed at the River Jordan, where he was baptised. We are told about a voice that spoke from heaven, affirming Jesus's identity and declaring that God was pleased with him (Mark 1:11). Jesus himself lets us know that he is not of this world. He tells us he and his Father are one (John 10:30). This statement would have echoed in the ears of the religious people listening to Jesus speak. Who would not think immediately of the verse 'Hear, O Israel: The LORD our God is one LORD' (Deuteronomy 6:4)? Or they might think of Jesus's other statement: 'And he said unto them, Ye are from beneath; I am from above: ye are of this world; I am not of this world' (John 8:23).

In this discourse, Jesus confronts the religious establishment of his day and tells the people of the choice before them: believe in him or die in their sins. Again, this laying out the truth in a black-and-white way should have brought to mind all that Moses had written. The children of Israel were constantly encouraged to choose life and not death, blessings and not curses, good and not evil.

Jesus went further in this discourse, knowing that the response to his teaching would be mixed. As we find later on in scripture, Jesus was willing that none should perish (2 Peter 3:9). That is why, in John's gospel, Jesus gives details about the manner of his death. It will not be the Jewish way of putting transgressors to death, which was by stoning (John 8:28). This detail is given to those who may have been wavering about Jesus's identity. When they saw his death, they would believe.

To reinforce this message, Jesus uses clear, concise words, so that there will not be any misunderstanding: 'Before Abraham was, I am'

(John 8:58). Later in his ministry, Jesus takes this truth further, stating, 'I am the way, the truth, and the life' (John 14:6).

In a way we should not be surprised by how astonished people were during the ministry of Jesus. When he was twelve years old, he was found in the Temple at Jerusalem, asking questions of and debating with the heads of the Jewish faith. They were astonished at his understanding and his answers (Luke 2:47).

Doctrine in the Bible covers personal conduct. When the apostle Paul writes to another of his prodigies, Titus, who was a minister in Crete, Paul exhorts him to 'speak thou the things which become sound doctrine' (Titus 2:1). Paul gives Titus instructions in line with those he gave to Timothy (1 Timothy 3). Notice that sound doctrine deals with the conduct of those who belong to Christ and how they might live right before God and man.

Look at why Paul stresses the importance of preaching sound doctrine: 'that the word of God be not blasphemed' (Titus 2:5). After Paul tells Titus how the believers should conduct themselves, he tells Titus how to conduct himself: 'In all things shewing thyself a pattern of good works: in doctrine shewing uncorruptness, gravity, sincerity' (Titus 2:7). In other words, Titus is being instructed not only to teach these things to his congregation, but to make an example of his life for others to follow—a pattern that honours God and brings glory to his name.

When we study the Pastoral Epistles, Timothy and Titus, it should be noted how much emphasis is placed on doctrine:

> Knowing this, that the law is not made for a righteous man, but for the lawless and disobedient, for the ungodly and for sinners, for unholy and profane, for murderers of fathers and murderers of mothers, for manslayers, For whoremongers, for them that defile themselves with mankind, for menstealers, for liars, for perjured persons, and if there be any other thing that is contrary to sound doctrine. (1 Timothy 1:9-10)

Now the Spirit speaketh expressly, that in the latter times some shall depart from the faith, giving heed to seducing spirits, and doctrines of devils. (1 Timothy 4:1)

If thou put the brethren in remembrance of these things, thou shalt be a good minister of Jesus Christ, nourished up in the words of faith and of good doctrine, whereunto thou hast attained. (1 Timothy 4:6)

Till I come, give attendance to reading, to exhortation, to doctrine. (1 Timothy 4:13)

Take heed unto thyself, and unto the doctrine; continue in them: for in doing this thou shalt both save thyself, and them that hear thee. (1 Timothy 4:16)

Let the elders that rule well be counted worthy of double honour, especially they who labour in the word and doctrine. (1 Timothy 5:17)

Let as many servants as are under the yoke count their own masters worthy of all honour, that the name of God and his doctrine be not blasphemed. (1 Timothy 6:1)

These things teach and exhort. If any man teach otherwise, and consent not to wholesome words, even the words of our Lord Jesus Christ, and to the doctrine which is according to godliness. (1 Timothy 6:2-3)

But thou hast fully known my doctrine, manner of life, purpose, faith, longsuffering, charity, patience. (2 Timothy 3:10)

All scripture is given by inspiration of God, and is profitable for doctrine, for reproof, for correction, for instruction in righteousness. (2 Timothy 3:16)

> For the time will come when they will not endure sound
> doctrine; but after their own lusts shall they heap to
> themselves teachers, having itching ears. (2 Timothy 4:3)

When we look over these passages given to Timothy, we see there are lifestyles that are inconsistent with sound doctrine. The moral character of these lifestyles does not reflect our heavenly Father. Paul tells Timothy they are contrary to sound doctrine.

Then there are doctrines that are not of God. These doctrines are satanic. They are there to entice you away from the living God and to rebel against him, with the final end being judgement. Jeremiah called them 'doctrine of vanities' (Jeremiah 10:8). Words of faith, the reading of scripture, and exhortation bring people to faith in Christ, for 'faith cometh by hearing, and hearing by the word of God' (Romans 10:17). Those who labour in the Word and doctrine are to be honoured. Others are warned to give honour to their masters so that the name of God and his doctrine be not blasphemed.

There is a warning not to preach any other doctrine. Paul reminds Timothy of how he has lived so that Timothy will do likewise. Paul finishes by saying all scripture is profitable for doctrine.

Paul writes similar words to Titus:

> For a bishop must be blameless, as a steward of God......
> Holding fast the faithful word as he hath been taught,
> that he may be able by sound doctrine both to exhort
> and to convince the gainsayers. (Titus 1:7, 9)

> But speak thou the things which become sound doctrine.
> (Titus 2:1)

> Young men likewise exhort to be sober minded. In
> all things shewing thyself a pattern of good works: in
> doctrine shewing uncorruptness, gravity, sincerity.
> (Titus 2:6-7)

> Exhort servants to be obedient unto their own masters, and to please them well in all things; not answering again; Not purloining (dishonest, stealing, theft), but shewing all good fidelity; that they may adorn the doctrine of God our Saviour in all things. (Titus 2:9-10)

Again Paul sets out the high standard for followers of Jesus: they should be able to preach 'sound doctrine'. Why? Followers of Jesus carry the reputation of God. They have been given the privilege to represent him and his goodness.

In the Temple, religious activities had become a business. The Temple was a good source of income. Paul told Timothy, 'the love of money is the root of all evil: which while some coveted after, they have erred from the faith' (1 Timothy 6:10). The scribes and priests had changed the order of priority. No longer was it to ensure that the people were instructed in the ways of righteousness and that their hearts conformed to the Law of Moses. Now the people took second place to the requirements of the Sanhedrin.

The scribes and priests sought how they might destroy Jesus. They conspired to kill him. Murder had entered their hearts. They had moved away from sound doctrine. They had become corrupt, just like their predecessors in the wilderness when God told Moses 'get thee down; for thy people, which thou broughtest out of the land of Egypt, have corrupted themselves' (Exodus 32:7).

The scribes and priests never operated in power like Jesus. Instead of humbling themselves, they felt threatened and allowed fear to dictate their subsequent actions of insecurity. They never rose to that place which John so eloquently unveiled in his epistle: 'There is no fear in love; but perfect love casteth out fear: because fear hath torment. He that feareth is not made perfect in love' (1 John 4:18).

CHAPTER 6

JESUS AT CAPERNAUM

And they were astonished at his doctrine
for his word was with power.

Luke 4:32

mmediately after the above passage, the Bible states, 'And in the synagogue there was a man, which had a spirit of an unclean devil, and cried out with a loud voice, Saying, Let us alone; what have we to do with thee, thou Jesus of Nazareth? art thou come to destroy us? I know thee who thou art; the Holy one of God' (Luke 4:33-34).

Here the rulers of the synagogue, as they watch and listen to Jesus, hear a remarkable confession from an unclean spirit before it is cast out by Jesus. The unclean spirit identifies and confesses Jesus as the one who has authority over it and is known to it as Jesus of Nazareth. Contrast this with the attitude of the Pharisees when the officers they had sent to arrest Jesus returned empty handed. They were included with the people, accused of not knowing the law, therefore are cursed (John 7:49). Yet the Pharisees themselves appear to be ignorant of the location of the place where Jonah was born, for it is in Galilee (John 7:52).

The unclean spirit trembles because Jesus has power to destroy it. The unclean spirit states a remarkable thing for all to hear, that Jesus is 'the Holy one of God.'

The person standing in front of the rulers of the synagogue is their Messiah. They see the demonstration of Jesus's power, and they hear the confessions given by the unclean spirit about Jesus's deity. Do you not think that some of the rulers were pricked in their consciences? Do you not think some would remember the reason Herod massacred the children aged two years and under at Bethlehem? It was because of the inquiry of the wise men: 'Where is he that is born king of the Jews?' Did not scripture foretell, 'A voice was heard in Ramah, lamentation, and bitter weeping; Rahel weeping for her children refused to be comforted for her children, because they were not' (Jeremiah 31:15). Notwithstanding, the rulers remained silent and stubbornly opposed to Jesus.

When we study the gospels, we find that not only are the words spoken by Jesus powerful, but they are followed by signs and wonders. The Hebrew Scriptures provide benchmarks to test prophets or dreamers. The first test is 'When a prophet speaketh in the name of the LORD, if the thing follow not, nor come to pass, that is the thing which the LORD hath not spoken, but the prophet hath spoken it presumptuously: thou shalt not be afraid of him' (Deuteronomy 18:22).

The second test is to do with a prophet or a dreamer of dreams performing signs and wonders. 'If there arise among you a prophet, or a dreamer of dreams, and giveth thee a sign or a wonder, And the sign or the wonder come to pass, whereof he spake unto thee, saying, Let us go after other gods, which thou hast not known, and let us serve them; Thou shalt not hearken unto the words of that prophet, or that dreamer of dreams' (Deuteronomy 13:1–3). The Lord allows this to happen 'for the LORD your God proveth you, to know whether ye love the LORD your God with all your heart and with all your soul' (Deuteronomy 13:3).

The instructions in Deuteronomy set out how to recognise true prophets and how to deal with false prophets. God expects his people to be able to distinguish between the profane and the holy, between the true prophet and the false prophet.

Now Jesus is a prophet—not just any prophet, but the one Moses spoke about: 'I will raise them up a Prophet from among their brethren, like unto thee, and will put my words in his mouth; and he shall speak unto them all that I shall command him. And it shall come to pass, that whosoever will not hearken unto my words which he shall speak in my name, I will require it of him' (Deuteronomy 18:18–19).

As the Pharisees listen to Jesus, we may ask the question, 'Who is being tested?' The Pharisees have scripture to stand upon to verify the authenticity of the one who speaks so powerfully. And yet at the same time they are the people under the spotlight as God proves their hearts to see if they love him. Scripture is a double-edged sword!

In another part of scripture, Jesus makes a statement that is very remarkable, the importance of which is often missed: 'But if I cast out devils by the Spirit of God, then the kingdom of God has come unto you' (Matthew 12:28). Luke records this also with the added information that if Jesus, with the finger of God, casts out devils, we do not need to doubt that the kingdom of God is now here (Luke 11:20).

It is insightful to note what Jesus did not say. Jesus never said the kingdom of God had come when he raised the dead, nor when he opened blind eyes, nor when the deaf were made to hear and the dumb to speak. He did not even say it when he healed people of leprosy and all kinds of other diseases. Yet when Jesus cast out devils, he said that now the cleansed person knew the kingdom of God had come. Furthermore, the expression 'finger of God' takes us back to Moses, when God wrote the ten commandments on a tablet of stone, and to Jesus, who wrote on the ground with his finger when the woman caught in adultery was brought before him.

The kingdom of God is a kingdom of righteousness. This kingdom deals firstly with the root of all rebellion and wickedness—that is, the demonic realm of Satan. 'For we wrestle not against flesh and blood, but against principalities, against powers, against the rulers of the darkness of this world, against spiritual wickedness in high places' (Ephesians 6:12). According to the book of Proverbs, life comes from walking in the paths of righteousness (12:28), and—one of the most important scripture passages for the destiny of a nation—'Righteousness exalteth a nation: but sin is a reproach to any people' (Proverbs 14:34). When the spiritual realm of the kingdom of God dominates the natural realm, then people experience the power of God in healings and miracles.

Jesus also revealed truth which far surpassed the expectation of the Pharisees. For all their opposition to Jesus, they still looked for a messiah to come and sit upon the throne of David. Their expectation was always confined to the natural realm; their messiah would set them free from the yoke of Rome or any other oppressor. However, Jesus goes further than this. He is not only the Messiah who will sit on David's throne, expressed in the kingdom of heaven, but he is Lord over all creation, principalities, and powers. Jesus is coming to redeem all mankind from the fall.

Notice the sequence in scripture: first the suffering, and then the glory. The suffering of Jesus is described by the prophet Isaiah: 'He is despised and rejected of men; a man of sorrows, and acquainted with grief: and we hid as it were our faces from him; he was despised, and we esteemed him not. Surely he hath borne our griefs, and carried our sorrows: yet we did esteem him stricken, smitten of God, and afflicted. But he was wounded for our transgressions, he was bruised for our iniquities: the chastisement of our peace was upon him; and with his stripes we are healed' (Isaiah 53:3–5).

He is coming as a double king: 'King of righteousness, and after that also King of Salem, which is, King of peace' (Hebrews 7:2). Righteousness is a spiritual kingdom. The apostle Paul tells us the 'kingdom of God is not meat and drink; but righteousness, and peace, and joy in the Holy Ghost' (Romans 14:17). Jesus is also the coming King of Salem, which is Jerusalem, the expectation of the rabbis. No world peace comes to this earth until Jesus comes and reigns and receives the glory and adoration which is due unto him.

Jesus had authority, and he had the power to exercise that authority. In Luke's account, the people are amazed at the words Jesus spoke (Luke 4:36). Jesus was releasing the authority and power of the 'word of God'

(Luke 4:4). Jesus spoke the Word and commanded the unclean spirit to come out of the man, and that unclean spirit came out.

As believers and followers of Jesus, we have been given a case study on how to meet the instructions given in Mark's gospel: 'these signs shall follow them that believe; In my name shall they cast out devils' (Mark 16:17). Another instance is found in Matthew's gospel: 'When the even was come, they brought unto him many that were possessed with devils: and he cast out the spirits with his word' (Matthew 8:16).

Scripture presents us with a contrast: those who believe the words of Jesus and those who do not believe the words of Jesus. This comes out clearly in the early part of the book of Acts. After Peter preached to the crowd, people received his words with joy and immediately were baptised. Three thousand were converted after hearing one sermon (Acts 2:41)! How different a picture from when Moses came down the mountain to find the people worshipping a golden calf. That day three thousand lost their lives (Exodus 32:28). This latter incident takes us back to Jesus's early ministry, when the people were told bluntly that God's Word was not in them, for if it had been, they would have recognised who Jesus was (John 5:38).

We find in the Psalms a constant reminder of the greatness of the Lord. Because he is great, we are to give him the glory due to his name (Psalm 29:2). Others are encouraged to worship and give praise to his name in the dance, singing and playing musical instruments such as the timbrel and harp (Psalm 149:3). We are also to honour his name for he is the one who rides 'upon the heavens by his name JAH' (Psalm 68:4). JAH is the abbreviation for Jehovah, first found in Exodus 15:2, where the Hebrew word translated as 'Lord' is given as 'Jah'. It is the first time in scripture we find this. It is associated with singing as the people rejoice over their deliverance from bondage in Egypt.

As we continue through the Psalms, in the midst of all the verses about honour and extolling his name, we come across 'for thou hast magnified thy word above all thy name' (Psalm 138:2). Why is this so important? The answer is found in John's gospel: 'In the beginning was the Word, and the Word was with God, and the Word was God' (John 1:1). 'The Word was made flesh, and dwelt among us' (John 1:14). Jesus is the Word, and in him is life. Jesus spoke the Word and deliverance followed. As the Word, he speaks words and all obey. Nature is subject to him, diseases are subject to him, and death is subject to him. All the powers of darkness are subject to him. He speaks, and the heavens and the earth come into being.

The psalmist wrote an incredible thing when he stated, 'for thou hast magnified thy word above all thy name' (Psalm 138:2). Two things go together in scripture: Word and truth, 'thy truth: thy word is truth' (John 17:17). John tells us that when God sent Jesus, the words that Jesus spoke were from God, and the Spirit that was in Jesus was without measure (John 3:34). It is not only Jesus who speaks the words of God. We are told that even as a branch receives its life from a tree, if our life is hid in God and we are abiding in him, then our prayers are effective, for we are praying according to the leading of the Spirit, and God answers prayer (John 15:7). The same Spirit that is in Christ is in every believer.

There is no higher name than the name of Jesus. 'That at the name of Jesus every knee should bow, of things in heaven, and things in earth, and things under the earth' (Philippians 2:10). The prophet Isaiah wrote, 'I have sworn by myself, the word is gone out of my mouth in righteousness, and shall not return, That unto me every knee shall bow, every tongue shall swear' (Isaiah 45:23).

The Word of God is a solid foundation for us to stand upon. We make decrees and proclamations in line with the Word. We stand upon the promises and declare God is faithful. We can take the Word and intercede before God. Above all, we should keep our lives in alignment with the Word.

Unlike the rabbis, who relied on the teachings and opinions that had been gathered, collated, and passed down the generations in their various Talmud's, Jesus spoke the authority of scripture. We should never, ever underestimate the authority and power of scripture, which, as we have just seen, is the Word of God.

When Jesus was led into the wilderness, he overcame the temptations by standing on the Word of God. His reply to Satan constantly was 'it is written' (Matthew 4:4). All of creation came into being through the 'word' being spoken. We are called to stand on the Word.

In the book of Leviticus, we have a chapter listing the blessings that follow obedience to the instructions given by God. Conversely, there is a list of the consequences of disobedience and turning away from the laws of God. 'But if ye will not hearken unto me, and will not do all these commandments; And if ye shall despise my statutes, or if your soul abhor my judgements, so that ye will not do all my commandments, but that ye break my covenant' (Leviticus 26:14-15). This is followed with specific consequences listed.

When we look at the history of Israel, it is as stated in Leviticus. When the Israelites turn from the Lord, their health is affected. They suffer disease of the lung, fevers, and sorrow of the heart. When they sow their seeds at harvest time, their enemies come and eat it. God removes his protection from them. If this is insufficient to cause them to repent, the punishment is multiplied seven times. The Lord states, 'And I will break the pride of your power; and I will make your heaven as iron, and your earth as brass' (Leviticus 26:19). Literally the heavens are closed, and no matter how much seeking is done, there is no reply.

God will humble the proud, for pride leads to deception and pride was at the root of Satan's fall. If this does not bring about repentance, then pestilence comes. Enemies besiege their cities and take them prisoner. 'And I will scatter you among the heathen, and will draw out a sword after you: and your land shall be desolate, and your cities waste' (Leviticus 26:33).

Throughout Jesus's lifetime, Israel lived under the authority of Rome. This was a continuation of the judgements Moses warned would happen if they forsook the Lord and turned from him. It is in this setting that Jesus comes as the Messiah, fulfilling scripture both in word and deed, and from the start he faces incredible opposition.

Failure to experience the reality of the Word of God produces a substitute. Pride takes over, and deception is complete. The antidote is found in scripture. We are told to fear the Lord, to hate evil, to hate pride, and to hate arrogance (Proverbs 8:13). The fear of the Lord covers both wisdom and knowledge. In contrast to the people, the Lord states, 'My covenant will I not break, nor alter the thing that is gone out of my lips' (Psalm 89:34).

When the apostle Paul writes to the church at Corinth, he acknowledges that they might not have been impressed by his speech, but he never used words to capture their imaginations with man's sophistry. He came in the demonstration of the power of the Holy Spirit (1 Corinthians 2:4). Paul explains that faith is based not on the wisdom of men, but on the Word of God and power of God (1 Corinthians 2:5).

Paul supplies us with a great contrast: the natural versus the spiritual. Man's wisdom is in opposition to the demonstration of the Spirit and of power. A great orator can captivate a crowd. He can gather a great following and stir up the people. But Paul is not out to impress anybody. He is not out to enhance his reputation before men. Instead, he comes in the power of the Holy Spirit to demonstrate the truth of the Word of God.

Notice what he says: 'I determined not to know any thing among you, save Jesus Christ, and him crucified' (1 Corinthians 2:2).

Paul realises that if people are saved by the power of God, they will be kept by the power of God. If people are drawn by good oratory, then they will need good oratory to keep them.

When Paul writes to the church at Thessalonica, he reiterates this same message: 'For our gospel came not unto you in word only, but also in power, and in the Holy Ghost, and in much assurance; as ye know what manner of men we were among you for your sake' (1 Thessalonians 1:5). Again, Paul lays out his priorities and highlights his conduct and character, emphasising that the Thessalonians saw a demonstration of God moving in their midst.

At Capernaum, in the synagogue, Jesus demonstrates his authority over an unclean spirit. The rulers of the synagogue hear the confession of the unclean spirit: that the one standing before them is the 'Holy one of God'. In their hand they have scripture telling them about the virgin birth, as well as the place and time of birth of their Messiah. They know the reason for the massacre of the children at Bethlehem thirty years earlier.

Thirty years later, the child whom Herod tried to kill has become a man. His name is Jesus. He preaches the Word of God with power, and the people are astonished at his doctrine. People are talking among themselves. They ask, 'What a word is this! for with authority and power he commandeth the unclean spirits, and they come out' (Luke 4:36).

Jesus comes demonstrating the power of God in signs and wonders, thereby giving the rulers ample opportunity to verify if he is the prophet like unto Moses. Their own scripture not only provides instructions for testing a true prophet but also gives details about their Messiah and what to look for to identify him.

As the Sanhedrin judges Jesus, the Sanhedrin also is being judged. The rulers are tested regarding what is in their hearts. Fear of God has given way to pride in those hearts, leading to deception.

When the apostle Paul comes along, he continues in the way of Jesus, preaching the Word of God, not with the wisdom of men. He demonstrates the power of the Holy Ghost in signs and wonders. This is an example to all believers.

CHAPTER 7

FEAST OF TABERNACLES

*Jesus answered them, my doctrine is not
mine, but his that sent me.*

John 7:16

*If any man will do his will, he shall know of the doctrine,
whether it be of God, or whether I speak of myself.*

John 7:17

The Jewish people have two calendars, one for secular purposes and one for religious observance. Religious events remind the Jewish people of how God has visited them in the past. Within the Jewish religious calendar the Feast of Tabernacles, also known as the Feast of Booths[31] is the final feast or the last of the holy days. It is called Sukkot in Hebrew and is held on the fifteenth day of the seventh month, Tishrei, which falls anywhere from late September to late October on the Gregorian calendar. The Feast of Tabernacles is an annual reminder to the people of Israel that God is the Great Shepherd who has chosen to tabernacle among them, to protect and bless them wherever they

---

[31] See appendix 4.

wander. Moses wrote that God would dwell among the children of Israel and that he would be their God (Exodus 29:45).

The Feast of Tabernacles is also called the Feast of the Lord, and in the Old Testament book of Hosea, it is very prominent.

> What will ye do in the solemn day, and in the day of the feast of the LORD? (Hosea 9:5)

> And I am the LORD thy God from the land of Egypt will yet make thee to dwell in tabernacles, as in the days of the solemn feast. (Hosea 12:9)

When Israel returned from their Babylonian captivity, this was the feast that they kept. 'They kept also the feast of tabernacles, as it is written, and offered the daily burnt offerings by number, according to the custom, as the duty of every day required' (Ezra 3:4).

This feast is connected to the name of the prophet Haggai, for his name means 'festive'. It celebrates the gathering of the harvest, a joyous time. Haggai, along with Zechariah, returned to Israel after the seventy-year captivity in Babylon. Both men prophesied when Zerubbabel was governor of Judah. Their immediate focus was the rebuilding of the Temple.

Look at Haggai's message to the people. He told them to look at all their effort and how much they had sown; they had little to show for it. They did not have enough to eat, they lacked water, and their clothes were so skimpy that they froze in them. They had holes in the bags that they put their wages in, yet they wondered why those wages disappeared (Haggai 1:6).

Haggai goes on to give a remarkable prophecy: 'The glory of this latter house shall be greater than of the former, saith the LORD of hosts: and in this place will I give peace saith the LORD of hosts' (Haggai 2:9). But peace only comes to this earth once peace is established by the Prince of Peace. That is why there is such a battle over Jerusalem. When peace comes to this earth, it will come to Jerusalem first.

It is at the Feast of Tabernacles that Jesus chooses to reveal himself and give his messianic credentials. John revealed how this was an appropriate feast by writing in the beginning of his gospel, 'And the Word was made flesh, and dwelt among us' (John 1:14). He reiterated what Moses wrote in Exodus. In other words, God in Christ physically tabernacled himself with the descendants of Abraham, Isaac, and Jacob. He came in the flesh. He is going to teach his people important doctrine, and he is going to do it in the flesh, where all can see him, hear him, and speak with him.

There are a number of other notable characteristics of this feast.

The Feast of Tabernacles is unique among the religious observances of Israel. Not only the Jewish people will hear from their Messiah; Gentiles are also invited to participate. Jesus is going to teach doctrine that Jew and Gentile can hear together! Doctrine is the truth about God. The book of Proverbs states, 'For I give you good doctrine' (Proverbs 4:2).

The prophet Isaiah states, 'And the Gentiles shall come to thy light, and kings to the brightness of thy rising' (Isaiah 60:3).

When Jesus was eight days old he was brought to the temple to be circumcised. In the temple there was a man called Simeon and the Holy Ghost was upon him. When he saw Jesus he began to prophesy over Jesus declaring that he would be 'A light to lighten the Gentiles, and the glory of thy people Israel' (Luke 2:32).

At the Feast of Tabernacles, Jesus, the Messiah, stands up and expounds how scripture is to be fulfilled. It is the unfolding of the most remarkable event in human history—the Creator of all things speaking face to face with man.

Moses wrote, 'Gather the people together, men, and women, and children, and thy stranger that is within thy gates, that they may hear, and that they may learn, and fear the LORD your God, and observe to do all the words of this law' (Deuteronomy 31:12). When the Temple was dedicated, Solomon prayed:

> Concerning the stranger, which is not of thy people Israel, but is come from a far country for thy great name's sake, and thy mighty hand, and thy stretched

out arm; if they come and pray in this house; Then hear thou from the heavens, even from thy dwelling place, and do according to all that the stranger calleth to thee for; that all people of the earth may know thy name, and fear thee, as doth thy people Israel, and may know that this house which I have built is called by thy name. (2 Chronicles 6:32-33)

The prophet Zechariah also speaks of a time coming when 'the nations which came against Jerusalem shall even go up from year to year to worship the King, the LORD of hosts, and to keep the feast of tabernacles' (Zechariah 14:16).

The feast is to last for seven days, but there is a peculiarity: the first day is a Sabbath, and so is the eighth day (Leviticus 23:39). Jonathan Cahn notes the prophetic implications by stating, 'It is the last of the holy days appointed by God, the final feast. So it speaks of what happens after the end of the end...after the end of days...the end of time. It's the very last of God's appointed days ... the mystery day.'[32] It has a prophetic element pointing to a future fulfilment. The feast, therefore, points to experiencing the exhilaration of the age to come.

The Feast of Tabernacles is an all-encompassing feast in nature. It is prophetic, which points to Christ's return. Gentiles are welcome to participate. It is revealing of how God wants to have an intimate relationship with all of his creation.

This is the feast when Jesus stands up and declares to those gathered in the Temple, 'My doctrine is not mine.' The question arises, whose doctrine is it? Who is Jesus, and what is this doctrine he is now going to share?

From Luke's testimony, Jesus is the promise given by the prophet Isaiah: 'Therefore the Lord himself shall give you a sign; Behold, a virgin shall conceive, and bear a son, and shall call his name Immanuel' (Isaiah 7:14). Therefore, Luke tells us, 'He shall be great, and shall be called the

---

[32] Jonathan Cahn, *Book of Mysteries* (Lake Mary: Charisma Media, 2016), 89.

Son of the Highest: and the Lord God shall give unto him the throne of his father David' (Luke 1:32).

That Jesus has come to do the will of his Father and to reveal his Father to us is recorded in Matthew's gospel: 'All things are delivered unto me of my Father: and no man knoweth the Son, but the Father; neither knoweth any man the Father, save the Son, and he to whomsoever the Son will reveal him' (Matthew 11:27). This is a significant revelation, for there is only One who can reveal to us God the Father, and that is Jesus Christ, the only begotten Son of God (John 1:18). Jesus is unique in the sense that the blood in his veins is God's blood. Hence the hymn writer would write, 'What can wash me whiter than snow? Nothing but the blood of Jesus.'[33] When Jesus states the doctrine is not his, scripture lets us know it is the doctrine of God the Father.

What is the will of the Father? Firstly, it is for us to believe that Jesus is who Jesus said he was—the Son of God. 'This is the work of God, that ye believe on him whom he hath sent' (John 6:29).

What is the importance of believing Jesus was sent by the Father? We can look at this question from a different angle, that of the question that was asked of Jesus by the rich young ruler. The young man wanted to know what good work he had to do to inherit eternal life (Matthew 19:16). The answer given to him was to believe in him whom God had sent. This answer is summed up for us in one of the most famous passages of scripture: 'For God so loved the world, that he gave his only begotten Son, that whosoever believeth in him should not perish, but have everlasting life' (John 3:16). God does not want anyone to perish and suffer eternal damnation. Jesus's death on the cross paid for all our sins.

This is further elaborated by John when he talks about the will of the Father. The Father wills that we believe in him whom the Father has sent. Everyone who believes in Jesus may have eternal life (John 6:40). The apostle Peter tells us the Lord does not want anyone to perish; all should come to repentance (2 Peter 3:9). Scripture is always clear: God's heart is towards you, and his message is to choose life!

---

[33] https://hymnary.org/text/what_can_wash_away_my_sin Robert Lowry

In John's gospel, we read about the great multitude that followed after Jesus. They saw miracles. They saw people healed of all kinds of diseases (John 6:2). Immediately after that was the feeding of five thousand people and the testimony of those who saw this fabulous miracle. It was their affirmation that Jesus was the prophet spoken of who was to come into the world (John 6:14).

The following day, discovering that Jesus was in Capernaum, the people came seeking after him. Jesus had so gripped their imagination that they wanted to be used in the same way. They wanted to know how to do the works of God (John 6:28). The key provided by Jesus stands for all time: 'This is the work of God, that ye believe on him whom he hath sent' (John 6:29). This truth has never diminished for those who have ears to hear and a heart open to God.

Notice how Jesus corrected the crowds by replacing the word 'works' with 'work', singular, just as he had corrected the rich young ruler. The first step is to believe in the Lord Jesus Christ.

When Jesus performed miracles—in this case, the feeding of five thousand the previous day—the people came and clamoured around him with one thing on their minds. They wanted to be able to do similar miracles. Before going any further, they asked Jesus for a sign to confirm his identity. They were looking for Jesus to do something beyond what they had already seen. In so doing, they brought up how their fathers, as they travelled through the wilderness, were fed with manna, the bread from heaven.

Jesus replied by informing them that Moses was not the one who gave their fathers manna from heaven. It was Jesus's Father who provided them with the true bread from heaven (John 6:32). Jesus thus revealed to them that he was the true bread from heaven who gave life to the world. The sad part of this episode came when Jesus told them that those who had seen the Son and believed would have everlasting life, but they who saw him now believed not.

On another occasion, Jesus was at the Temple during the Feast of Dedication. He was besieged by the Jews to tell them plainly if he was the Christ. He told them bluntly that they had seen the miracles which were done by his Father as a witness that Jesus had not come on his own, but had been sent by his Father. They had not believed because they were not of the sheep his Father had given Jesus.

What really provoked the Jews was Jesus's confirmation that he and the Father were one (John 10:30). What a powerful statement! The creator God stood in their midst in human form. We can catch a glimpse of the turmoil this revelation brought.

From a Jewish perspective, the significance of believing and following what Jesus was telling them is given in Matthew's gospel. It provides details about how entrance to the kingdom of heaven is achieved through obedience to the will of the Father (Matthew 7:21). The kingdom of heaven is the physical kingdom where Jesus will sit on the throne of David, as told by Luke: 'He shall be great, and shall be called the Son of the Highest: and the Lord God shall give unto him the throne of his father David' (Luke 1:32).

Furthermore, just as Jesus had a relationship with his Father, his people can have a relationship with Jesus. 'For whosoever shall do the will of my Father which is in heaven, the same is my brother, and sister, and mother' (Matthew 12:50). This again speaks of God dwelling with us. It is intimacy, and it is being part of a family—God's family.

This relationship between Jesus and his Father is emphasised throughout scripture. We are told clearly that if we deny Jesus in front of men, then Jesus will deny us before his Father in heaven (Matthew 10:33). Jesus reminds us of the intricacies of this relationship and its importance: 'All things are delivered unto me of my Father: and no man knoweth the Son, but the Father; neither knoweth any man the Father, save the Son, and he to whomsoever the Son will reveal him' (Matthew 11:27).

According to scripture, Jesus delayed his coming to the Feast of Tabernacles and his entering the Temple in Jerusalem. Meanwhile, lots of rumours circulated among the people. The rumours were wide-ranging, covering the full spectrum of people's opinions. Some said Jesus was a good man. Others said he deceived the people (John 7:12). So the people of Israel were divided, and this division was only exacerbated by the Sanhedrin, who had oversight in the teaching of the Law and the Prophets. The Sanhedrin resolutely opposed Jesus. The most influential of them were the most vociferous opponents of Jesus. As a result, any who did believe in Jesus kept it quiet.

When Jesus eventually showed up and demonstrated his credentials, both in the words he spoke and the authority he exercised, the division did not diminish among the people. Some accused Jesus of having a devil (John 7:20). Others asked if their religious leaders knew that Jesus was the very Christ (John 7:26). Then we read of all the commotion as people's opinions fly back and forth. Some declared Jesus a prophet (John 7:40). Others voiced their belief that he was the Christ (John 7:41). Still others rebutted this view and accused the believers of being deceived (John 7:47).

Although Jesus's identification of himself as the Messiah stunned those who heard him, in the midst of this controversy, nobody seems to have paid attention to Jesus's words. 'If any man will do his will, he shall know of the doctrine, whether it be of God, or whether I speak of myself' (John 7:17) provides the foundation to test if Jesus doctrine is true or false. There is this sequence 'do his will' and then 'you will know'. The first step for those who are wavering, for those seeking to know the truth, and for those who are custodians of scripture is to follow the instructions given here by Jesus.

If you pay close attention to this event, you will note that many people had opinions, but no one availed themselves of the means to verify Jesus's credentials as the true Messiah.

Jesus repeatedly let it be known of his dependence upon his Father, and that he could do nothing of himself. What his Father reveals to him is what he declares to the people. Therefore, any judgments he makes are true, for they are not his own will but that of his Father (John 5:30). Jesus repeats this message, stating, 'For I came down from heaven, not to do mine own will, but the will of him that sent me' (John 6:38). This speaks of the incarnation—'God became flesh'—and the humanity of Jesus Christ. In his humanity Jesus experienced all the emotions of this life: the pain, suffering, joy, sorrows, and temptations. He thereby was able to identify with every temptation that a person experiences here on earth.

This is important. We have a scene from heaven described to us in the book of Zechariah:

> And he shewed me Joshua the high priest standing before the angel of the LORD, and Satan standing at his right hand to resist him. And the LORD said unto Satan, The LORD rebuke thee, O Satan; even the LORD that hath chosen Jerusalem rebuke thee: is not this a brand plucked out of the fire? (3:1–2)

This scene from heaven is remarkable. In heaven, Jesus does not rebuke Satan. At this juncture, Satan can easily make accusations against God and taunt God, asking him what he knows about suffering and pain and living in a body of flesh. Satan stands before the Lord— that is, he stood before Jehovah. Satan is very brash. He thinks nothing of accusing the Lord to his face.

Then Jesus turns up, and he turns up as a man in a body of flesh. And in a body of flesh, after forty days of fasting, Jesus stands his ground against Satan. When Satan tempts him, he resists and rebukes Satan by speaking the words of scripture. As a man, Jesus shows us how to defeat Satan!

The major event that Jesus spoke about over and over was the sacrifice that he was going to make by laying down his life. This was in fulfilment of the promise God gave when he said, 'I will put enmity between thee and the woman, and between thy seed and her seed; it shall bruise thy head, and thou shalt bruise his heel' (Genesis 3:15). Jesus is born to die, but not just any ordinary death—the sinless Son of God is going to take our place and receive the punishment that is rightly ours. 'For he hath made him to be sin for us, who knew no sin; that we might be made the righteousness of God in him' (2 Corinthians 5:21). Jesus suffers in our place, and the wrath of God is poured upon him!

Jesus confidently tells us, 'Therefore doth my Father love me, because I lay down my life, that I might take it again' (John 10:17). Jesus also says some other things to his disciples in advance of the crucifixion. He uses the phrase 'then shall ye know' (John 8:28). He talks of a specific day when that will come to pass (John 14:20). Jesus is telling his disciples how he will be lifted up and crucified. When that day comes, they will know that everything he has taught and done was according to scripture and what his Father taught him. Not only that, they will understand the unity of the Father and himself, and his disciples will become part of that unity.

In Gethsemane the full revelation of the wrath of God was revealed to Jesus. The extremity of what lay before him caused him to sweat great drops of blood. Angels had to come to minister unto him. A full revelation of the wrath of God was given to him, because Jesus had to be willing to go to the cross to be offered up for sin. He was not going in ignorance. The death on the cross is described in Hebrew as 'deaths'. The singular cannot contain nor describe the death that Jesus suffers for humanity.

The gift of eternal life comes at a great cost. The gift is offered to everyone who wants eternal life. If you do not want this gift, in effect, you are willing to pay the price of your own sin. Scripture states you will perish. In scripture, to perish never means annihilation. Scripture emphasises that each individual is an eternal being. Life does not end when one's body is put in a grave.

The Lord Jesus Christ himself continually emphasised that man is an eternal being. Jesus during his ministry quotes one verse from Isaiah more often than any other verse: 'And they shall go forth, and look upon the carcases of the men that have transgressed against me: for their worm shall not die, neither shall their fire be quenched; and they shall be an abhorring unto all flesh' (Isaiah 66:24). These quotations are as follows:

Where their worm dieth not, and the fire is not quenched (Mark 9:44)

Where their worm dieth not, and the fire is not quenched (Mark 9:46)

To be cast into hell, into the fire that never shall be quenched (Mark 9:45)

He will burn up the chaff with unquenchable fire (Matthew 3:12)

Shall be in danger of hell fire (Matthew 5:22)

Every tree that bringeth not forth good fruit is hewn down, and cast into the fire (Matthew 7:19)

As therefore the tares are gathered and burned in the fire; so shall it be in the end of this world (Matthew 13:40)

And shall cast them into a furnace of fire: there shall be wailing and gnashing of teeth (Matthew 13:42)

And shall cast them into a furnace of fire: there shall be wailing and gnashing of teeth (Matthew 13:50)

It is better for thee to enter into life halt or maimed, rather than ... to be cast into everlasting fire (Matthew 18:8)

It is better for thee to enter into life with one eye, rather than two eyes to be cast into hell fire (Matthew 18:9)

Depart from me, ye cursed, into everlasting fire prepared for the devil and his angels (Matthew 25:41)

If a man abide not in me, he is cast forth as a branch, and is withered; and men gather them, and cast them into the fire, and they are burned (John 15:6)

Mark's gospel and Luke's gospel also have many of the teachings of Jesus recorded on this subject.

At the centre of all that Jesus taught, the most powerful message was that of forgiveness. When Peter asked Jesus how often he should forgive a person who did him wrong, Jesus answered that he should forgive seventy times seven. This is significant in itself, but there is something much more profound. Jesus explains that if you are unwilling to forgive men their sin who sin against you, then your Father in heaven is not going to forgive you of your sin (Matthew 6:15).

This passage in many ways matches up with Paul's writing to the Philippian church. He tells them to work out their own salvation and to do it in fear and trembling (Philippians 2:12). Paul, when he writes to the Ephesians, also emphasises the importance of forgiveness when he lays out how they should forgive one another and be kind to one another even as Christ has forgiven them (Ephesians 4:32).

Many people struggle and find it hard to forgive. There are some crimes which are horrific and leave people's lives in ruins. People can be thrown into situations that are not of their own making and are outside their control. The thought of offering forgiveness may look and feel totally unachievable, let alone reasonable. In fact, bitterness and hatred can easily take root as a person reacts to and tries to come to terms with what they have experienced.

In scripture, when you forgive a person, you are not saying what they did was right. Forgiveness in scripture is actually a mechanism for setting you free. It is meant to stop bitterness and hatred becoming your prison and consuming your whole life. Forgiveness does not come easily, and in the end it is a choice you make. Offering forgiveness is really an exchange that takes place. You are handing over to God, the righteous judge, the person who caused you pain. That person is God's to deal with, so that healing can begin to take place in your heart and in your life.

The first mention in scripture of such forgiveness is found in the story of Joseph. Joseph was betrayed by his brothers and sold as a slave. Many years later, a severe famine arose, and his brothers came to Egypt. By this time Joseph's position was second to Pharaoh. After his brothers learned who he was, out of fear they beseeched Joseph to forgive them. I once heard R. D. Kendall preach a powerful sermon on how Joseph not only forgave his brothers, but gave them the words to speak to their father Jacob. Jacob never found out what really happened to Joseph. The sins of Joseph's brothers were covered by forgiveness.

One of the more well-known verses of scripture concerns our responsibility to humble ourselves before God, pray, seek his face, and turn from our wicked ways. If we do this, God says he will hear us from heaven. He will forgive our sin, and he will heal our land (2 Chronicles 7:14).

The apostle Paul, writing to the church at Thessalonica, tells them that the will of God for them is sanctification and to keep clear from fornication (1 Thessalonians 4:3). In a Christian context, sanctification literally means to be set apart for the purposes of God. It is tied in with being holy.

We can get an understanding by looking at the Old Testament. Israel was called to be a holy nation separate from all other nations. Within their ranks they had people set apart for different functions, such as the Levites, the priests, and the high priest. Each had a holy calling.

In the New Testament, every Christian is called into a life of holiness. Peter unpacks this by declaring, 'But ye are a chosen generation, a royal priesthood, an holy nation, a peculiar people; that ye should shew forth the praises of him who hath called you out of darkness into his marvellous light' (1 Peter 2:9). This passage clearly gives the reason why God wants you to be sanctified: it is for his glory. Jesus states the means by which sanctification takes place in our lives when he prays to his Father, 'Sanctify them through thy truth: thy word is truth' (John 17:17).

The Feast of Tabernacles is the occasion for Jesus to come and tabernacle with his people. He provides evidence of his messianic identity. He chooses this particular feast because it is open to all people of all races. This was spelled out in the Old Testament by Moses and Solomon. Jesus is fulfilling scripture by bringing light to the Gentiles and glory to Israel, a sign of a time to come when all the nations will worship God at Jerusalem.

Jesus makes it abundantly clear that his words are the words of his Father and gives his commission: 'For I came down from heaven, not to do mine own will, but the will of him that sent me' (John 6:38). That will is that they should believe in the Lord Jesus Christ, for he came with the signs and wonders according to the word of Moses. A condition is given by Jesus whereby they might know for certain that Jesus is the promised Messiah: 'If any man will do his will, he shall know of the doctrine, whether it be of God' (John 7:17). Furthermore, entrance to the kingdom of heaven is by 'doing the will of the Father' (Matthew 7:21). The physical kingdom of heaven is at hand if the words of Jesus are believed.

Jesus comes to fulfil scripture and to eradicate forever the sin problem. 'Therefore doth my Father love me, because I lay down my life, that I might take it again' (John 10:17). The enormity of the cost for God to redeem man can never be underestimated. 'In whom we have redemption through his blood, the forgiveness of sins, according to the riches of his grace' (Ephesians 1:7). The enormity of what man is being saved from likewise can never be underestimated: eternal damnation. The gift is offered to all, forgiveness of sins and a calling to be separate and follow Jesus into a destiny indescribable. The greatest gift of all and the unveiling of this truth took place at the Feast of Tabernacles.

CHAPTER 8

QUESTIONING OF JESUS BY THE HIGH PRIEST

*The high priest then asked Jesus of his
disciples, and of his doctrine.*

John 18:19

The questioning of Jesus by the high priest took place when Jesus was taken from the garden of Gethsemane to be tried by the Sanhedrin for what they believed to be blasphemy: Jesus making himself out to be the Son of God. By the time this trial took place, the priests no doubt had collated a portfolio of all of Jesus's teachings and doctrines.

If there was one thing that really upset the whole religious establishment, it came down to their own ideas of what was permissible and what was not permissible to be done on the Sabbath day. From their perspective, miracles were not to take place on the Sabbath— full stop! When the disciples plucked some corn on the Sabbath, 'the Pharisees saw it, they said unto him, Behold, thy disciples do that which is not lawful to do upon the Sabbath day' (Matthew 12:2). On another occasion, in the middle of Jesus preaching in the Temple, the chief priests and elders interrupted him, demanding to know who gave him authority (Matthew 21:23).

Therefore, when Jesus healed a person or did some miracle on the Sabbath, it always, inevitably, degenerated into a major confrontation. The question would then arise: Whose authority gives you the right to heal on the Sabbath? It was only a small step from that to bringing up and questioning Jesus's doctrine.

In a way, this questioning of Jesus reminds us of the story of the blind man who received his sight after Jesus made mud by spitting on some dirt and then anointed the blind man's eyes with it (John 9:6). We are told this man was brought to the Pharisees on the Sabbath. It is insightful to follow the interrogation this man went through, for it gives a picture of the intensity of the interrogation that Jesus would endure at the hands of these same people.

Some of the Pharisees who questioned the formerly blind man denied that Jesus was a man of God. The reason? The miracle took place on the Sabbath day (John 9:16). It is amusing to note that the Pharisees demanded that this man tell them what he thought of Jesus. A formerly blind man, uneducated, unable to read or write, a beggar all his life, untrained in theology, was asked to give his opinion about Jesus after receiving his sight. Incredible!

The harshness of the Pharisees' response to such a wonderful miracle is revealed in the way they called this man's parents. They were called because the Jews did not believe the man had been blind. So the man was subjected to the most intense bombardment of questioning, and that bombardment continued when his parents were brought before the Pharisees: Is this your son? Was he born blind? How is it he can now see (John 9:19)?

On a further two occasions the man was brought before the Pharisees. They did not like the man's responses, so he was reviled and accused of being one of Jesus's disciples (John 9:28). The people who did this had no compassion. They were cruel and heartless. They could not rejoice with this man over the miracle he had received.

The story of the blind man's sight being restored and the reaction it provoked from the Pharisees lets us know the Pharisees' attacks on Jesus were scathing. They were out to pull him down and besmirch his name. Their hardness of heart warped their questioning of the Saviour about his doctrine.

When it came to Jesus's disciples, the Pharisees found them a thorn in their flesh. We know from the book of Acts what the Pharisees thought about Peter and John: they were unlearned and ignorant fishermen (Acts 4:13). How is it possible that they could be used of God? Were they Levites? Were they priests? As mentioned, we also know when the disciples plucked the ears of corn, they were accused of doing 'that which is not lawful to do upon the Sabbath day' (Matthew 12:2).

From this, we have a good idea how vicious the questioning of Jesus would be. We know Jesus was challenged many times on his authority, for we read, 'When he was come into the temple, the chief priests and the elders of the people came unto him as he was teaching, and said, By what authority doest thou these things? and who gave thee this authority?' (Matthew 21:23).

Earlier on in Jesus's ministry, the question that arose was the legality of undertaking healings on the Sabbath (Matthew 12:10). We know the Pharisees did not ask this question from any other motive than that they might have something to accuse Jesus with. Jesus had already dealt with that issue. He told the Pharisees in plain words that the Sabbath was given for man, not the other way around (Mark 2:27). He further told them of his lordship over the Sabbath as the Son of Man (Mark 2:28). Jesus gave them his credentials. They were supposed to be the people of the Book, knowing all that was in the Law, the Prophets, and the Writings.

Jesus had one question after another thrown at him: Why did you heal on the Sabbath? Why are you constantly breaking the Sabbath and not keeping it holy? Who gives you that authority? Where did you come from? What did you mean when you stated you are not of this world? How can you rebuild the Temple in three days? Jesus was more than able to withstand their onslaught. And the onslaught was continuous!

When Jesus was taken before Annas and Caiaphas, the high priests, they had already let it be known it was expedient that one man should die for the people (John 18:14). This was said by Caiaphas even before the questioning of Jesus began. This is what we call a kangaroo trial:

give an appearance of following the law though in fact the decision has long been made. Before Jesus was even interrogated, the outcome had already been decided.

Every year the high priest went into the Holy of Holies to offer a sacrifice for the sins of the people. But when Jesus came before the priests, they said one man should die for the people. That one man was the sinless Son of God, for the blood that flowed through Jesus was not the blood of Adam but the blood of God. 'Take heed therefore unto yourselves, and to all the flock, over the which the Holy Ghost hath made you overseers, to feed the church of God, which he hath purchased with his own blood' (Acts 20:28).

Scripture goes on to state, 'Neither by the blood of goats and calves, but by his own blood he entered in once into the holy place, having obtained eternal redemption for us' (Hebrews 9:12). The same idea is captured by the hymn writer who wrote, 'What can wash away my sin? Nothing but the blood of Jesus; What can make me whole again? Nothing but the blood of Jesus.'[34]

But Caiaphas did not believe Jesus was the Son of God nor that the blood that flowed through Jesus's veins was God's blood. Even when Caiaphas asked Jesus about his deity directly and received an answer in the affirmative, Caiaphas did not believe and went on to rent his clothes (Mark 14:63).

From time to time in the history of the Jewish nation, we find two high priests serving at the same time. This was the case at the time of Jesus. Scripture informs us that both Annas and Caiaphas were serving as high priests when John the Baptist was in the wilderness (Luke 3:2). When Jesus was brought before them, it is worth paying particular attention to what transpired. Their verdict on Jesus was one of blasphemy against God (Matthew 26:65). Then they began to abuse Jesus, spitting in his face and buffeting him while others smote Jesus with their hands (Matthew 26:67). Annas and Caiaphas declared over Jesus the sin of blasphemy while they laid their hands on him.

---

[34] https://hymnary.org/text/what_can_wash_away_my_sin Robert Lowry

This was a remarkable, really a stunning action by these men, especially since we know the role and duties of priests. When a person came before a priest with an animal to be sacrificed, the priest would put his hand on the sacrifice and declare the person's sin over the animal before it was killed. The animal, being a substitute to cover the person's sin, literally stood in that person's place. Here, before Jesus was crucified, the high priests laid hands on him. They pronounced their own sin on the Messiah—their blasphemy—and then had Jesus led away to be tried by Pontius Pilate and crucified.

In reply to the Pharisees' question about his doctrine, Jesus responded that he preached openly in the synagogues (Luke 4:44) and taught in the Temple while the feast was being celebrated (John 7:14). By bringing this up, Jesus was highlighting the wickedness of the ruling religious elite. He had not been hiding from them. They could have sent soldiers to arrest him at any time. Instead, Jesus was arrested and brought before the Sanhedrin when the city was asleep.

Jesus was interrogated, abused, and tortured. False witnesses were bribed to testify against him. The Law of Moses was nowhere to be seen; instead, it was flagrantly ignored.

At this interrogation, something else remarkable took place. How many times have you heard that you should turn the other cheek as a Christian? It is found in Jesus's Sermon on the Mount, when Jesus taught that when you are smitten on your right cheek, you should turn your head so that your attackers can smite you on the other cheek (Matthew 5:39).

It is good to be reminded that this is part of the constitution of the kingdom that was at hand. Scripture tells us to rightly divide the word of truth (2 Timothy 2:15). At his interrogation, Jesus did not turn the other cheek when he was hit by his abusers. He turned and said that if he had spoken or done some evil, they should tell him what it was. If he had not done evil, they should tell him why they smite him (John 18:23).

Is that not interesting? Jesus refused to turn the other cheek! Jesus brought up the law before them!

This encounter reminds us to have our hearts right with God. The high priests Annas and Caiaphas were not interested in knowing the true identity of Jesus. Nor were they really interested in his doctrine and that of his disciples. They had already made up their minds that they wanted Jesus to be killed. We know they consulted discreetly about how this could be achieved (Matthew 26:4). Throughout Jesus's ministry, this was a major objective. 'After these things Jesus walked in Galilee: for he would not walk in Jewry, because the Jews sought to kill him' (John 7:1).

In fact we read:

- How they might destroy him (Matthew 12:14)
- How they might entangle him (Matthew 22:15)
- How they might destroy him (Mark 3:6)
- How they might take him by craft (Mark 14:1)
- How they might kill him (Luke 22:2)

When people's hearts are so wicked, no number of miracles and no amount of preaching the Word of God makes any impact. We find written that the more they hear the Word and continually reject the Word, the more hearts harden. They reach a place where there is no remedy (Proverbs 29:1). The end result is that revelation becomes hidden from their eyes, and they go on to commit the greatest catastrophe imaginable. The psalmist David tells us what it is when he states emphatically, 'I shall be innocent from the great transgression' (Psalm 19:13). The custodians who were to teach the people the paths of righteousness and truth ended up committing the great transgression: they crucified their own Messiah.

Jesus's words to the scribes and Pharisees were direct and devastating. Notice that Jesus never minced his words. Jesus exposed their hypocrisy. 'Woe unto you, scribes and Pharisees, hypocrites! for ye are like unto whited sepulchres, which indeed appear beautiful outward, but are within full of dead men's bones, and of all uncleanness' (Matthew 23:27). Their outward appearance displayed all the paraphernalia of the life of God. They projected themselves as being holy while in fact there was no life in them; they were dead. They had nothing to give. They were like the fig tree Jesus cursed. From the outside, they looked the part, but inside, they bore no fruit.

How did they get into that position? Well, we know what happened when the remnant of the Jews returned from Babylon. Ezra brought out the book of the Law of Moses in the sight of all the people. The people stood up to listen as the Word was read out to them (Nehemiah 8:5). Certain men and Levites fulfilled their duties by helping the people to understand and comprehend the Law (Nehemiah 8:7). The result of understanding God's 'words' brought 'great mirth' (Nehemiah 8:12).

They went on to keep the commandment to keep the Feast of Booths, known as Sukkot, which they had not kept since the days of Joshua (Nehemiah 8:14). This feast was kept for seven days, under the leadership of Nehemiah and Ezra, by all those who returned to Israel and Jerusalem.

From the days of Ezra and Nehemiah, a deterioration certainly set in. Was it due to the space of four hundred years with no prophet showing up? Possibly. One thing is for certain: not in a million years would they have imagined that when the Messiah showed up, they would not recognise him. That would have been the furthest thing from their minds. Yet, when their Messiah did show up, they did not recognise him as such. They did not believe his words. His replication of miracles their forefathers experienced in the wilderness made no impact. Seeing extraordinary miracles never moved them. When they heard the confessions of unclean spirits as to who Jesus was and what his authority was, they closed their ears. They rebelled against the Holy One of Israel, just like their forefathers, and broke the Law of Moses in the process.

How did they get into that condition? The Pharisees no doubt began with good intentions, probably wanting to separate themselves from the things of the world and seek a life of holiness. They separated themselves to have encounters with God, remembering all the miracles God had done in their nation throughout their history.

However, as generations came and went and no prophet arose in the land, changes could have imperceptibly taken place without the people being fully conscious of their impact. When the power of God is not visible, religion puts alternatives in place to explain the change. It only takes small, imperceptible steps to head in a direction that ends up living in the flesh, having an outward form of religion, and relying on self-righteousness.

This self-righteousness led the Pharisees to oppose their own Messiah. This self-righteousness separated them from their God. They finished up with the audacity to question the authority and doctrine of their Messiah. Worse still, they connived with false witnesses to put to death their Messiah on a Roman cross.

PART II

THE MYSTERIES OF GOD TO BE PROCLAIMED BY FAITHFUL STEWARDS

CHAPTER 9

MYSTERY OF GODLINESS

And without controversy great is the mystery of
godliness: God was manifest in the flesh.

1 Timothy 3:16

W hen Paul writes to young Timothy, he shares with him one of the most amazing revelations that has ever been written: 'God was manifest in the flesh' (1 Timothy 3:16). It is an incredible revelation. Paul is saying that God turned up on this earth and lived in a body of human flesh. From scripture, we have witness statements of how people saw him. They touched him and handled him, 'That which was from the beginning, which we have heard, which we have seen with our eyes, which we have looked upon, and our hands have handled, of the Word of life' (1 John 1:1).

The outstanding thing about the mystery of godliness is that God appeared in the flesh. It spanned the time horizon from Jesus's birth till he was caught up to glory. John attested to this when he declared, 'In the beginning was the Word, and the Word was with God, and the Word was God' (John 1:1). John unravels this statement: 'the Word was made flesh, and dwelt among us, (and we beheld his glory, the glory as of the only begotten of the Father,) full of grace and truth' (John 1:14).

It is the greatest verse in the Bible that speaks of the deity of the Lord Jesus Christ.

Spurgeon, who is known as the 'Prince of Preachers' writes, 'This is one of the most extraordinary doctrines declared in human hearing, for were it not well attested, it would be absolutely incredible that the Infinite God who fills all things, who Was and Is, and Is to Come, the Almighty, the Omniscient, and the Omnipresent, actually condescended to veil Himself in the garments of our inferior clay.' He goes on to say, 'This is a mystery surpassing all comprehension.'[35]

No wonder Paul told Timothy, 'Without controversy great is the mystery of godliness.' How could it be that the One who created all things and maintains all things by the Word of his power took on the form of man and was born into this world as a helpless babe (Hebrews 1:3)? The God of eternity was manifested in time, from a world where time is non-existent into a world where everything is constrained by time and where everything waxes old and decays.

The Son of God, the Creator of the world, came into this world as a baby. He was born in a stable in Bethlehem, Judea, as foretold by the prophet: 'But thou, Bethlehem Ephratah, though thou be little among the thousands of Judah, yet out of thee shall he come forth unto me that is to be ruler in Israel; whose goings forth have been from of old, from everlasting' (Micah 5:2).

Jesus's birth is extraordinary. It is a virgin birth. Jesus does not carry the DNA of Adam; he carries the DNA of God. His birth was prophesied in the days of Ahaz, king of Judah, by Isaiah: 'Therefore the Lord himself shall give you a sign; Behold, a virgin shall conceive, and bear a son, and shall call his name Immanuel' (Isaiah 7:14). Immanuel mean 'God is with us'. Mary, his mother, and Joseph, his stepfather, are given the incredible responsibility to protect and oversee the growth of this child. No wonder the angels look on in such awe. Scripture states Jesus never took on the nature of angels, but he took on the seed of Abraham (Hebrews 2:16).

---

[35] The Spurgeon Center, https://www.spurgeon.org/resource-library/sermons/the-great-mystery-of-godliness.

We read of Jesus's supernatural birth, the visit of the wise men, Herod's attempt on his life, and his family fleeing to Egypt. These events make us aware that Jesus is no ordinary person. The next instalment of his life occurs at the Temple in Jerusalem, when he is twelve years old. Those with whom he debated or who heard him were taken aback by his answers and were astonished at his understanding of scripture (Luke 2:47).

There are no other records of any youthful preaching, nor did he do any miracles during his early years. The only other information on Jesus's life before his ministry began is that he apprenticed to become a carpenter.

Jesus began his ministry in Cana of Galilee, where he turned water into wine. However, before that miracle took place, scripture describes how he increased in wisdom and stature, having favour with both God and man (Luke 2:52).

A further insight into Jesus's life is provided by the writer to the Hebrews, who states that Jesus, though being the Son, still had to learn obedience by the things he suffered (Hebrews 5:8). Jesus in his humanity, man of very man, experiences what it is like to live in a body of flesh. Therefore, it is written, 'For we have not an high priest which cannot be touched with the feeling of our infirmities; but was in all points tempted like as we are, yet without sin' (Hebrews 4:15).

When John the Baptist was baptising people at the River Jordan, Jesus came to be baptised. This was when John the Baptist made a bold statement: 'Behold the Lamb of God, which taketh away the sin of the world' (John 1:29). How does Jesus take away sin? We are 'purchased with his own blood' (Acts 20:28). We are not purchased by the blood of bulls, nor the blood of goats, nor the blood of any other animal. Animal blood does not take away our sin. But the blood of God does. It washes us clean. It is eternal blood! There is power in the blood of Jesus, and the great news for sinners is that his blood never loses its power.

Furthermore, the one who declared Jesus to be the Lamb of God was not only a prophet, he was a priest in the lineage of Aaron. His priestly duty was to ensure that the sacrifice to be offered for sin was without blemish. At the River Jordan, John the Baptist declared Jesus the perfect sacrifice—there was no blemish, no sin in him.

Many remarkable things can be highlighted in the life of Jesus. He feeds the multitude but allows himself to suffer hunger. He casts out devils but goes into the wilderness and is tempted by the Devil. Scripture states Jesus was 'in all points tempted like as we are, yet without sin' (Hebrews 4:15). God allows himself to be tempted. It is unfathomable.

Therefore, Jesus can identify with each individual's temptation. More than that, Jesus demonstrates how to get the victory over temptation by using the Word of God as a sword. Peter encourages us to submit ourselves to God and resist the devil. In this way, we will see how powerful God's Word really is (James 4:7). We resist by quoting the Word of God just like Jesus did.

When thinking about Jesus, a number of things can capture our imagination. There are the miracles that people saw, the preaching that people heard, his authority over nature, and his power over the demonic realm. What an extraordinary a privilege for the disciples to be in the company of Jesus for a space of three and half years.

Yet scripture reveals to us a glimpse that few consider: 'He is despised and rejected of men; a man of sorrows and acquainted with grief' (Isaiah 53:3). It is very hard for us to comprehend how people see incredible miracles before their eyes, marvel at the words spoken, and yet reject the Son of God. He is despised. He experiences rejection. Amid the healings and miracles people see performed, they are unaware of the sorrow and grief Jesus endures. People have contempt for him. Scripture states he came to his own and they rejected him. He experiences deep stress and disappointment. There is grief. There is intense sorrow. He weeps over Jerusalem, for he knows the destruction that is to come and the plight its inhabitants will find themselves in. His entire ministry is one of conflict and opposition. Yet the Saviour of the world came with one purpose: to lay his life down for us.

Paul expands on the mystery, telling us that not only was God manifest in the flesh, but also 'justified in the Spirit' (1 Timothy 3:16). The work of redemption, the sacrifice of Jesus on the cross at Calvary—in the eyes of those involved in the crucifixion, they were getting rid of a troublemaker who did not fit into their religious world. They condemned Jesus. On the cross, Jesus cried out that it was finished (John 19:30). This was the culmination of his earthly ministry, which began by him being conceived when the Holy Spirit overshadowed Mary. Therefore, scripture tells us Jesus was 'declared to be the Son of God with power, according to the spirit of holiness, by the resurrection from the dead' (Romans 1:4).

When it came to the day of Pentecost, Spurgeon notes, 'The Holy Spirit bore witness with signs and miracles, and wondrous gifts, that he who professed to be the incarnate Deity was most surely God and the saviour of men.'[36]

Angels beheld God's plan of redemption being put into action. They saw the birth of Jesus and the wise men who came to the stable to worship. They participated in announcing the good news to shepherds watching their sheep. They must have been completely amazed as they pondered what scripture revealed about man in relation to God's plan. They asked what was so special about man that God would lift him up and set his heart upon him (Job 7:17). The psalmist asked a similar question (Psalm 8:4). The psalmist comes back to the same question in Psalm 144, asking what is so special about man that God takes account of him.

Those same angels ministered to Jesus during his three and half years of ministry. Firstly, they came to him in the wilderness after he had fasted forty days and overcome the temptations laid before him by Satan (Matthew 4:11). An angel ministered to Jesus in the garden of Gethsemane, where 'being in an agony he prayed more earnestly: and his sweat was as it were great drops of blood falling down to the ground' (Luke 22:44).

This was after Jesus had prayed to his Father with a request that, if possible, the cup before him be removed. Yet he submitted not to his own will, but to the will of his Father (Luke 22:42). In Gethsemane, the full revelation of the judgement and wrath of God on sin was revealed to Jesus. Therefore, Jesus went up Mount Calvary willingly, knowing

---

[36] Ibid.

what was to come. He did not go up in ignorance. The extremity of the revelation caused great drops of blood to fall onto the ground. No wonder he needed an angel to strengthen him!

That this message of the cross is preached to the Gentiles is just incredible. It was to the Jewish nation the oracles of God were given. Paul, writing to the church at Ephesus, reminds them of this and says, 'ye were without Christ, being aliens from the commonwealth of Israel, and strangers from the covenants of promise, having no hope, and without God in the world' (Ephesians 2:12). Jewish apostles declared this message to the Gentiles.

Spurgeon writes, 'If you had told an intelligent Jew that some of his fellow countrymen would become apostles to the Gentiles, to declare that the wall which surrounded the favoured nation was broken down, he would have smiled incredulously, and exclaimed, "Impossible!"'[37] Yet the apostle to the Gentiles, when he gives his credentials, states that he was 'Circumcised the eight day, of the stock of Israel, of the tribe of Benjamin, an Hebrew of the Hebrews; as touching the law, a Pharisee' (Philippians 3:5).

For over two thousand years the preaching of the cross has been believed throughout the world. What began with a handful of disciples obeying the command of Jesus to take this good news into all the world has changed the destiny of individuals and the destiny of nations (Mark 16:15). Perhaps the earliest disciples' commitment to spreading the gospel is best summed up by Andrew, a fisherman, who brought his brother Peter to Jesus. It is recorded in *Foxe's Book of Martyrs* that, when faced with death and commanded not to preach, Andrew stated that he 'would not preach the honour and glory of the cross, if he had feared the death of the cross.'[38]

Scripture informs us God's method of reaching people is through the preaching of his Word (1 Corinthians 1:12). The result of the early disciples obeying the instructions of the Saviour was the demise of Diana of the Ephesians; Apollo, the god of the sun; Mars, the Roman

---

[37] Ibid.

[38] W. G. Berry, *Foxe's Book of Martyrs* (Grand Rapids, MI: Baker Book House, 1997), 8.

god of war; and Venus. Along with them were destroyed Bacchus, Ceres, Cupid, Fauna, Flora, Fortuna, Janus, Juno, Jupiter, Mercury, Minerva, Neptune, Pluto, Saturn, Vesta, Vulcan, and a whole host of lesser deities—and that was only in the Roman Empire. Though preaching the cross was considered foolish by the world, it was God's ordained way of demonstrating his power (1 Corinthians 1:18).

Jesus, scripture tells us, was received into glory. Before this event took place, 'he shewed himself alive after his passion by many infallible proofs, being seen of them forty days, and speaking of the things pertaining to the kingdom of God' (Acts 1:3). His instruction to his followers was to wait in Jerusalem until they received power. On the day of Pentecost, one hundred and twenty were gathered together, praying, when the Holy Spirit came upon them. Before that took place, 'they looked stedfastly toward heaven as he went up, behold, two men stood by them in white apparel; Which also said, Ye men of Galilee, why stand ye gazing up into heaven? this same Jesus, which is taken up from you into heaven, shall so come in like manner as ye have seen him go into heaven' (Acts 1:10- 11).

CHAPTER 10

MYSTERY OF THE DIVINE INDWELLING

Even the mystery which hath been hid from ages and from
generations, but now is made manifest to his saints:
To whom God would make known what is the riches
of the glory of this mystery among the Gentiles;
which is Christ in you, the hope of glory.

Colossians 1:26–27

In the letter to the Colossians, Paul brings to them a mystery which had been concealed and unknown to past generations: 'Christ in you the hope of glory'. It's a revelation that had remained dormant and hidden up to the time of the apostle Paul, but now, the Holy Spirit, removed the veil of this wonderful truth which we will now look at.

The gospels reveal two aspects of the work of Christ: that which is done for us and that which is done in us. Writing in 1895, James M. Campbell states:

> Many think almost exclusively of what Christ has done
> for them, and overlook what He is doing in them; they
> look at redemption upon the divine side as a finished
> work, and fail to look at it upon the human side as a

continuous work; they are so much taken up with the idea of Christ dying upon the cross for their offences as almost to forget that He is living in their hearts to guide, to inspire, to bless, to save.[39]

This revelation makes it clear that we do not look outside ourselves to find God's direction and guidance for our lives. We do not look outside ourselves to find answers to prayer, for Christ is in us. He is the indwelling Christ and 'in him dwelleth all the fullness of the Godhead bodily' (Colossians 2:9). We need this inward revelation of Christ to produce the life of God in us.

What Paul writes is also his testimony of the reality in his own life. It is how he was transformed. 'But when it pleased God, who separated me from my mother's womb, and called me by his grace, To reveal his Son in me, that I might preach him among the heathen; immediately I conferred not with flesh and blood' (Galatians 1:15-16). For God's Son to be revealed in each one of us, it requires that we as individuals have our own personal encounter with Christ.

Sadly, it is common to find people who have a knowledge of the historical Christ and have studied the biblical narrative in a similar fashion as any academic subject. The unveiling of the Word of God goes beyond head knowledge to believing with the heart. It is with the heart that we believe Christ has been raised from the dead. It is with the heart that we believe unto righteousness. Head knowledge is knowing about Christ, but when the heart believes, it brings us into the realm where we trust him. We trust his righteousness to be sufficient to enable us to stand in the presence of God without condemnation.

Jesus taught a second birth, whereby our human spirits are made alive to God. This birth is a prerequisite, for scripture teaches us that 'God is a Spirit' (John 4:24). When we come to worship, we are to do so in spirit and in truth (John 4:24). Our spirits must be quickened by God and made alive so that we have fellowship with our Creator. The process

---

[39] J. M. Campbell, *The Indwelling Christ* (Chicago: Fleming H. Revell, 1895), Livingtemples. org/books/indwelling_christ.htm,

begins with the Holy Spirit, who is the one to bring conviction of sin and reprove the world. It is God's standard of righteousness and God's standard of judgement that are revealed, and no person is excluded from them (John 16:8). Therefore, when we hear the Word of God preached, our conscience is pricked. It is the Holy Spirit's way of convicting us of sin and making us aware of our need for a Saviour.

When Paul writes to the church at Corinth, he explains the change of identity that occurs at conversion. We become a new creation in Christ due to our spirits being made alive. The outcome is a new perspective on life. Old things lose their importance, and everything is new because we have been changed (2 Corinthians 5:17).

John, the disciple, worded it slightly differently when he said, 'Behold, what manner of love the Father hath bestowed upon us, that we should be called the sons of God: therefore the world knoweth us not, because it knew him not' (1 John 3:1).

Peter puts it in black-and-white terms when he writes about the mercy God has extended to those who did not know him so that they can now proclaim they are the people of God: 'which had not obtained mercy, but now have obtained mercy' (1 Peter 2:10).

These are three great ways of summarising the enormity of the transformation provided in the new birth. We are a new creation, adopted into God's family and called sons of God. Once strangers to the promises of God, we have become the recipients of his great love and have obtained mercy.

When Paul writes to the church at Philippi about how they should live, he encourages them to operate and think like the Lord Jesus Christ, for we have the ability to let Christ's mind function in us (Philippians 2:5). Not only are those who are born of the Holy Spirit a new creation, but they can have the mind of Christ.

In the book of Romans, Paul writes a similar exhortation: 'And be not conformed to this world: but be ye transformed by the renewing of your mind, that ye may prove what is that good, and acceptable, and perfect, will of God' (Romans 12:2).

Dr. Henry W. Wright explains how you renew your mind: it is 'cleansed from Satan's lies and thought patterns by the washing of the water of the Word.[40] He quotes Paul's words to the church at Ephesus: 'That he might sanctify and cleanse it [the church] with the washing of water by the word' (Ephesians 5:26). Dr. Wright elaborates upon the transaction that takes place as we meditate on the Word of God: it moves from our short-term memory to our long term memory. Dr. Wright explains the outcome: 'After time that thought becomes permanently part of your soul. It becomes a part of your mind, your will, and your emotions, a part of your personality—a part of your biology. Good thoughts become a part of your biology. The Word of God permanently becomes a part of your biology.'[41] He references the book of Proverbs: 'For as [a person] thinketh in his heart, so [are they]' (Proverbs 23:7). He adds, 'It is a biological truth that the things we think about and dwell on actually become part of who we are. Science discovered the mind-body connection long ago.'[42]

This process is explained by Paul to the Corinthians. Paul uses the analogy of looking into a mirror. As you would gaze into a mirror, gaze into Christ and see the glory of the Lord. You will be changed into the likeness of the Lord and go from glory to glory by the Spirit of the Lord (2 Corinthians 3:18).

When we think of the life of Christ as told in the Bible, it unveils a life spent fully meditating on the Word of God. Take the story of Jesus sleeping in the boat crossing the Sea of Galilee. A storm arose. The disciples panicked, but Jesus was completely calm. It reminds us of the words of the prophet telling us that the way to have perfect peace is to keep your mind upon God, for that is the way you demonstrate your trust in him (Isaiah 26:3).

The new birth makes it possible to display the love of God. It is the work of the Spirit of God. Through this work, Christ's divine nature is implanted in us. The Bible describes this as an 'incorruptible seed' (1 Peter 1:23). This divine nature constitutes our core essence. The growth

---

[40] Henry W. Wright, *Exposing the Spiritual Roots of Disease* (New Kensington: Whitaker House, 2019), 74.
[41] Ibid., 69.
[42] Ibid., 68.

of the new life is described in the gospel of John: 'I am the vine, ye are the branches: He that abideth in me, and I in him, the same bringeth forth much fruit: for without me ye can do nothing' (John 15:5). The life of Christ flows into us, for we are grafted into the source of divine life.

We are not only to believe who Jesus is and what he says, but we are also to walk in alignment with the Word of God as his disciples. We are called to demonstrate the resurrection power of our Saviour. God's destiny for us is revealed in Christ.

Scripture gives us more details of why we want to 'put on the new man', and the apostle Paul makes it very plain that the new man is modelled after the Lord Jesus Christ, 'put on the new man, which is renewed in knowledge after the image of him that created him' (Colossians 3:10). The Bible tells us that Jesus 'is the image of the invisible God' (Colossians 1:15). Therefore, the new man is Christ in you. This is in opposition to the 'old man', the flesh, which Paul calls the 'carnal man' (Romans 8:7).

So a Christian has two natures. There is the new man, and there is the old man. There is enmity between them. Scripture exhorts us to feed the new man, the spiritual man, and to starve the old man, the carnal, fleshly man. The conflict challenges every Christian as they pursue God's destiny for their life.

The depth of a person's conversion can reflect a person's ongoing walk with Christ. It is said about the Lewis revival in Scotland, from 1948 to 1949, that people came under such terrifying conviction of their condition before a holy God that, once they got up from their knees, they were trembling at the encounter that had taken place. It was not uncommon for men to be in agony of the soul throughout a whole night, crying to God for mercy. To those individuals surrendering their wills and conscience and yielding to the call of God, it reflected the depths of the work of grace done in their lives. There was no turning back.

One should always seek deep encounters, for such encounters have an impact on your God-given destiny. When yielded to God and walking in righteousness, the conscience is clear of guilt. Consecration to God and holiness of life puts the brakes on the works of the flesh. God's presence and holiness become a great method that brings constraints to how we walk. Christ in us literally produces a clearer vision of God's glory, authority, and ongoing love for us.

The revelation of the indwelling Christ made such an impact upon Paul that we see it reflected in his writings to the various churches:

> The first man Adam was made a living soul; the last Adam was made a quickening spirit. (1 Corinthians 15:45)

> Examine yourselves, whether ye be in the faith; prove your own selves. Know ye not your own selves, how that Christ Jesus is in you. (2 Corinthians 13:5)

> And if Christ be in you, the body is dead because of sin; but the Spirit is life because of righteousness. (Romans 8:10)

> But we have this treasure in earthen vessels, that the excellency of the power may be of God, and not of us. (2 Corinthians 4:7)

> But when it pleased God, who separated me from my mother's womb, and called me by his grace, To reveal his Son in me, that I might preach him among the heathen; immediately I conferred not with flesh and blood. (Galatians 1:15-16)

> I am crucified with Christ: nevertheless live; yet not I, but Christ liveth in me: and the life which I now live in the flesh I live by the faith of the Son of God, who loved me, and gave himself for me. (Galatians 2:20)

> My little children, of whom I travail in birth again until Christ be formed in you. I desire to be present with you now, and to change my voice; for I stand in doubt of you. (Galatians 4:19-20)

That Christ may dwell in your hearts by faith. (Ephesians 3:17)

Look at what Paul is saying to the churches: prove the truth of it in your own life, experience life that comes from the Spirit, the treasure is within, there is no need to confer with flesh or blood, the life is lived by the power of God, and become like Christ because it is God's love that we are grounded in. To crown it all, God's Spirit quickens us and makes all this a reality.

This is the literal outcome of what Jesus taught while he was with his disciples: 'Jesus answered and said unto him, If a man love me, he will keep my words: and my Father will love him, and we will come unto him, and make our abode with him' (John 14:23).

Compare this with how Jesus sums up human nature: 'For from within, out of the heart of men [men used here covers all people], proceed evil thoughts, adulteries, fornication, murders, Thefts, covetousness, wickedness, deceit, lasciviousness, an evil eye, blasphemy, pride, foolishness: All these evil things come from within, and defile the man [person]' (Mark 7:21–23). It is remarkable. We begin to discover the greatness of this mystery and how incomprehensible it is. It is an amazing statement: 'Christ in you'. It is not just the Holy Spirit that lives in us, but Christ himself.

The enormity of this revelation can be put into context when we read through the Old Testament. From the very beginning of the Old Testament, we are introduced to the work of the Holy Spirit, beginning with how the Spirit moved upon the waters covering the earth (Genesis 1:2). The Holy Spirit 'filled the heavens' (Job 26:13). The passage emphasises the power of God as Creator. The heavens are filled with galaxies, stars, planets, suns, moons, dust clouds, shooting stars, and asteroids. The psalmist tells us how the heavens were made and elaborates by saying it was done by God's breath (Psalm 33:6).

There is a further interesting revelation given by the psalmist about the Holy Spirit's work. The Holy Spirit is sent to restore the earth and make it new. The Holy Spirit renewed the face of the earth after two floods, the first flood being that described in Genesis chapter 1, and the second flood being the flood in the days of Noah.

In addition to the work of creation, we are told the Holy Spirit interacted with man. The first account recorded is that the Spirit of God will not always contend with man (Genesis 6:3). Then we read of the Holy Spirit dealing with Abraham and his descendants. During the time of the Old Testament, the coming of the Holy Ghost upon a person can be seen as temporary or occasional. We see how revelation was revealed to the prophets.

The Holy Spirit not only came upon people in Old Testament times, but filled people too. It is said of Bezalel that God filled him with the Spirit of God and gave him wisdom, understanding, and knowledge to produce design and work of exceptional quality (Exodus 31:3). Aholiab worked with him. The Holy Spirit was given to those men as a gift and was in them.

Moses elaborated on Bezalel's experience and reiterated that he was filled with God's Spirit (Exodus 35:31). Moses was another person whom the Holy Spirit was in. Isaiah asked where the God who put the Holy Spirit in Moses was (Isaiah 63:11). Nehemiah let us know that this was not a few isolated cases. He pointed out that when the prophets spoke on behalf of God to the nation, it was through God's Spirit in them (Nehemiah 9:30).

The work of the Holy Spirit in the Old Testament can be seen in creation. Everything that has life is a result of the operation of the Holy Spirit. All life on the planet Earth is a result of the moving of the Holy Spirit. All life in the heavens above, everything seen, and everything unseen is evidence that the Holy Spirit has been intimately involved.

The Holy Spirit has been involved in human history, disclosing revelations of God to men. In particular, revelations were given about the coming Messiah, some as typology, so that the people could identify the Christ when he appeared. Sometimes the Holy Spirit came upon a person; at other times the Holy Spirit filled the person. Sometimes the characters of the people were in question; others were regarded as righteous. The Holy Spirit would be given for a set purpose and did not indwell anyone permanently. Even with regard to the birth of Jesus, we see that the Holy Spirit came upon Mary.

In all the examples we have in the Old Testament, no one had 'Christ in them'. It is only after Jesus rose from the dead did this become possible. As Paul states it was hidden from past generations. No one in the Old Testament were aware of this great revelation of a Saviour who would die and rise again and then indwell them, live in them.

Paul writes about the glory of this mystery among the Gentiles. What a mystery! The riches of the glory of this mystery are elaborated in many parts of scripture. 'In whom we have redemption through his blood, the forgiveness of sins, according to the riches of his grace' (Ephesians 1:7). It is in Christ we find the treasures of wisdom and of knowledge (Colossians 2:3). Paul is telling the Gentiles that they have come from a place of having no hope and being without God to this glorious position of Christ being in them.

There is much more to this mystery, especially in light of what Jesus says in the gospels, which we have noted above. 'For from within, out of the heart of men, proceed evil thoughts, adulteries, fornications, murders, Thefts, covetousness, wickedness, deceit, lasciviousness, an evil eye, blasphemy, pride, foolishness. All these evil things come from within, and defile the man' (Mark 7:21–23). How is it possible that God, who is holy, can come and live in a body of flesh with such corruption? How is it possible that God, who is holy, can come and dwell in all who believe in him simultaneously? Yet scripture goes on to state that is the work the Holy Spirit does in us. He establishes himself in our hearts, with no guilt attached, so we can live in holiness before our God (1 Thessalonians 3:13).

The apostle Paul, in his letter to the Romans, writes that 'all have sinned, and come short of the glory of God' (Romans 3:23). The message of scripture reveals the true nature of man, and it is not a pleasant picture that is painted. It is a picture of depravity, corruption, wickedness, and self-interest. Above all it is a picture of hatred towards God. In other words, contrary to what you may think or hear or believe about how good man is, it never lines up with the condition of man set out in the Bible. The Bible paints man in a fallen condition, which many refuse to believe. Filmmakers like to portray man as primitive species in the universe. When confronted with beings of a higher intelligence, man is not destroyed by these beings. Why? They see human society as replicating their own society and slowly progressing. The Bible simply states, 'Let them alone: they be blind leaders of the blind. And if the blind lead the blind, both shall fall into the ditch' (Matthew 15:14).

The apostle Paul preached the gospel 'all have sinned!' (Romans 3:23). It is not the message people are looking to hear, nor is it the message people want to hear. However, it is good to ponder the question Job asked. He wanted to know what man could take something unclean and make it clean. He answered for himself that he could not do it (Job 14:4).

Who can cleanse themselves? The obvious answer is that nobody can. Job stated a further truth: it was the breath of Almighty God, the Spirit of God, that made him and gave life to him (Job 33:4). The prophet Isaiah expressed this same thought: 'Thus saith God the LORD, he that created the heavens, and stretched them out; he that spread forth the earth, and that which cometh out of it; he that giveth breath unto the people upon it, and spirit to them that walk therein' (Isaiah 42:5).

The prophet Jeremiah spoke of the sheer magnitude of the corruption of the heart. It is deceitful. Wickedness that you cannot believe flows from it. Who among us can fathom it (Jeremiah 17:9)?

When Jesus came to Jerusalem for the Feast of Passover, a great multitude believed in him when they saw the miracle he performed. But Jesus knew how easily men's hearts could be swayed and the condition of those hearts. Therefore, he never allowed men to interfere in the destiny already prepared for him by his Father (John 2:23–25). So it is a great mystery—Christ in you, the hope of glory.

The apostle Paul explained how sin came into the world by the disobedience of Adam, causing death to reign over men in all subsequent generations due to sin, for all are guilty, all have sinned (Romans 5:12). Then we get this great revelation: just as one man, Adam, by his disobedience made many sinners, so by the obedience of another man, Christ Jesus, many shall be made righteous (Romans 5:19). The obedience of Jesus—he who knew no sin becoming sin for us—enabled a great transaction to take place, so that we who are under condemnation can be rescued and clothed in God's righteousness. God humbled himself, obedient unto death, nailed to a cross (Philippians 2:8). It is a mystery of mysteries, the salvation purchased by Jesus for us—Christ in you, the hope of glory!

Paul told the Corinthian church that in Christ they had a new nature. The old nature and desires passed, for they were now changed, and the incorruptible seed planted in them made everything new (2 Corinthians 5:17). Scripture tells us when we are 'born again' (John 3:3) by the Spirit of God, we become new creations. Our spirits become alive and can commune with God, for God is Spirit. Our worship flows from our spirits and ascends to the throne of God.

To close this chapter, one verse which has already been highlighted is worth remembering and meditating upon. The Bible reveals to us a great mystery to lift us up to a higher level of intimacy with our Saviour. It tells us that Christ comes and lives in us and 'in Him dwells all the fullness of the Godhead bodily' (Colossians 2:9). God is Father, Son, and Holy Spirit—one God, three persons. Maybe as Christians we don't appreciate this enough—that we are indwelt by the Godhead. If nothing else gets us excited, this certainly should.

CHAPTER 11

MYSTERY OF THE ONE UNION OF JEWS AND GENTILES

How that by revelation he made known unto me the mystery;
That the Gentiles should be fellow heirs, and of the same body.

Ephesians 3:3...6

The inauguration of the church is recognised as having taken place on the day of Pentecost, when the Holy Spirit was poured out in the upper room in Jerusalem. All of the believers were Jewish with no Gentiles involved. The Distinguished Professor Emeritus of Bible and Theology Stanley M Horton notes, 'No other prejudice, no other barrier to fellowship was ever so great as that between Jews and Gentiles.'[43] Here we are given another mystery, and that is how Gentiles should share and be partakers with Jews to come together to be one body called the church.

The obstacles to this seemingly impossible truth are highlighted by Konstanty Gebert, particularly when he expounds on Leviticus 22:32–33, when God took Israel out of Egypt.[44] Gebert points out that the

---

[43] Stanley M. Horton, *What the Bible Says about the Holy Spirit, Fifth Printing* (Springfield, MO: Gospel Publishing House, 1989), 156.
[44] Konstanty Gebert, *54 Commentaries to the Torah* (Krakow: Publishing House Austeria, 2005), 146.

Exodus was personal to Israel; therefore, to a convert to Judaism, it does not have the same impact. When speaking both of the descendants of Abraham and of converts to Judaism, he remarks, 'One is tempted to think that the former are a little closer to the Lord. After all, only those who went out of Egypt were sanctified by the Lord; the others joined later.' For example, how can a convert celebrate the crossing of the Red Sea when his descendants did not take part in this deliverance?

Gebert also highlights Rashi teaching from the Talmud when discussing the difference in meaning attributed to the phrase 'in Israel' between a person born Jewish and a proselyte. Rashi says God expects more from the Jewish people than from proselytes. Gebert quotes Rashi as saying, 'The decision to convert to Judaism does not seem reasonable: it is well-grounded only when the potential convert wishes not only to participate in the Jewish faith, but also in the Jewish fate.'[45] These comments give us a flavour of how massive this mystery is and the shift in thinking that is required so that Jew and Gentile can be brought together to worship the living God and become one body.

Horton also points out how Jesus prepared the disciples before the Great Commission was given to take the gospel to all nations. They initially understood their audience to be Jews scattered among these nations. Something supernatural had to take place in order for the mind-set of the early church to be changed.

Horton highlights the working of the Holy Spirit in the life of Peter. Cornelius, a Roman centurion who loved the Jewish people and feared God, received a vision from the Lord with instructions to send for Peter, who was in Joppa. As Cornelius's servants drew near to Joppa, Peter went on the roof of a house to pray at the sixth hour. As Peter prayed, he began to feel hungry and fell into a trance. While he was in the trance, the heavens opened and a large sheet was lowered, containing all sorts of creatures. Then a voice came to Peter, instructing him to get up, kill, and eat (Acts 10:10–13). Because he was Jewish and the animals in the vision were classified as unclean in Jewish law, Peter's initial reaction was to refuse. Three times this vision was given to Peter. The Lord

---

[45] Ibid., 147.

used this illustration to prepare Peter for the visit of three uninvited guests approaching the property where he was (Acts 11:5-9). At that exact moment, the Holy Spirit spoke to Peter of the men who had come seeking him, with the instruction go with them.

Peter obeyed the instructions of the Holy Spirit to go to the house of Cornelius, and took with himself six other believers. Once the formalities were over at Cornelius's house, Peter began to preach the Word of God to a house full of people that Cornelius had gathered together. Peter began by introducing his audience to the one who was widely known as Jesus of Nazareth. He explained how Jesus was anointed of the Holy Spirit. Everywhere he went, he exposed the works of the devil, set people free who were oppressed by the demonic, healed people of all manner of sickness and disease, and declared how God was with him.

Then Peter shared his personal, first-hand experiences of what he had seen and experienced as he travelled around the country and in Jerusalem while in the presence of Jesus. Peter spoke of the crucifixion of the Lord Jesus Christ and how God raised him from the dead after three days. Jesus appeared openly to his followers in ten separate appearances, with over five hundred seeing him on one occasion. Peter referenced the words of the prophets as witness to Jesus's true identity. He described how forgiveness of sins was given to those who believed in Jesus's name (Acts 10:38–43).

As Peter preached, something remarkable took place. 'While Peter yet spake these words, the Holy Ghost fell on all them which heard the word' (Acts 10:44). Peter and the men with him were left amazed as 'they heard them speak with tongues, and magnify God' (Acts 10:46). Horton notes, 'The evidence that convinced them, they heard them speak with tongues, and magnified God.'[46]

Peter rehearsed the events at Cornelius's house, for he knew there would be opposition from some of the believers back in Jerusalem. And this opposition did come—not so much that he spoke to Gentiles, but rather that he ate non-kosher food with them! Peter related to them what had taken place at Cornelius's house and what he had said to the

---

[46] Horton, What the Bible Says about the Holy Spirit, 156.

people Cornelius gathered together. He spoke of them being filled with the Holy Spirit and speaking in tongues. It was like the day of Pentecost all over again! Then we have this fabulous verse of scripture: 'When they heard these things, they held their peace, and glorified God, saying, Then hath God also to the Gentiles granted repentance unto life' (Acts 11:18).

Jesus made a statement that is important for us to pick up. He stated that the Law and the Prophets finish with John the Baptist (Luke 16:16). He was talking about a transition that was in the process of taking place. With the benefit of hindsight, we understand that the period of time we are living in is no longer under the dispensation of law but under the dispensation of grace. Indeed, the apostle Paul writes to the church at Ephesus that he was the one who got this revelation from God and was making it known unto them (Ephesians 3:2).

Paul wrote something similar to the church at Rome: 'Now to him that is of power to stablish you according to my gospel, and the preaching of Jesus Christ, according to the revelation of the mystery, which was kept secret since the world began' (Romans 16:25).

In the early church, there were priests who came to believe that Jesus was their Messiah. However, they were still trying to come to terms with the new reality. Scripture records them saying that Gentile believers should be circumcised and comply with the Law of Moses (Acts 15:5). This was the great discussion that Paul and Barnabas had with the Council at Jerusalem. After much deliberation, James spoke, and all agreed that Gentiles should not be circumcised nor should they be brought under the Law of Moses. The only requirements would be that the new believers did not become polluted with idols, did not commit fornication, and did not eat animals that were strangled nor anything made with blood (Acts 15:20). And so it is to this day.

The combination of Peter describing what happened at Cornelius's house, Paul and Barnabas giving testimony of God working among the Gentiles during their travels, and James being inspired by the Holy Spirit brought about the dismantling of prejudices between Jewish and Gentile believers. It was the work of the Holy Spirit. Paul and Barnabas were given letters to be taken to the churches, reporting the decisions reached at the Council in Jerusalem and stating the matter seemed good not only to them but to the Holy Ghost. They did not want to lay upon people regulations and burdens that were unnecessary (Acts 15:28).

Erich Sauer (1898-1959), a German theologian remarks, 'The mystery of which Paul speaks of in Ephesians chapter 3 was that the Gentile believers should receive a completely equal standing in the Christian church with Jewish believers. They are fellow heirs, fellow members of the body, and fellow partakers of the promise in Christ Jesus through the gospel.'[47] The integration is so complete that it is impossible to distinguish Jew from Gentile. Sauer relates that this principle of equality would not have been seen by the Old Testament prophets. Therefore 'its composition, nature, and principle of organic fellowship, was in the Old Testament a 'mystery' not yet revealed.'[48]

However, the greater mystery is the love that Christ has for his church. 'And walk in love, as Christ also hath loved us, and hath given himself for us an offering and a sacrifice to God for a sweet smelling savour' (Ephesians 5:2).

The early church began with Jewish believers; then Gentiles were added. As time passed, the church comprised only Gentile believers. As C. Peter Wagner points out, 'since the time of the Nicene Council in the 4th century we have refused the right of the Messianic church to exist, insisting that Jewish converts live as Gentiles until the 20th century.'[49] It is in recent times that this situation has been overturned. Today, we can gladly proclaim that there are more messianic Jews than at any time since the days of the early church.

Paul in his Roman epistle highlights that it has always been God's purpose to reach the Gentiles: 'There shall be a root of Jesse, and he that shall rise to reign over the Gentiles; in him shall the Gentiles trust' (Romans 15:12). This verse quotes from the prophet Isaiah: 'And in that day there shall be a root of Jesse, which shall stand for an ensign of the

---

[47] Erich Sauer, *From Eternity to Eternity* (Carlisle: Paternoster Press and Erdman Publishing, 1994), 174.

[48] Ibid, 175.

[49] C. Peter Wagner, *The Queen's Domain* (Colorado Springs: Wagner Publications, 2000), 75.

people; to it shall the Gentiles seek: and his rest shall be glorious' (Isaiah 11:10).

The Jewish rabbis through the centuries have always looked back at the great events in their history, when God showed himself strong on their behalf. Gentile believers can share in the miraculous works of God that have been done in the past. However, in always looking back, the rabbis have become so focused that they have been blinded to the fact that the Gentiles, who were without Christ and without hope, look forward and rejoice in the great work of salvation accomplished at Mount Calvary. As we draw near to the end of this age, once again the church is more and more reflecting the make-up of the early church, Jew and Gentile.

CHAPTER 12

MYSTERY OF THE SEVEN STARS

The mystery of the seven stars which thou sawest in my right hand, and the seven golden candlesticks.

Revelation 1:20

This mystery was given to the disciple who was close to Jesus's heart (John 21:20). He was the apostle John, writing on the Isle of Patmos, a small island in the Aegean Sea, where he was held as a prisoner. The focus of the mystery given to John is centred on seven specific churches which were located in Asia Minor, what is modern-day Turkey.

We will begin with the interpretation given to him of what the seven stars and seven candlesticks represented. This will be followed by looking at the number seven given in the book of Revelation, the imprint of the divine trademark—a trademark which, we will see, is firmly implanted in Christ's own genealogy. This uniqueness lets us know that the message that unfolds from the revelation is itself of a divine origin. But more than this, John gives us the seven glorified attributes of Jesus himself.

We will also look at the condition of the seven churches by bringing together teaching from Jesus, James, and Paul, along with John, in order to provide a comprehensive picture. In order to do this, we shall look at the following:

- Seven kingdom parables in Matthew 13
- James's epistle to Jewish believers in the Messiah
- Paul's epistles to the seven churches
- John's message to the seven churches

The book of Revelation opens by telling us it 'is the Revelation of Jesus Christ' (Revelation 1:1). It states there is a special blessing to those who read the book or hear the words of the prophecy (Revelation 1:3). So this mystery is connected with prophecy, and the prophecy is defined as near at hand (Revelation 1:3). It 'must shortly come to pass' (Revelation 1:1). These statements point to events to come on God's calendar.

The portion of the revelation given to John which we will cover is found in chapters 2 and 3. Chapter 4 onwards details what will take place on the earth during the seven years running up to Christ's return at his Second Coming. This period is also known as the time of Jacob's troubles.

Jacob's troubles are first mentioned by the prophet Jeremiah: 'Alas! for that day is great, so that none is like it: it is even the time of Jacob's trouble; but he shall be saved out of it' (Jeremiah 30:7). Jesus, discussing events at his Second Coming, tells us, 'And except those days be shortened, there should no flesh be saved: but for the elect's sake those days shall be shortened' (Matthew 24:22). Those elect are defined: 'For Jacob my servant's sake, and Israel mine elect, I have even called thee by thy name' (Isaiah 45:4).

On Patmos, John gives details of a supernatural encounter and states that on the Lord's day he was in the Spirit (Revelation 1:10). 'The Lord's day' can either be understood to mean the Sabbath day or alternatively, that John was taken in the Spirit or transported to the Day of the Lord. If the latter happened, then John saw events from the perspective of Jesus's return at the Second Advent.

The key to the book is expressed by John when he gives details of what he has just seen—those things which are present and those which are to come (Revelation 1:19). He saw the glorified Christ in all his splendour. The churches were in existence at the time of the revelation, and an unveiling of events after the church age unfolds. John also describes a similar experience not long after this one, during which he is once more taken in the Spirit and sees a throne in heaven and one on the throne (Revelation 4:2).

John was exiled by Domitian, who was the Roman emperor from AD 81 to 96. John tells us he was sent to Patmos for testifying to the truth of the Word of God and for the testimony of Jesus Christ (Revelation 1:2). The testimony of Jesus Christ is defined as the spirit of prophecy (Revelation 19:10).

In his first supernatural encounter, John saw seven golden candlesticks. Standing in the midst of them was the Lord Jesus Christ, the Son of Man (Revelation 1:13). John says Jesus was holding seven stars in his right hand (Revelation 1:16). Immediately, John received an explanation. The seven stars are the angels of the seven churches: and the seven candlesticks which thou sawest are the seven churches (Revelation 1:20).

The candlesticks were made of gold. Gold normally stands for deity and speaks also of value and of purity. The function of the candlesticks was to bring light. Light encapsulates what the church is to be, a light in the world. It also goes beyond this and represents to us a God who is holy. There is no darkness in him. Therefore, as God is holy, those who are called to follow him are required to be holy in their lifestyle—specifically in their conversations with one another (1 Peter 1:15–16). In the midst of the candlesticks, the church of the Lord Jesus Christ, we find the Son of Man.

Each of the churches is given a word from the Lord Jesus Christ. In them you find a strong correlation to Israel's history, which Gentiles may not fully appreciate, for they highlight where Israel stumbled. In these messages there are embodied strong warnings to the churches not to disregard what they are being told.

It is also worth pointing out that the Bible gives its own definitions, and here a star is defined as an angel. This opens up other parts of scripture. It gives us insight to such verses as 'And his tail drew the third part of the stars of heaven, and did cast them to the earth' (Revelation 12:4). Scripture is not alluding to planets being cast to the earth; it is the third of the angels who rebelled against God. 'And the great dragon was cast out, that old serpent, called the Devil, and Satan, which deceiveth the whole world: he was cast out into the earth, and his angels were cast out with him' (Revelation 12:9). This event happens during the last seven years before the return of Jesus Christ. It is also known as Daniel's seventieth week of years, and commonly described as the Tribulation.

John was exiled close to the end of the first century, and wrote to seven churches: Ephesus, Smyrna, Pergamos, Thyatira, Sardis, Philadelphia, and Laodicea. The number seven introduces the signature of God in the book of Revelation, letting us know how supernatural this message is. Seven is the number of completion, and it is found throughout scripture. In the book of Revelation alone, there are seven churches, seven Spirits of God, seven golden candlesticks, seven stars, seven angels, seven lamps of fire, seven seals, seven horns, seven eyes, seven trumpets, seven thunders, seven heads, seven crowns, seven last plagues, seven golden vials, seven mountains, and seven kings.

John's description of Jesus is also seven-fold, but he can only give it in relationship to what can be understood. Describing the appearance of Jesus in his glorified body, John states his head and hair were white 'like' wool, white 'as' snow (Revelation 1:14). The eyes of Jesus he speaks 'as' a flame of fire (Revelation 1:14). Jesus's feet are 'likened' to fine brass 'as if' burned in a furnace (Revelation 1:15). Jesus's voice is 'as' the noise of many waters (Revelation 1:15). He holds the seven stars in his right hand (Revelation 1:16). When he speaks, from his mouth goes forth a two-edged sword (Revelation 1:16). His countenance 'was as' seeing the sun shining in all its strength (Revelation1:16).

As mentioned, the book of Revelation 'is the Revelation of Jesus Christ' (Revelation 1:1). Jesus's genealogy is constructed on a base of seven. We find the genealogy of Jesus in Matthew's gospel. Think of designing a genealogy where everything about its construction is to be divided by seven, i.e., words, letters, vowels, consonants, words beginning with a vowel, words beginning with a consonant, words that occur more than once, words that occur in more than one form, words that occur in one form, nouns, generations, and so on. For an individual to construct a genealogy that would accomplish the complete breakdown of language such that more than seventy hepatic structures are found divisible by seven, a person would have to live for three thousand years. Yet the One who gave us a book based on sevens has a genealogy that conforms to this pattern.[50]

In the gospels, it is recorded seven times that John the Baptist gives witness of Jesus Christ: see Matthew 3:11, Mark 1:7, Luke 3:16, John 1:15, John 1:26, John 1:29, and John 1:36.

Let us pause for a moment to understand how we arrived at the point in history, AD 90 to 96, when John wrote these letters. In scripture, there are a number of jigsaw pieces that we can bring together to obtain greater insight into these churches, and indeed a template for a healthy church. We will begin at the first hint given by Jesus that God is going to work among the Gentiles, so that the Gentiles will come to faith and believe that Jesus is the Son of God. This is found in Matthew's gospel where Jesus has one of his many confrontations with the Pharisees.

Jesus's Confrontation with the Pharisees

In Matthew chapter 12, we arrive at a pivotal point in the ministry of Jesus. The chapter begins with the perennial accusations of Sabbath-breaking: 'thy disciples do that which is not lawful to do upon the Sabbath day' (Matthew 12:2). Mark and Luke record this same confrontation. Immediately after it takes place, we read, 'And, behold, there was a man which had his hand withered. And they asked him, saying, Is it lawful to heal on the Sabbath days? That they might accuse him' (Matthew 12:10). Feeling vindicated in their own minds that God would never do any such thing on the Sabbath, 'the Pharisees went out, and held a council against him, how they might destroy him' (Matthew 12:14).

From there it was a short step to committing the unpardonable sin—and this was much deeper than attributing the works of God to the

---

[50] Chuck Missler, *Hidden Treasures in the Biblical Text*, (Coeur d' Alene: Koinonia House, Eleventh Printing), 26-29.

Devil. It was speaking against the Holy Spirit, which scripture says will not be forgiven, not in this world nor in the world to come (Matthew 12:32). Mark in his gospel lays out what the unpardonable sin is, so that no one will have an excuse: 'But he that shall blaspheme against the Holy Ghost hath never forgiveness, but is in danger of eternal damnation: Because they said, He hath an unclean spirit' (Mark 3:29-30).

Notice carefully how this great sin is committed and how easy it is for people in a crowd, getting riled up by others, to speak out. Before they realise what they have spoken through their lips, they have blasphemed against the Holy Ghost. This should stop us in our tracks. Consider the words found in James chapter 3 about the unbridled tongue, how it is capable of defiling one's body, how it is like a fire, a world of iniquity, and a deadly poison. Therefore it is not surprising to find scripture warning us that we will give an account for our words 'in the day of judgement' (Matthew 12:36).

In the middle of this heated clash, Jesus dropped a further revelation. After he had been rejected as Messiah, Jesus told the Pharisees that 'in his name shall the Gentiles trust' (Matthew 12:21). The ferocity of the reply was quick in coming. They accused Jesus of casting out 'devils by Beelzebub the prince of the devils' (Matthew 12:24). Thus they committed the unpardonable sin, blaspheming the Holy Ghost by accusing him of being Beelzebub, the Lord of Flies!

In Matthew chapter 13, Jesus's method of preaching changed. He began to speak in parables. Jesus only interpreted the parables to his disciples. This was not to make it easier for people to understand, but that scripture might be fulfilled.

> All these things spake Jesus unto the multitude in parables; and without a parable spake he not unto them: That it might be fulfilled which was spoken by the prophet, saying, I will open my mouth in parables; I will utter things which have been kept secret from the foundation of the world. (Matthew 13:34-35)

Jesus provided parables, what can be described as secrets or revelation that no one had any ability to interpret without the help of the Holy Spirit, for that revelation had been kept secret from the foundation of the world.

We now know the seven parables as the kingdom parables, and they are specific for Gentiles. That alone gets our attention. How did God engineer circumstances for the gospel to be made known to Gentiles? Let's take a short journey through the book of Acts.

James the Apostle

The spread of the gospel is first seen in the letter of James Zebedee, whose death we read of in Acts 12. James was the brother of John, and Herod had him killed by the sword (Acts 12:2). This was around AD 43–44. James wrote his letter fairly early in the life of the church, before Paul's conversion. Hence James addresses his epistle to the twelve tribes of Israel, which had been scattered among the nations (James 1:1). It is still early days in the spreading of the good news of Jesus, and at this stage of development it is purely a Jewish church with no Gentile involvement. However, here is a strange thing. Caiaphas never believed Jesus to be the Messiah, but he still 'prophesied that Jesus should die for that nation [Israel]. And not for that nation only, but that also he should gather together in one the children of God that were scattered abroad' (John 11:51-52). He references the Saviour and the dispersion of the Jewish people!

James's greeting is not to churches nor to individuals. At that time, there were no Gentile churches or Gentile believers. We know from scripture that some were preaching the message of John the Baptist. Once more it is worth emphasising how the early church was very much a Jewish church. It is important to bear this point in mind, for it can easily be overlooked due to the exposure—and rightly so—of Paul's missionary journeys. This gives further weight to why John's warnings contained in his message to the churches are skewed to Jewish believers.

Around this time, Saul of Tarsus began to persecute the church. Our introduction to him is when he stands consenting to the stoning of

Stephen as a heretic. Scripture records great persecution of the church, resulting in many disciples fleeing to other parts of Judea and Samaria, leaving only the apostles at Jerusalem (Acts 8:1). Paul continued to search out Christians, entering houses, placing men and women in prison, and bringing much havoc to the church. As the persecution intensified, believers spread throughout the Roman Empire, and those fleeing preached the Word of God everywhere they went (Acts 8:3–4).

The first Gentile we know to have been converted is Cornelius, a Roman centurion, along with his household. The report taken back to Jerusalem by Peter caused the disciples to be astonished, for it was the furthest thing from their minds. When they heard of the gift of the Holy Ghost being given to Gentiles, that was like an earthquake, requiring a major paradigm shift in their thinking and understanding (Acts 10:45). By this time the church was already scattered abroad due to the persecution.

Apostle Paul

It is Paul's conversion and calling to preach the gospel to the Gentiles that we are most familiar with. Along with Barnabas and others, Paul embarked on missionary journeys, establishing churches everywhere he went. Our interest is drawn to Paul because he writes seven epistles to believers in seven churches: Ephesians, Philippians, Corinthians, Galatians, Romans, Thessalonians, and Colossians.

As mentioned above, those from an earlier dispersion were continuing to preach in line with what John the Baptist taught, which was similar to what Peter preached on the day of Pentecost: 'repent and be baptized … for the remission of sins' (Acts 2:38). When Paul arrived at Ephesus, he came across some of John's disciples and asked them if they had received the Holy Ghost. Their reply was negative, for they did not know what Paul was talking about. Paul asked about their water baptism and found out they were disciples of John the Baptist (Acts 19:1–3). This incident highlights to us the transition that had been ongoing since the time of John the Baptist's preaching.

Apostle John

When we come to the time of John's writing, what we would call the mother church, the church at Jerusalem, was no longer in existence. It had been scattered due to the destruction of Jerusalem in AD 70 by the Roman general Titus. The city was completely demolished, fulfilling the words of Jesus about Jerusalem's complete destruction so that no stone would be left upon another (Matthew 24:2).

For the first thirty years of church history, the church at Jerusalem was very prominent. When questions arose, such as whether Gentile believers should be circumcised, it was the church council at Jerusalem who dealt with those issues. It was at Jerusalem that the church council agreed what should be preached to the Gentiles, and this is found in Acts 15.

When Paul went on his missionary journeys, he returned to Jerusalem, reporting back to the church. He provided details of churches established, the impact of the gospel everywhere it was preached, and his experience of the providence of God. With the development and expansion of the church, Jerusalem remained at its centre. Yet when John writes, that church is no longer in existence.

Other churches did exist at the time of John's writing, such as Colosse, Hierapolis (where Philip was crucified upside down during the reign of Domitian), and Troas. It is estimated from the day of Pentecost to the time of John's writing, over sixty churches were established throughout the Roman Empire. It is interesting to note which churches are NOT mentioned.

The glaring exemption that stands out is Rome. This is particularly revealing, for the Roman Catholic Church propagates apostolic succession through Peter. In John's writing, it is completely ignored by the Spirit of God. The Roman church assumed the mantle of Christianity and gave to itself all the powers, authority, and influence that such a responsibility implied. With the transfer from Jerusalem complete, it introduced an ecclesiastical set-up that has come down through two thousand years of intrigue, politics, and outward religion!

A second church not mentioned which has prominence in scripture is Antioch. This is the city were the disciples were called Christians first (Acts 11:26). We read of the church at Jerusalem hearing good reports from Antioch, so they sent Barnabas there (Acts 11:22). We then read that Barnabas left to go to Tarsus, to seek Paul. 'And when he had found him, he brought him unto Antioch. And it came to pass, that a whole year they assembled themselves with the church, and taught much people' (Acts 11:26). We get a little postscript telling us prophets were sent from Jerusalem in these days to Antioch (Acts 11:27).

Three major locations are passed over in silence by John: Jerusalem, the founding church; Rome, the church that claimed apostolic succession; and Antioch, a church blessed by mighty men of God such as Barnabas, Paul, and the prophets from Jerusalem. Yet none of these churches were mentioned in the letters John writes.

There is one further piece of information to be aware of. When John writes, Paul is no longer alive to exhort, to encourage, and to give input to the churches. Once Domitian was dead, the Roman senate repealed his acts, and John was released from his captivity on Patmos.[51] John then went to Ephesus and governed the churches in Asia. It was from Ephesus that John wrote his gospel and epistle. These writings re-emphasised the teachings and instructions previously given to the churches.

Seven Churches

We can now look at the seven churches found in the book of Revelation. There are a number of general observations which we can make.

Every church received these letters, which collectively give a picture of the condition of the churches at the end of the era of the last apostle. They provide details of those things commended by the Lord and highlight the things that brought displeasure. They are a record of commendations and rebukes to these churches. They show us what the Lord Jesus Christ values and give insight into how Satan operates

---

[51] W. Grinton Berry, *Foxe's Book of Martyrs* (Grand Rapids, MI: Baker Book House, Twentieth Printing, 1997), 14.

to make a church ineffectual. They provide a template, if you like, to measure how well a church is performing. This template can be applied to any church in any time period.

Each church receives an update from the one who walks in their midst, evaluating their condition and standing from God's perspective. Some churches who think they are not doing well are commended; others, thinking they are doing well, discover they are falling short. Each church receives a critical instruction: 'He that hath an ear, let him hear what the Spirit saith unto the churches' (Revelation 2:7,11,17,29;3:6,13,22).

The churches are not to be ignorant of Satan's devices. To emphasise this point, Old Testament examples are brought up so that the churches know what they are dealing with and the action they need to take.

The order in which the churches are given provides an outline of church history. If the churches had been laid out in any other order, this would not have been the case. Broadly speaking Ephesus covers the period up to AD 200, Smyrna 200 to 325, Pergamos 325 to 500, Thyatira 500 to 1000, Sardis 1000 to 1500, Philadelphia 1500 to 1900, and Laodicea 1900 to present. This certainly would have been a mystery hidden from all the churches, but it is well documented in Christian writing today.

At first it is easy to dismiss this level of revelation from the Bible as unimportant. Some may consider it rare. However, the order found is much more prevalent than one may realise. Another good example is the genealogy of the first ten names listed in Genesis. They are Adam, Seth, Enosh, Kenan, Mahalalel, Jared, Enoch, Methuselah, Lamech, and Noah. The meaning of their names and the order in which they are placed actually give the plan of redemption: 'Man, appointed mortal sorrow, the Blessed God shall come down teaching, His death shall bring the despairing rest.'[52] This means we cannot simply ignore the churches as providing history in advance as just coincidence.

When Jesus returns for his church, these letters indicate that not everyone will be ready. There will be people who are religious but do not know Jesus as their personal Saviour. The consequences for people

---

[52] Missler, *Hidden Treasures in the Biblical Text*, 16.

in such a condition is that they will enter into a time when the wrath of God is poured out on the earth. This stands out as we look at individual churches.

Bringing together the seven churches of Revelation, the kingdom parables given by Jesus, and Paul's letters to seven churches, we can lay out a table as follows:

Church	Time Period	Kingdom Parables	Paul's Letter
Ephesus	Up to AD 200	The Sower	Ephesians
Smyrna	200–325	Tares/Suffering	Philippians
Pergamos	325–500	Grain of Mustard Seed	Corinthians
Thyatira	500–1000	Leaven	Galatians
Sardis	1000–1500	Treasure in a Field	Romans
Philadelphia	1500–1900	Pearl	Thessalonians
Laodicea	1900 to present	Net Cast into the Sea	Colossians

Looking at the seven churches of Revelation, we find references to the Old Testament that we have already alluded to, both positive and negative, that make these letters by John peculiarly Jewish. This reminds us that the themes brought up by John would not readily resonate with a Gentile; their historical relevance would be obscure. It might remind some of the Jewish believers how Ezekiel saw the presence of God lifting from the temple. The doctrinal statements should be given close scrutiny as well, for they do not all align with the teaching given to the church by the apostle to the Gentiles, the apostle Paul.

Ephesus

The church at Ephesus was blessed by the ministry of Paul. They were commended for standing for the truth, their labour in the gospel, and hating the things God hated. However, in all of these activities, they lost their first love for Christ. The Lord gives them an exhortation, that to the ones who overcome he will grant access to the tree of life (Revelation 2:7). The tree of life is in the garden in the book of Genesis, and it is found again at the end of the book of Revelation. Take a moment to stop and ask yourself this question: How does a Christian obtain eternal life?

The gospel message can be summed up as follows: 'all have sinned' (Romans 3:23). The penalty for sin is death—that is, eternal death—but God's gift is eternal life through the Lord Jesus Christ (Romans 6:23). When we are born again by God's Spirit, we are adopted into his family and we are called sons of God. When Jesus appears, we are going to have a body like his glorious body, for we shall see him in his glorious body (1 John 3:2).

A Christian receives eternal life not from the tree of life, but from the Lord Jesus Christ himself. 'For by grace are ye saved through faith; and that not of yourselves: it is the gift of God' (Ephesians 2:8). When we ask Jesus to forgive our sins and come into our hearts, he gives us power to become sons of God (John 1:12). That is why scripture reinforces this truth: if you have been born again and Christ lives in you, then you have the life of the Son of God (1 John 5:12).

Furthermore, a person's position once they have been born again by God's Spirit is that of an overcomer, for the same Spirit that raised Christ from the dead now dwells in us, and he is greater than he that is in the world (1 John 4:4). It is only those believers in the dispensation of the church who do not need access to the tree of life, for they already have the life of Christ.

Let us look at the parable associated with Ephesus.

The parable of the wheat and tares transcends the church age. This is made plain when Jesus says to let them grow together until it is the time of the harvest. The reapers will gather the harvest and bundle together the tares to be burned. The wheat they shall gather and put into the barn (Matthew 13:30). When John the Baptist preached at the River Jordan, he gave insight into Jesus's ministry by stating his own baptism in water was for repentance, but the one to come after him would baptise in the Holy Ghost and with fire. He was the one who would thoroughly purge and gather the wheat into the barn, while the chaff would be burned by unquenchable fire (Matthew 3:11–12).

In the Tribulation before the Second Coming of Jesus, we read about an angel coming out of the temple to one who is sitting on a cloud, and with a loud voice cries, 'Thrust in thy sickle, and reap: for the time is come for thee to reap: for the harvest of the earth is ripe' (Revelation

14:15). James wrote about the gardener who waits for the precious fruit of the earth to ripen (James 5:7). Scripture goes on to say the one sitting on the cloud thrust his sickle into the earth, and the earth was reaped (Revelation 14:16). The angels are the reapers of the harvest; they gather the wheat into the barn.

The description of the tares that are gathered for the fire is also given. An angel from the temple in heaven comes with a sharp sickle, along with another angel from the altar who has power over fire. The second angel cries out to the first angel to thrust in the sickle and gather the clusters of the vine of the earth, for her grapes are now ripe. 'And the angel thrust in his sickle into the earth, and gathered the vine of the earth, and cast it into the great winepress of the wrath of God' (Revelation 14:19).

Wine comes from the vine. In the book of Deuteronomy, wine appears to have a twofold identification. Firstly it is the wickedness of men connected with the demonic: 'For their vine is of the vine of Sodom, and the fields of Gomorrah: their grapes are grapes of gall, their clusters are bitter: Their wine is the poison of dragons, and the cruel venom of asps' (Deuteronomy 32:32-33). The vine of the earth encapsulates all the unsaved people on the earth—the tares from the parable. This is in opposition to Jesus, who is the true vine: 'I am the vine' (John 15:5).

Smyrna

Jesus provides the Smyrna church with a perfect commendation, telling them he knows all about their works, what they have had to go through, and their poverty. He tells them they are in fact rich. He says that he knows them who blaspheme say they are Jews, but they are actually of the synagogue of Satan (Revelation 2:9). One well-known faithful witness at Smyrna was Polycarp, who was bishop of Smyrna. He was burned alive under the fourth persecution of Christians by Rome.[53]

The Word of God that this church sowed is described as good seed. Jesus talked about the kingdom of heaven, likening it to the sower who

---

[53] Berry, *Foxe's Book of Martyrs*, 20.

sowed good seed in his field (Matthew 13:24). The church that sowed good seed was the Philippian church, which sowed into the ministry of Paul. When Paul writes to them, he gives them the accolade that when he left them to preach the gospel in other places, they were the only church that kept in touch concerning giving and receiving (Philippians 4:15).

Pergamos

Looking at the church at Pergamos, it corresponds to the condition of the church broadly from AD 325 to 500. John notes there are those who have remained faithful, but others have followed the doctrine of Balaam and committed fornication.

There are three things to know about Balaam. Firstly, his way is described by Peter as forsaking the true and right way, for Balaam loved money, whether he got it above board or by other means. Such money is described as the wages of unrighteousness (2 Peter 2:15). Secondly, the error of Balaam was to disobey God and return privately to Balak (Numbers 31:16). Thirdly, the doctrine of Balaam was to show Balak how Israel could be cursed without any help from any prophet: his way, his error, and his doctrine. This led the people of Israel into sin, eating food sacrificed to idols and committing fornication.

This period of time also saw the development of a clergy who ruled over the laity. It is known as 'the doctrine of the Nicolaitans' (Revelation 2:15).

There is a parable of the mustard seed and the tree full of birds. The mustard seed usually refers to faith, but the birds are about demons. (Jesus defined the birds for us in the parable of the sower.) There is faith at this time, for there is 'Antipas my faithful martyr' (Revelation 2:13). But corruption has already set in, the doctrines of demons where Satan has his seat.

Pergamos is a church married to the world. Paul writes to the church at Corinth, and he has to deal with worldly issues of morality and carnality.

Thyatira

The warning of Balaam was given to the church at Pergamos, for he helped Balak to trap the children of Israel, which caused them to sin. Similarly, the church at Thyatira was warned about Jezebel. John brings up their tolerance of Jezebel, who called herself a prophetess. In actuality she seduced God's people to commit fornication and taught them to eat food sacrificed to idols (Revelation 2:20). These were the very things the church at Jerusalem advised believers to abstain from and sent letters to the churches by the hand of Paul and Barnabas to this effect.

Jezebel was one wicked woman. She was queen of the northern state of Israel, alongside her husband, King Ahab. Jezebel replaced the worship of Jehovah by killing God's prophets and introduced the worship of Baal, bringing in all the immorality associated with Baal worship. The Jezebel spirit, probably the strongest spirit mentioned in scripture, is a spirit of intimidation and control, and is usually behind divisions that take place in churches. It is a spirit that can operate at the highest level of government.

The parable associated with this church was that of leaven, which begins small but ends up corrupting everything.

Balaam and Jezebel were extreme warnings to the early church. The Jewish believers in the dispersion would have fully understood the seriousness of these warnings as representing places where Israel had stumbled.

Paul wrote to the Galatians and asked who had bewitched them. They were foolish, for they listened to those telling lies and deceiving them. They departed from the truth. They should have known better after what they saw and heard when Paul was among them (Galatians 3:1).

Sardis

The condition of the church at Sardis was one of great disappointment. It had a name, but there was no life. Only a few had been found faithful. The overcomer would be clothed in white raiment (Revelation 3:5).

The parable is that of a treasure in a field. Treasures are hard to find. They require due diligence and discipline to search them out. In this parable, once the treasure has been found, it costs everything to obtain. Hence we find only a few people have held true to the Word of God and have not defiled themselves (Revelation 3:4).

The book of Romans is the great book centred on those who hunt for this treasure.

Philadelphia

The church at Philadelphia was given the opposite type of message. This church received commendations, and nothing negative was said of it. The one who is holy and true and has the key of David is the Lord Jesus Christ (Revelation 3:7). This is very Jewish, for the key of David is connected with the Davidic Covenant and the promise of a Jewish kingdom. This is not something on a Gentile's radar.

The Lord also gives them a wonderful promise of keeping them secure when the hour of temptation comes upon the whole world. This temptation to come is designed to try those who dwell on the earth (Revelation 3:10). In other words, the Philadelphians will escape the tribulation and the time of wrath, which Jesus defined as a time like no other that has ever been on the earth nor will ever come again to the earth (Matthew 24:21).

The parable for the church at Philadelphia is the pearl of great price. Jesus, their Messiah, is that pearl!

Paul wrote to the church at Thessalonica:

> For the Lord himself shall descend from heaven with a shout, with the voice of the archangel, and with the trump of God: and the dead in Christ shall rise first: Then we which are alive and remain shall be caught up together with them in the clouds, to meet the Lord in the air: and so shall we ever be with the Lord. (1 Thessalonians 4:16-17)

This church is removed before the wrath of God is poured out on the earth.

Laodicea

The church at Laodicea held a view of themselves which was the opposite of how the Lord saw them. They thought they were rich, but God said they were poor. This was a church that sat on the fence, neither hot nor cold. Their condition was such that we find Christ telling them that he was standing outside their door, knocking. The call goes out to those who hear his voice to open the door and let him in. If they do that, then they will have intimate fellowship with the Lord (Revelation 3:20). This is a lukewarm church, and the parable provides warnings of what is to come.

The parable attached to this church is found in Matthew 13:47–52. This parable talks about a net being cast into the sea. What is caught in the net will be separated at the end of the world, when the angel comes forth. It is the separation of the wicked from the just. The wicked will be cast into the furnace of fire. Screams of torment with great wailing and gnashing of teeth will take place (Matthew 13:49–50). It is the only place in scripture we find related to this kind of net. The net is dragged along the bottom, and the two ends slowly come together, catching everything in its path.

The gospel is to be preached to all humanity. However, the parable also shows a separation of people due to their response to the Word of God. The net is pulled in to shore once it is full, and the catch is separated between that which is good and that which is bad. The bad is cast away (Matthew 13:48). This parable ends with judgement.

Paul wrote to the church at Colosse. A major warning he left with them centred on philosophy, vain deceit, and the tradition of men. Paul warned them about coming under those influences and following after basic things of this world, not after Christ (Colossians 2:8).

Summary

In the letter to the churches, Jesus is speaking to those Jews who have believed that he is the Son of God, their Messiah. Therefore, his warnings take them back in their history to important events that caused much turmoil and distress. By providing churches with doctrine that transcends the church age, Jesus is letting them know that the time of Jacob's troubles follows God's dealing with the Gentiles. Therefore, the tree of life is brought up.

The rejection of Jesus by the religious hierarchy in Israel resulted in Jesus's declaration that the Gentiles would trust in his name. The process by which this took place is described in the book of Acts. Persecution scattered the Jewish believers to different parts of the Roman Empire. It was purely a Jewish church at that time. There was no Gentile church, for the apostle to the Gentiles had still to begin his missionary journeys.

This is around the time we read about the first Gentile convert, which took the church in Jerusalem by surprise. 'When they heard these things, they held their peace, and glorified God, saying, Then hath God also to the Gentiles granted repentance unto life' (Acts 11:18). It is not until the conversion of Saul, whose name was changed to Paul that the gospel was taken to the Gentiles.

We find that Paul encountered Jewish believers converted under John the Baptist's ministry. When we read the seven letters of Revelation, their Jewishness stands out due to the Old Testament comparisons made to the condition of the churches. This is not surprising, for we are in the early days of the gospel being preached to the Gentiles. Jewish believers are still the predominant members. Gentiles are not going to be familiar with Jewish history, nor are Gentiles at the stage of understanding the significance of the key of David to the Jewish believer's expectation of the Davidic Covenant being fulfilled and a Jewish Messiah reigning from Jerusalem.

The layout of church history that is derived from John's letter to the churches we can see in retrospect, but unless given as a revelation to the early church, this would have been a hidden mystery. These are different aspects of the mystery associated with the seven stars.

CHAPTER 13

MYSTERY OF THE KINGDOM OF HEAVEN

*Because it is given unto you to know the
mysteries of the kingdom of heaven.*

Matthew 13:11

O nly in the gospel of Matthew do we find any reference to the kingdom of heaven. In fact Matthew mentions it thirty-two times. The book of Matthew heralds the arrival of the King, and Jesus's lineage is given to confirm his credentials. The arrival of the king suggests the setting up of a kingdom for the king to rule over. The expectation of all Israel, even today, is the visible return of their Messiah to set up his kingdom on earth. Notice the question the disciples asked the risen Christ before his ascension: Is this the time that you are going to set up your kingdom in Israel? (Acts 1:6). Ever since the fall of Jerusalem to Nebuchadnezzar, Israel has been looking and waiting for this kingdom.

Before we go any further, it is good to point out that scripture talks about the kingdom of heaven, the kingdom of God, and the millennial kingdom. It is common for commentators to treat the kingdom of heaven and the kingdom of God interchangeably. Yet heaven is not God, and God is not heaven. Paul defined for us the kingdom of God. It 'is not meat and drink; but righteousness, and peace, and joy in the

Holy Ghost' (Romans 14:17). In other words, the kingdom of God is a spiritual kingdom. The millennial kingdom is the one-thousand-year reign of Christ on earth, talked about in Revelation chapter 20. This leaves us to look at and to define the kingdom of heaven.

God took Israel as a nation back at the time of their wanderings in the wilderness. When they entered the land of Canaan, God raised up judges to rule over them. When they turned from God, their enemies prevailed against them. Eventually they cried out to the Lord for help. Then God sent them a deliverer.

However, there came a time when the Israelites wanted to be like other nations and asked for a king. Moses prophesied that this would come to pass. The kingdom only lasted till the death of Solomon. Then it split between the Northern Kingdom and the Southern Kingdom. The Northern Kingdom, known as Israel, quickly fell into idolatry. Eventually the Assyrians invaded, and they were taken from their land and dispersed. The Southern Kingdom, Judah, survived for a much longer period, but they succumbed to wickedness and idolatry, resulting in the Babylonian captivity. A remnant of the captives returned from Babylon. When Jesus came on the scene, Israel was subjugated to Rome.

The descendants of Abraham through the lineage of Isaac and Jacob have always looked for a physical, tangible kingdom on this earth. The disciples looked for it, and we know it will be established at the Second Coming of Jesus. The message of the angel to Mary is that Jesus 'shall be great, and shall be called the Son of the Highest: and the Lord God shall give unto him the throne of his father David' (Luke 1:32). The message John the Baptist preached was one of repentance, for that kingdom was near at hand (Matthew 3:2). When John gives this message, he is telling his audience how close their hope of the messianic kingdom is.

How do we know this? Jeremiah the prophet tells us, 'Behold, the days come, saith the LORD, that I will raise unto David a righteous Branch, and a King shall reign and prosper, and shall execute judgement and justice in the earth' (Jeremiah 23:5). When Matthew gives Jesus's genealogy, he ties it in with the covenant to Abraham given in Genesis chapter 17. The prophet Isaiah prophesied, 'For unto us a child is born, unto us a son is given: and the government shall be upon his shoulder:

and his name shall be called Wonderful, Counsellor, The Mighty God, The everlasting Father, The Prince of Peace' (Isaiah 9:6).

The branch is not only the son of David. Isaiah tells us he is 'the branch of the LORD' (Isaiah 4:2).

> In the beginning was the Word, and the Word was with God, and the Word was God. (John 1:1)

> God was manifest in flesh. (1 Timothy 3:16)

> Behold, I will bring forth my servant the Branch. (Zechariah 3:8)

> Behold the man whose name is The BRANCH; and he shall grow up out of his place, and he shall build the temple of the Lord. (Zechariah 6:12)

The messianic promises of the Old Testament with regards to setting up a Jewish kingdom began to be unfolded to the Jewish people. The message of Jesus is identical to that of John the Baptist: 'From that time Jesus began to preach, and to say, Repent for the kingdom of heaven is at hand' (Matthew 4:17). Jesus travelled throughout Galilee, he taught in the synagogues, he ministered to those who were sick of all manner of diseases, and his message was the gospel of the kingdom (Matthew 4:23). As the Jewish people were looking for a prophet like unto Moses, Jesus demonstrated the power of God that belongs to this kingdom. The people were witnesses to the signs and wonders wrought by the hand of Jesus.

Jesus demonstrated his credentials to Israel as the Branch spoken of by the prophets, so that they might believe in him. From scripture we know his message was gladly received by the ordinary people. A common man in the street, who was physically blind at that, declared one of the greatest revelations given during Jesus's ministry. Two blind men had a stunning revelation, for they identified Jesus as the Son of David. Therefore they cried out for mercy (Matthew 20:30).

Jesus not only verified that John the Baptist was a prophet, but he went further, telling the people, 'Verily I say unto you, Among them that are born of women there hath not risen a greater than John the Baptist: notwithstanding he that is least in the kingdom of heaven is greater than he' (Matthew 11:11). It is important to point out this statement is about the kingdom of heaven and not the kingdom of God. Among them born of women would certainly be included those born under the banner of the Law and the Prophets. The new birth, on the other hand, refers to a person born by the Spirit of God.

Two prophets in particular lay out what the kingdom of heaven will look like. Isaiah provides the details in chapter 11 of his book: 'there shall come forth a rod out of the stem of Jesse, and a branch will grow out of his roots: And the spirit of the LORD shall rest upon him, the spirit of wisdom, and understanding, the spirit of counsel and might, the spirit of knowledge and the fear of the LORD' (Isaiah 11:1- 2). There is no place for the wicked in this kingdom, where the wolf will dwell with the lamb, and the leopard shall lie down with the kid, and the calf and the young lion together. The cow and the bear shall feed together, and the young child will not be bitten by the asp.

Throughout Isaiah chapter 11, we have 'in that day, in that day'. Zechariah lays out this kingdom and expands on 'in that day' by letting us know a fountain will be opened up for the house of David and to the people of Jerusalem for sin and uncleanness (Zechariah 13:1). 'In that day' there is no need for any prophet in Israel, for the Lord will be in the midst of them as their king, ruling over all the earth. 'In that day' the Lord will be known by the name one (Zechariah 14:9). The least in this kingdom will have Christ in their midst; they will be dwelling in a kingdom that Jesus spoke about to his disciples: 'Verily I say unto you, That ye which have followed me, in the regeneration when the Son of man shall sit in the throne of his glory' (Matthew 19:28).

When Jesus chooses his disciples, he sent them out to preach. The message centred on the nearness of the kingdom of heaven (Matthew 10:7). Notice the command Jesus gave to those disciples: 'Go not into the way of the Gentiles, and into any city of the Samaritans enter ye not' (Matthew 10:5). Instead they were commanded to go to the 'the lost sheep of the house of Israel' (Matthew 10:6). Those are the people to whom Jesus had come to in fulfilment of scripture. 'I am not sent but unto the lost sheep of the house of Israel' (Matthew 15:24).

What is so specific about the kingdom of heaven that it ended up becoming a mystery? At the River Jordan, John was interrogated by the Pharisees, who wanted to know his identity and his authority. In reply, John brought up the words of the prophet Isaiah and declared that he was a voice speaking out in the wilderness, giving instructions to all who heard him to prepare the way of the Lord and to make straight in the desert a road for their God (Isaiah 40:3).

The Pharisees had before them the scripture passage from Malachi about sending the prophet Elijah before the great and terrible day of the Lord (Malachi 4:5). The Pharisees enquired of John, asking a number of questions centred on who they expected to show up. When John told them directly he was not Elijah, they were perplexed, especially, since John threw in a passage that appears not to have been on their horizon.

They had their theology rigidly fixed. They were never able to distinguish between the first coming and the second coming of their Messiah. Peter highlights this and gives us the difference: 'Searching what, or what manner of time the Spirit of Christ which was in them did signify, when it testified beforehand the sufferings of Christ, and the glory that should follow' (1 Peter 1:11).

This failure to distinguish between the two comings detailed in the Old Testament overflowed into Jesus's ministry. The Pharisees accused Jesus of blasphemy because he said he was the Son of God. Hence we read of them quoting their law and stating it demanded the death penalty for such blasphemy (John 19:7).

We get an insight into this conflict when Jesus states, 'John came unto you in the way of righteousness, and ye believed him not: but the publicans and the harlots believed him: and ye, when ye had seen it, repented not afterward, that ye might believe him' (Matthew 21:32).

It is not until the Sermon on the Mount that we come across 'the 'kingdom of God' (Matthew 6:33). Matthew gives five instances in which the kingdom of God is mentioned:

- 'Seek ye first the kingdom of God' (Matthew 6:33)
- 'But if I cast out devils by the Spirit of God then the kingdom of God is come unto you' (Matthew 12:28)
- 'It is easier for a camel to go through the eye of a needle, than for a rich man to enter the kingdom of God' (Matthew 19:24)
- 'That the publicans [tax collectors] and the harlots go into the kingdom of God before you [Pharisees]' (Matthew 21:31)
- 'The kingdom of God shall be taken from you, and given to a nation bringing forth the fruits thereof—go to Gentiles' (Matthew 21:43)

The kingdom of God is associated with the righteousness of God. So we find it in Mark's gospel after Jesus is baptised in the River Jordan: 'The time is fulfilled, and the Kingdom of God is at hand: repent ye, and believe the gospel' (Mark 1:15).

There is a condition to enter the kingdom of God which you do not find to enter the kingdom of heaven. This was given to Nicodemus by Jesus. A person must be born again or he cannot enter and see this kingdom (John 3:3). This is a spiritual birth, and it is the work of the Holy Spirit. Larkin, the well-known Bible teacher and author on Dispensationalism, defines the kingdom of God as the 'reign of God in the universe over all his creation, covering heaven and earth, time and eternity.'[54]

The kingdom of heaven is described by Jesus in what are known as the kingdom parables. These parables, contrary to what is often taught, are not intended to make things easy to understand. The parables deal with Israel. There are twelve parables, the number connected with Israel, and the first seven can be applied to the period of the seven churches. This is the period from when the church came into being through to the rapture of the church, given in a mystery form. The final five parables cover Israel through the Tribulation up to the Jewish expectation, which is the physical return of their Messiah. Notice that when the disciples

---

[54] Clarence Larkin, *Dispensational Truth*, (Santa Fe: Sun Publishing, 1998), 133.

asked Jesus about the parables, their application was very specific. The parables were not designed nor given to teach general principles!

Let's take one of those parables as an example: the parable of the ten virgins. Three things stand out about this parable which guide us in the direction to go for interpretation. Firstly, it is a continuation of the Olivet discourse in Matthew chapter 24, when Jesus returns to set up his kingdom. The church is not in existence. The subject is when Jesus will set up his kingdom. It is a very Jewish question.

Secondly, the parable is about virgins, plural. This distinguishes the parable from that of the bride of Christ, for scripture tells us Jesus marries a chaste virgin, singular. Revelation chapter 14 says that in the time of the Tribulation, you will find virgins. In the Old Testament, the role of the virgins is given: 'She shall be brought unto the king in raiment of needlework: the virgins her companions that follow her shall be brought unto thee' (Psalm 45:14).

Luke puts it like this: 'And ye yourselves like unto men that wait for their lord, when he will return from the wedding; that when he cometh and knocketh, they may open unto him immediately' (Luke 12:36).

Thirdly, in this context it is the bridegroom, the Son of Man, whom they are waiting for. They are commanded to watch, for they do not know the time when the Son of Man will come—not the day and not the hour (Matthew 25:13). He will come with his bride from the marriage supper of the Lamb.

The events we read about in Matthew chapter 12 culminate in the catalyst for the kingdom of heaven going into a mystery form. What was permitted on the Sabbath became a point of contention in Jesus's ministry. The Pharisees always found fault with Jesus or his disciples when anything was done on the Sabbath. Here they confront Jesus when the disciples have been plucking corn on the Sabbath: 'Behold, thy disciples do that which is not lawful to do upon the Sabbath day' (Matthew 12:2).

In another place it says these scribes and Pharisees were paying close attention to see if Jesus would heal on the Sabbath day, looking for an occasion to find fault and make a case against Jesus (Luke 6:7).

This obsession with refusing to accept Jesus, although he came with signs and wonders to demonstrate his credentials as the prophet like unto Moses, blinded the Pharisees and led them eventually to commit the unpardonable sin. And it all began with an incomplete understanding of their own scripture, followed by rejecting the testimony of one of their own priests, John the Baptist, who identified Jesus as the 'Lamb of God' (John 1:29).

The grace and mercy of God is seen on the cross, where Jesus makes a most remarkable request to his Father. Jesus prays that their sin will be forgiven them, for they have no idea what they are doing (Luke 23:34). Peter, when preaching to the crowd after the lame man was healed, told them it was Jesus who healed the man. Peter echoed the same message of forgiveness that Jesus spoke on the cross: 'And now, brethren, I wot that through ignorance ye did it, as did also your rulers' (Acts 3.17). It is an amazing opportunity for the rulers to repent and acknowledge the grave error they committed in crucifying their Messiah. Peter goes on to say, 'Repent ye therefore, and be converted, that your sins may be blotted out, when the times of refreshing shall come from the presence of the Lord' (Acts 3:19).

We must remember that after Jesus was risen from the dead, Peter was still preaching the message of John the Baptist, with the additional proviso that he preached in the name of Jesus: 'Repent, and be baptized' (Acts 2:38). In the early part of Acts, Israel is being extended a second opportunity to receive Jesus as their Messiah. At this point the only scripture passages that required fulfilment were those concerning the Second Advent and the purposes of Daniel's seventieth week.

However, the Jewish hierarchy remained stubbornly opposed to acknowledging Jesus as their Messiah. The kingdom that was at hand never materialised.

When we go back into the Old Testament, we find a similar situation regarding 'when I would have healed Israel' (Hosea 7:1). This was in the days of King Jehoahaz. We read that he continued in the ways of King Jeroboam, who caused Israel to sin. God raised up Benhadad against him, for the Lord was angry against Israel as a result of their iniquity (2 Kings 13:3). This prompted King Jehoahaz to seek the face of the Lord, and the Lord responded positively to him, seeing the oppression the people were under. The king of Syria oppressed Israel greatly (2 Kings 13:4).

God was ready to move. God was ready to heal Israel. Yet healing did not take place. King Jehoahaz sought the Lord, but then we find the answer why God did not heal Israel. It lacked any action to remove the iniquity of Ephraim, and wickedness remained in Samaria (Hosea 7:1) and the groves (2 Kings 13:6). King Jehoahaz was not prepared to turn away from his sin and serve the Lord. He was not willing to have the false idols removed. The nation was not healed, but continued in apostasy until their dispersion.

We can only surmise what would have taken place had Israel repented, humbled itself, and acknowledged the great sin, the crucifixion of the Messiah. This past two thousand years of being despised and scattered among the nations, wandering with no homeland, could have been different.

We often find ourselves, like Israel, forgetting our history and the dealings of God with our nation. The kingdom of heaven, the physical throne of David in Jerusalem, was so close, yet so far. Failing to distinguish the suffering Messiah from the triumphant king and refusing to acknowledge Christ as their Jewish Messiah meant that the Jews would hear but not understand, and they would see but not perceive (Matthew 13:14). The kingdom of heaven awaits the return of the Lord Jesus Christ at the Second Advent. Then will be fulfilled all the expectation of Israel that they have held on to throughout their history.

CHAPTER 14

MYSTERY OF THE TRANSLATION OF THE LIVING SAINTS

Behold, I show you a mystery; we shall not
all sleep, but we shall be changed
In a moment, in a twinkling of an eye, at the last
trump: for the trumpet shall sound, and the dead shall
be raised incorruptible, and we shall be changed
For this corruptible must put on incorruption,
and this mortal must put on immortality.

1 Corinthians 15:51–53

In chapter 2, which covered the resurrection of the dead, we traced the progressive revelation given to the writers of the Old Testament on this subject. Jesus in his ministry verified the truth of what had been written and then went on to give a further revelation, saying, 'I am the resurrection, and the life' (John 11:25). The chapter concluded with the sequence of events revealed up to the time of the gospels, as follows:

- There is a redeemer. God himself is the redeemer (Job 19:25–27).
- Jesus (God manifest in the flesh) provides his credentials, stating, 'I am the Resurrection' (John 11:25).

- Jesus demonstrates this truth by rising from the dead, bringing all of the Old Testament saints with him (Matthew 27:52) and he led captivity (those in Paradise) captive (Psalm 68:18).
- Many of these Old Testament saints walked through the streets of Jerusalem. It is a wild scene! (Matthew 27:53).
- Those not resurrected with Jesus will be resurrected at a future time and will see God face to face. That will cover all the unrighteous from the time of Adam (Isaiah 26:19; Job 19:26)).
- The time when this will take place is defined as 'at the latter day on the earth' (Job 19:25) or 'last day' (repeated in John 11:24).
- This will result either in a person being raised to 'everlasting life', or resurrected to 'shame and everlasting contempt' (Daniel 12:2). The context is the when the Jewish Messiah comes. Jesus confirms Daniel's words: 'resurrection of life' and 'resurrection of damnation' (John 5:29).

It is from the story told by Jesus about the rich man and Lazarus that we learn that paradise is also called Abraham's bosom. Jesus depicts the conditions of the two men once they had died. The beggar, Lazarus, was taken by the angels to Abraham's bosom, but the rich man ended up in hell, where we find him tormented. We also discover this rich man could look across a great gulf and see both Lazarus and Abraham (Luke 16:22–23).

At Calvary, while Jesus hung on the cross, one of the thieves asked Jesus to remember him when he came into his kingdom. The reply from Jesus was that the man would be with him in paradise that very day (Luke 23:43). Paradise and Abraham's bosom are synonymous with each other; it is the same place.

Although many Old Testament saints walked through Jerusalem, scripture makes it clear that all those in paradise (Abraham's bosom) were resurrected. It is prophesied by the psalmist: 'Thou hast ascended on high, thou hast led captivity captive: thou hast received gifts for men; yea, for the rebellious also, that the LORD God might dwell among them' (Psalm 68:18).

At the time of Jesus's teaching, the church did not exist. No one had any revelation about the church. Even the disciples, who were Jesus's closest confidants, were completely in the dark. When we examine Jesus's ministry, we find his teaching on the resurrection is to Israel. Look at the instructions he gives to his disciples: 'Go not into the way of the Gentiles ... Go rather to the lost sheep of the house of Israel' (Matthew 10:5, 6).

Turning to the letter of the apostle Paul to the church at Corinth, we find a resurrection and a rapture being taught. Along with Paul's teaching found in 1 Thessalonians 4:14–17, it provides the foundational verses used to teach the rapture of the church.

The ministry of Paul and the calling of God on his life was stated by Paul in the book of Romans: 'For I speak to you Gentiles, inasmuch as I am the apostle of the Gentiles' (11:13). With the mystery of the church revealed, Paul's teaching is to the Gentiles who have been converted, and they are presented here to the church at Corinth.

To summarise, Jesus's ministry was to the lost sheep of the House of Israel, whereas Paul was called to be an apostle to the Gentiles. Jesus taught that there would be a rapture of his people when he returned to earth, and Paul taught the Gentile believers about a resurrection and a rapture.

We now have a clear starting point to unravel the teachings of Jesus and the teachings of Paul and to see how they fit together in scripture.

Before Jesus was taken and crucified, we find him on the Mount of Olives along with four of his disciples: Peter, James, John, and Andrew. In response to the disciples asking, 'what shall be the sign of thy coming, and of the end of the world' (Matthew 24:3), Jesus furnishes them with details of a rapture: 'And he shall send his angels with a great sound of a trumpet, and they shall gather together his elect from the four winds, from one end of heaven to the other' (Matthew 24:31). He elaborates, 'Then shall two be in the field; the one shall be taken, and the other left. Two women shall be grinding at the mill; the one shall be taken, and the other left' (Matthew 24:40-41). His elect in this passage of scripture are Jewish believers as found in the Old Testament: 'For Jacob my servant's sake, and Israel mine elect' (Isaiah 45:4).

The context of this briefing by Jesus to his disciples was to be always ready, for when they least expected it, the Son of Man would come (Matthew 24:44). This refers to the Second Coming of the Lord Jesus Christ as we shall see.

Let's look at placing this rapture Jesus spoke of into our timeline before proceeding to look at the mystery revealed to the apostle Paul.

To begin this journey, we need an understanding of the outworking of two Old Testament prophecies in particular: Daniel's vision of seventy weeks, and the peculiar instructions God gave to Ezekiel to enact before the Jewish captives in Babylon. Daniel was provided with a map of God's future plan for Israel. Ezekiel gives the answer to why Israel has had such a long period scattered among the nations. As part of this journey, we will bring up the dealings of God with Israel, which are unique to that nation.

Daniel's Supernatural Encounters

Daniel was taken captive to Babylon after Nebuchadnezzar captured Jerusalem. He rose to prominence due to his ability to provide the details of a dream given by God to Nebuchadnezzar and the interpretation of that dream. Daniel had a long career in Babylon and was elevated above all the wise men in Nebuchadnezzar's empire. In his later years, he came across the prophecy of Jeremiah stating that the captivity in Babylon would last for seventy years (Jeremiah 25:11). As the seventy years of captivity were drawing to a close, Daniel set his face to seek God—by prayer and supplication, with fasting, and with sackcloth—to get revelation about how God would bring this prophecy to fruition.

In the first year of Darius, the son of Ahasuerus, Daniel confesses his sins and the sins of his people. While he is continuing in prayer, an angelic encounter with Gabriel occurs. This was not the first time Gabriel had appeared to Daniel. Around seventeen years earlier, Daniel had been given a vision of a he-goat with a notable horn, and the vision was interpreted to Daniel by Gabriel. This latest encounter was to impart the knowledge and understanding required for the promise of God to be fulfilled. Daniel sought the face of God for understanding of Jeremiah's prophecy, and in the encounter with Gabriel, he received his answer.

It is prudent to note that Daniel had a number of supernatural encounters and was not always given full or complete revelation. In the last chapter of Daniel, he writes about not understanding everything he had heard (12:8).

In the study of scripture, there is a law called the law of first mention, which usually sets the stage for interpretation thereafter. The significance of Gabriel's visit and the implications which come from it cannot be overstated. The subject of the vision concerned the future of Jerusalem, the Jewish people, and the death of their Messiah, who 'shall be cut off' (Daniel 9:26). It also reveals when their Messiah will show up and establish his kingdom. It is crucial to grasp the context: 'thy people, thy holy city' (Daniel 9:24).

The full context of the vision Daniel received is as follows:

> Seventy weeks are determined upon thy people and upon thy holy city, to finish the transgression, and to make an end of sins, and to make reconciliation for iniquity, and to bring in everlasting righteousness, and to seal up the vision and prophecy, and to anoint the most Holy. Know therefore and understand, that from the going forth of the commandment to restore and to build Jerusalem unto the Messiah the Prince shall be seven weeks, and threescore and two weeks: the streets shall be built again, and the wall, even in troublous times. And after threescore and two weeks shall Messiah be cut off, but not for himself: and the people of the prince that shall come shall destroy the city and the sanctuary; and the end thereof shall be with a flood, and unto the end of the war desolations are determined. And he shall confirm the covenant with many for one week: and in the midst of the week he shall cause the sacrifice and the oblation to cease, and for the overspreading of abominations he shall make it desolate, even until the consummation, and that determined shall be poured upon the desolate. (Daniel 9:24–27)

Out of all the visitations and revelations given to the prophets throughout Israel's history, Missler describes this passage of scripture as the most astonishing in the Bible.[55] The prophecy encompasses all that has to take place with the nation of Israel and the city of Jerusalem before God's kingdom will be set up on earth 'to bring in everlasting righteousness'.

It is good to break this prophecy down into its particular parts.

The first thing to notice is the length of time this prophecy covers: 'seventy weeks are determined upon thy people and upon thy holy city.' Each week represents a seven-year time period; therefore, in total it covers a period of 490 years. It is worthwhile examining the significance of the number 490 in Israel's history, for it reveals to us how God has dealt with Israel in the past and how we can apply it to Israel today.

In the gospels, Peter asked Jesus a question about forgiveness. He wanted to know how many times he must forgive a person who did wrong to him. Peter suggested seven times (Matthew 18:21). Jesus's answer bears some attention, for it matches the number of years in Daniel's vision. Jesus tells Peter to multiply his answer by seventy (Matthew 18:22). That is four hundred and ninety times. When studying Israel's history, we find that it can be broken down into 490-year periods. But there is a peculiarity: the clock stops when Israel is in disobedience. This can be seen as follows:

- The period from Abraham to the Exodus is 505 years. If we subtract the age of Ishmael (15) when Isaac was born, because Ishmael was not the son of promise, it comes to 490 years.
- The period from the Exodus to the dedication of the Temple is 591 years. If we deduct the number of years of Israel's servitude in the book of Judges, we come back to 490 years.
- The period from the dedication of the Temple to the edict of Artaxerxes Longimanus is 560 years. If we subtract the 70 years' captivity in Babylon, we come back to 490 years.

---

[55] Chuck Missler, *Learn the Bible in 24 Hours* (Nashville: Thomas Nelson, 2002), 108.

- The period from the edict of Artaxerxes Longimanus to the crucifixion of Jesus covers 69 weeks of Daniel's vision, a period of 483 years.
- The clock stopped when Messiah was cut off after 483 years, leaving one seven-year period still to take place 'to finish the transgression, and to make an end of sins, and to make reconciliation for iniquity, and to bring in everlasting righteousness' (Daniel 9:24). This has been the longest period in Israel's history that God's clock has been stopped.

The second thing to note is the time when the prophecy starts. It begins with the commandment to rebuild Jerusalem, and it concludes when the Messiah is cut off—that is, when the Messiah is crucified. This is a period of 69 weeks in Daniel's vision, which equates to 483 years.

From history we can place this date: it is 14 March 445 BC. That tells us that the end of 483 years, when 'Messiah be cut off', is on 6 April AD 32.[56] This is the date of the crucifixion of the Lord Jesus Christ. We are told it is 'not for himself'. Jesus lays down his life to redeem mankind from sin.

The detail in the Prophet Zechariah's prophecy is such that no one should have been ignorant when it happened. He says, 'thy King cometh unto thee: he is just, and having salvation; lowly, and riding upon an ass, and upon a colt the foal of an ass' (Zechariah 9:9). When Jesus enters Jerusalem before his crucifixion, he enters the city riding on an ass. The word goes out to the daughters of Zion that they should behold their King (Matthew 21:5).

Jesus was crucified in the 69th week of Daniel's prophecy, to the exact date and exact time of the afternoon sacrifice in the temple.

The third thing to note is that Daniel's prophecy states, 'And the people of the prince that shall come shall destroy the city and the sanctuary.' The Romans crucified the Lord Jesus Christ, and the Romans destroyed Jerusalem in AD 70. It was also prophesied that none of the bones of the Lord would be broken. Under Jewish law, a person

---

[56] Ibid, 110.

would have been stoned to death. It is amazing to see how everything is orchestrated to fulfil scripture!

Fourth and finally, the prophecy states, 'And he shall confirm the covenant with many for one week: and in the midst of the week he shall cause the sacrifice and the oblation to cease, and for the overspreading of abominations he shall make it desolate, even until the consummation, and that determined shall be poured upon the desolate.' This is the final week of Daniel's vision, a period of seven years, which still has to be fulfilled. This seven-year period will start when a covenant is signed with Israel. This period is well documented in scripture, known as the time of Jacob's troubles. It is the time when the Antichrist will be revealed to the world.

This covenant to be signed will reflect the conditions that are going to prevail on the earth, causing Israel to make the treaty. The prophet Isaiah tells us:

> Because ye have said, We have made a covenant with death, and with hell are we at agreement; when the overflowing scourge shall pass through, it shall not come unto us: for we have made lies our refuge, and under falsehood have we hid ourselves ... And your covenant with death shall be disannulled, and your agreement with hell shall not stand; when the overflowing scourge shall pass through, then ye shall be trodden down by it. (Isaiah 28:15, 18)

It is at the fulfilment of Daniel's vision that God brings in 'everlasting righteousness' when Jesus returns to this earth to reign as King of Kings and Lord of Lords.

From the crucifixion until now has been the longest period when God's clock has been stopped in Israel's calendar. After the resurrection of Jesus, the Sanhedrin did not acknowledge their great transgression. The Sanhedrin, even after being confronted with the evidence of the resurrection of Jesus, remained hostile to the gospel message and compounded their sin by persecuting those who believed. The result has been two thousand years of the Jews wandering throughout the nations of the earth, with Daniel's prophecy of the final seven years awaiting fulfilment.

Why has this period of time been so much longer than those of the past in Israel's history? Let us look at the word given to Ezekiel.

Ezekiel's Acts in Babylon

Like many of the prophets in the Old Testament—who were required to demonstrate prophetically what the Lord was going to do—Ezekiel is instructed to act out the siege of Jerusalem to the captives at the River Chebar in Babylon. In addition, he is told to lie on the ground: so many days on his right side and so many days on his left side. These were all prophetic acts to be done openly in front of the people, laying out the consequences of their idolatry. As we shall see, they have a bearing on Israel's history after the Babylonian captivity.

The rise of the Babylonians saw them conquering Nineveh in 606 BC. There are two battles with Pharaoh Neco. The first was 609 BC, but the most significant was in 606 BC at the battle of Carchemish. At this battle, Nebuchadnezzar defeated Pharaoh Neco. Nebuchadnezzar then went on to conquer Jerusalem. This was the first of three sieges that Nebuchadnezzar undertook at Jerusalem.

'The Servitude of the Nation'[57] begins with the first siege of Jerusalem by Nebuchadnezzar. Many captives are taken to Babylon. Daniel and his three friends Shadrach, Meshach, and Abednego are among those taken to Babylon. By the time Gabriel appears to Daniel to give him the vision, Daniel is an old man. The important thing to note is that the seventy years of captivity starts from this invasion by Nebuchadnezzar. The nation goes into captivity, and the Babylonians put in place a vassal king to rule on their behalf.

However, only nine years later, in 597 BC, Nebuchadnezzar returns to Jerusalem. This second siege arises due to a rebellion against his rule.

---

[57] Missler's terminology for Israel being brought under the control of the Babylonians.

After the city is taken, a further group of captives are taken to Babylon. This time a priest named Ezekiel is included.

As mentioned, Ezekiel is called to demonstrate prophetically the future of the Jewish people. He is given revelations from God that assist our understanding and help open up the vision Gabriel gives Daniel.

Ezekiel is taken to Telabib, which lay outside of Babylon, beside the River Chebar (Ezekiel 3:15). There are no records that Daniel or Ezekiel ever met. Daniel is in the palace, among the higher echelons of society, whereas Ezekiel is stationed with many of the captives from Jerusalem who are working on the land. Ezekiel is 25 years old when taken as a captive. After another five years, at the age of 30, Ezekiel is called by God to be a prophet.

Ezekiel is told to enact the siege of Jerusalem by setting his face against it and demonstrating before the people as a sign to the house of Israel (Ezekiel 4:3). In 586 BC, Nebuchadnezzar once more brings his armies to Jerusalem. His anger and frustration with the constant rebellions result in the city of Jerusalem being razed to the ground.

The 'Desolation of Jerusalem'[58] takes place at the third siege of the city, when Jerusalem is completely destroyed and left in rubble. However, Ezekiel highlights further potential consequences if there is no repentance. Once more he is required to act out in front of the people. This time he lies on his left side for the sin of Israel, and a given number of days are specified. The days Ezekiel has to lie on his left side represent the number of years the house of Israel will bear their iniquity. The number of years given is 390 (Ezekiel 4:4–5). Once Ezekiel does this, he is told to lie on his right side, bearing the sin of Judah for forty days, each day representing a year (Ezekiel 4:6). In total, Ezekiel lies on his sides for 430 days, which represents a period of 430 years.

However, unlike the captivity in Babylon for seventy years, as described by Jeremiah, this period does not stand out. It is worth noting that Israel's seventy years in captivity matches the disobedience of Israel over a 490-year period, during which they did not keep the seventh year as a Sabbath to rest the land. The people of Israel did not willingly

---

[58] Missler's terminology for the complete destruction of Jerusalem.

obey the instructions given to them. The Lord removed them from the land and laid it desolate. They were put in a position that they could not cultivate the land until full restitution was made.

In the book of Leviticus, it states the consequences for continuing to disobey the Lord. Disobedience results in the punishment for sin being multiplied seven times (Leviticus 26:18). Should the people walk in disobedience and refuse to hear the words of the Lord, then punishment is multiplied seven times (Leviticus 26:21). This message is repeated again in verse 24, and culminates a fourth time with the statement that they will suffer God's fury for their sins and be chastised seven times (Leviticus 26:28). This gives us an explanation as to why, when the people returned to Jerusalem, they were still subjugated to another nation.

When we subtract the seventy-year captivity in Babylon from the Ezekiel's 430 years, we have 360 years remaining.[59] When this is multiplied by seven, it gives us a period of 2,520 years. The Jewish calendar is based on 360 days in a year. On this basis, Missler provides the time period as 2,483 years, 9 months, and 21 days.[60]

At the end of the seventy years following Nebuchadnezzar's first invasion of Israel, there is the Decree of Cyrus. From the time of this decree, adding on the additional years prophesied by Ezekiel, we reach the exact day Israel is restored as a nation: 14 May 1948.

From the time Jerusalem was rendered desolate at the third siege, seventy years passed. Then came the Decree of Artaxerxes. Again, adding the additional years given by Ezekiel, we arrive at 7 June 1967, which is when Israel recaptured Jerusalem.

In 2018, for the first time in over two thousand years, Jerusalem was once again recognised as Israel's capital. This is important because Daniel's vision cannot be completed until the Jewish people are back in their land and Jerusalem is their capital. It is a further step pointing towards the imminent arrival of the events of Daniel's final seven years.

---

[59] Grant R. Jeffrey, *The Signature of God* (Toronto: Frontier Research Publications, 2002), 175.
[60] Missler, *Learn the Bible in 24 Hours*, 133.

If you pay particular attention, everything that has been covered is centred on Israel, Jerusalem, and the coming of the Jewish Messiah to reign at Jerusalem. There has been no mention of the church, for it is not part of the vision given to Daniel.

Before Jesus appears as King of Kings and Lord of Lords, scripture details Daniel's seventieth week. It is also known as the Tribulation. The last three and a half years will be unlike anything that has ever taken place before. Jesus states, 'Except those days should be shortened, there should no flesh be saved: but for the elect's sake those days shall be shortened' (Matthew 24:22). Again, a quick reminder: do not be misled by the word 'elect' as found in Paul's writings. Here it refers to the elect of Israel, a usage similar to that found in the writings of the prophet Isaiah and other places in the Old Testament, as well as in Jesus's discourse.

Now we have an answer to our question why God's clock has been stopped for such a long time. It is the punishment for the Israelites' disobedience and a lack of repentance while in captivity in Babylon.

When we go back to when only a small remnant remained in the land of Israel, after the third siege by the Babylonians, this hardness of heart is graphically displayed. They had seen the fulfilment of all of the words of Jeremiah and all the evil that befell Jerusalem, yet they did not humble themselves. They asked Jeremiah to inquire of the Lord if they should go down to Egypt, but then told Jeremiah they would not obey the word God gave them. Those who stood against Jeremiah and their wives offered incense to idols. They blamed their predicament on the worship of the queen of heaven coming to a stop. Those who went down to Egypt died in Egypt.

The importance of the nation of Israel existing today is simple. The return of the Jewish people to their homeland is a prerequisite for the completion of Daniel's vision—'upon thy people and thy holy city'.

Jesus's Teaching on a Rapture

Let's turn again to the Mount of Olives discourse. 'And as he sat upon the Mount of Olives, the disciples came unto him privately, saying, Tell us, when shall these things be? and what shall be the sign of thy coming, and of the end of the world' (Matthew 24:3). Notice the questions concern the return of Christ at the Second Advent and the events that will take place at the end of the world. The events will be those of Daniel's seventieth week, which was interpreted for us as a period of seven years which the book of Revelation covers in detail. At the end of the seven years, a rapture happens. Jesus tells us that 'he shall send his angels with a great sound of a trumpet, and they shall gather together his elect from the four winds, from one end of heaven to the other' (Matthew 24:31).

God's kingdom is set up on the completion of Daniel's vision, which brings in 'everlasting righteousness'. Immediately preceding this, a rapture takes place.

The psalmist tells us:

> Our God shall come, and shall not keep silence: a fire shall devour before him, and it shall be very tempestuous round about him. He shall call to the heavens from above, and to the earth, that he may judge his people. Gather my saints together unto me; those that have made a covenant with me by sacrifice. (Psalm 50:3–5)[61]

In Matthew's gospel, a reference to the final harvest (typified by wheat) is given. Jesus speaks of a thorough cleansing before this can take place. The leftovers (typified by chaff) get thrown into the fire to be consumed (Matthew 3:12). Matthew also advises us that when Jesus comes, it will be swift, like the lightning. Matthew indicates Jesus will come from the east to the west (Matthew 24:27).

Let us summarise what we have gleaned so far:

Daniel's timeline provided the details as to when the Jewish Messiah would be cut off. The prophecy of Zechariah highlighted how they would recognise their Messiah. Jesus, the Messiah, was crucified on Mount Calvary, fulfilling this prophecy to the exact day and to the exact time of the afternoon sacrifice.

---

[61] Strong's Hebrew Lexicon, https://blueletterbible.org/lexicon/h622/rvr60/wic/0-1, 'gather' (H622) means to gather and take away, remove, withdraw.

We have learned that God's clock stops when Israel is in disobedience, and a further seven-year period is still to come to complete Daniel's vision.

The length of the Jewish dispersion is explained to us through Ezekiel's unusual behaviour and the application of the punishments given in the book of Leviticus for when the nation does not turn away from sin. The prophet Jeremiah laid out God's case against the people of Jerusalem. Chapter 25 is a good example. Hardness of heart and lack of repentance were the final catalyst that led to the downfall of the nation. The city of Jerusalem was laid waste, and those who survived the siege were carried off to Babylon.

Jesus speaks of the end time as a period unlike any other time in human history. It will never be repeated again.

Daniel tells at the end of this final seven-year period, God will bring in everlasting righteousness. As Christians, we understand this event as the Second Advent or Second Coming of the Lord Jesus Christ. This will be the time of the rapture spoken of by Jesus.

We can place this rapture in our timeline as follows:

- There is a redeemer. God himself is the redeemer (Job 19:25–27).
- Jesus (God manifest in the flesh) provides his credentials and states, 'I am the Resurrection' (John 11:25).
- Jesus demonstrates this truth by rising from the dead, bringing all of the Old Testament saints with him (Matthew 27:52) and He led captivity (those in Paradise) captive (Psalm 68:18; repeated in Ephesians 4:8).
- Many of these Old Testament saints walked through the streets of Jerusalem. It is a wild scene! (Matthew 27:53).
- Those not resurrected with Jesus will be resurrected at a future time and will see God face to face. That will cover all the unrighteous from the time of Adam (Isaiah 26:19; Job 19:26).
- There is a rapture immediately before God brings in everlasting righteousness (Matthew 24:31; Psalm 50:3-5). This will be at the Second Coming of Jesus.

- The time when this will take place is defined as 'at the latter day on the earth' or 'last day' (Job 19:25; repeated in John 11:24).
- This will result in a person either being raised to 'everlasting life', or resurrected to 'shame and everlasting contempt' (Daniel 12:2). The context is when the Jewish Messiah returns. Jesus confirms Daniel's words: 'resurrection of life' and 'resurrection of damnation' (John 5:29).

Jesus revealed a rapture to his disciples on the Mount of Olives but did not mention anything about the dead being raised—that is, a resurrection. However, when we turn to the book of Revelation, we find a reference to martyrs who were killed for testifying and declaring the Word of God (Revelation 6:9). Later in the book of Revelation, we discover they have been resurrected out of great tribulation. They are standing clothed in white raiment, which speaks of God's righteousness. They have been washed clean by the blood of the Lamb (Revelation 7:14). They 'lived and reigned with Christ a thousand years' (Revelation 20:4).

Immediately after this rapture takes place, Jesus returns to earth and lands upon the Mount of Olives. He sets up his kingdom and reigns for a thousand years with Jerusalem as his capital. Let us look at this for a moment.

When Jesus returns to reign in Jerusalem, we are told he will come down the king's highway and land on the Mount of Olives. When Israel was in Kadesh, they enquired of Edom for permission to pass through their country. They promised not to touch the harvests or the vineyards, nor even to help themselves to water from any of their wells. They would keep strictly to the king's highway (Numbers 20:17). When a search is made through the historical records, we do not find the name of any king travelling on this highway. It is a highway reserved only for the King of Glory!

The details of this route were given to Moses, with the various landmarks along the route clearly set out: from Sinai to Seir to Mount Paran. We have a prophecy that states he will come with ten thousand of his saints (Deuteronomy 33:2). This prophecy is quoted by Jude.

It reminds us of the prophecy that has lain dormant since before the days of Abraham. The prophecy was given by Enoch, the seventh man from Adam. He prophesied the coming of the Lord with ten thousand of his saints. It is the Second Coming of the Lord to establish righteousness on the earth. Judgement is going to fall upon all the ungodly for the deeds they have committed and the words they have raised against God Almighty himself (Jude 14–15). When the Second Advent takes place, Jesus will come along this route, which is the same route we read that the Ark of the Covenant followed to the crossing of the Jordan River.

The Second Advent is an appearance of Jesus to the whole world. Every person who is alive is going to see him. It will be particularly painful for the Jewish people. Their eyes will be opened, and they will see the one they rejected (Revelation 1:7). As Jesus comes in the clouds, all his enemies will flee before him.

Paul's Teaching on a Resurrection and a Rapture

We are now in a place to unpack the apostle Paul's revelation that he received from the Lord. To the church at Corinth, Paul wrote:

> Behold, I shew you a mystery; We shall not all sleep, but we shall be changed, In a moment, in the twinkling of an eye, at the last trump: for the trumpet shall sound, and the dead shall be raised incorruptible, and we shall be changed. For this corruptible must put on incorruption, and this mortal must put on immortality.
> (1 Corinthians 15:51–53)

As we study this passage, there are a number of revelations Paul shares with Christian believers. Firstly, he is going to unveil the mysteries surrounding what happens to a Christian who is alive when Jesus returns, what happens to a Christian who has already died, and what type of body a Christian will inherit in eternity.

When scripture states 'we will not all sleep', that is scripture's way of stating we will not all die. There will be those alive when Jesus returns, and they will meet the Lord 'in the air' (1 Thessalonians 4:17).

For those who have died, Paul explains, they leave their bodies to go to be with the Lord (2 Corinthians 5:8). That is, their souls and spirits go into his presence. The opposite is true when we are still in our bodies; we have not entered into that heavenly place, for our souls and spirits are still together in our earthly bodies (2 Corinthians 5:6). In other words, when you die, your body is going to go into the grave, but your spirit and soul are going to go into the presence of God, to await a resurrected body.

Paul repeats this message to the Christians at Thessalonica when he tells them that he does not want them to be ignorant about what happens at death. Paul does not want them to be like other people who have no hope, for one day they will be reunited (1 Thessalonians 4:13). This hope is the resurrection of the body. When Paul writes to Titus, he calls this hope the 'blessed hope' (Titus 2:13).

At the time of this rapture, 'the dead shall be raised incorruptible, and we shall be changed. For this corruptible must put on incorruption, and this mortal must put on immortality' (1 Corinthians 15:52-53). To the church at Philippi, Paul tells them how we look for our Saviour to come from heaven. He explains how our earthly, corrupt bodies will be exchanged for glorious bodies like that of the Lord Jesus Christ (Phil. 3:21–22). We get a glimpse of what this glorious resurrection body looks like as we meditate on the appearances of Jesus after his resurrection. Furthermore, when we have put on this new body we can make a great declaration: death has lost its power over us, and the grave is not going to be able to hold us when Jesus comes (1 Corinthians 15:54–55).

The whole process is done and completed 'in the twinkling of an eye' (1 Corinthians 15:52). Paul details it thus:

> For the Lord himself shall descend from heaven with
> a shout, with the voice of the archangel, and with the
> trump of God: and the dead in Christ shall rise first.
> Then we which are alive and remain shall be caught

up together with them in the clouds, to meet the Lord
in the air: and so shall we ever be with the Lord. (1
Thessalonians 4:16-17)

The apostle Paul also provides the sequence to the resurrection, likening it to a farmer gathering in his crops: first fruits, the main harvest, and then the gleanings. The gleanings come at the end. 'Christ the firstfruits' is at the beginning (1 Corinthians 15:23).[62] Jesus rose from the dead, and all the Old Testament saints held in paradise (Abraham' bosom) rose with him. Many of these Old Testament saints walked through the streets of Jerusalem. Those who rose with Christ were part of the first fruits.

Next, Paul expands on his exegesis and states, 'But every man in his order: Christ the firstfruits; afterward they that are Christ's at his coming' (1 Corinthians 15:23). In the context of Paul writing to Gentiles, this points to when Jesus returns for his church. Paul likens this to the main harvest.

Paul brings the matter to a conclusion by stating the end comes, and the kingdom of God is delivered to the Father. All rebellion in the earth, their powers, and their authority will be put down (1 Corinthians 15:24). This is the return of the Lord Jesus Christ at the Second Advent. The period from the rapture of the church to the Second Advent is the end-time harvest during the last seven years of this age. It is the gleanings at the end of harvest.

We can summarise Paul's teaching on the rapture of the churches as follows: at the rapture of the church, there will be a resurrection from the grave of the bodies of those who have died. Together with those who are still living, they will be caught up in the air to meet Christ. In that moment, their corruptible bodies will put on incorruption—that is, they will receive a resurrected body like the Lord Jesus Christ's resurrected body.

---

[62] Erich Sauer, *From Eternity to Eternity* (Carlisle: Paternoster Press and Erdman Publishing, 1994), 78.

When Do the Events of Paul's Mystery Take Place?

To answer this question, we will look at how theologians interpret Paul's teaching and the teaching of the early church. We will be looking at the three main theological positions that the church has adopted since its inception. These positions are categorized as premillennial, postmillennial, and amillennial. In Revelation chapter 20, we are told six times about a one-thousand-year period known as the millennium, a word which means 'one thousand years'—hence the term in these theological categories. It is an important doctrine, for whatever position is taken, interpretation of scripture will be seen through that lens.

During this one-thousand-year period, we are informed, the Devil—who is also called Satan and described as a dragon—is going to be bound up in chains and cast into the bottomless pit (Revelation 20:1–2). We then have unveiled to us those who will reign with Christ throughout the millennium:

> And I saw thrones, and they sat upon them, and judgment was given unto them: and I saw the souls of them that were beheaded for the witness of Jesus, and for the word of God, and which had not worshipped the beast, neither his image, neither had received his mark upon their foreheads, or in their hands; and they lived and reigned with Christ a thousand years. (Revelation 20:4)

Notice two important elements stated in these passages, Satan is bound for a thousand years and Christ reigns (on earth) for a thousand years.

The theological question that arises centres on when the events Paul shares are going to take place. Is it before the one-thousand-year reign of Christ on earth? Or is it after the one-thousand-year reign of Christ on earth? Or is the millennium to be understood simply as an allegorical expression meaning an indeterminate period of time, with Christ coming at the close of that time?

Theologians clash on whether scripture should be interpreted at face value—that is, whether it is literal or whether it is to be taken allegorically.

As a backdrop, historically, the premillennial view was held by the early church up until the time of Origen (AD 182–254), who introduced the allegorical method of interpretation. This method of interpretation was made popular by Augustine. It eventually became the dominant church position, known as amillennialism. It is appropriate to look at these theological positions, starting with amillennialism.

The Amillennialist Position

Amillennialism became the major position of the church at the time of Augustine, after adopting Origen's allegorical method of interpretation. The term 'amillennial' means 'no millennium.'[63] Amillennialism maintains the Second Coming of Christ will occur at the end of the millennium period, which is effectively an unknown length of time. It covers the time from the resurrection of Jesus until he comes again.

Viewed from an allegorical perspective, the one thousand year millennium is not taken literally, but rather spiritually. After this allegorical one-thousand-year period, they see the fulfilment of Paul's words to the Corinthians.

This position maintains Satan has been bound since the resurrection of Jesus. Importantly, however, this binding does not mean that Satan is inactive in the world. Rather, during this period, Satan cannot deceive the nations. He cannot prevent the spread of the gospel. Jesus is reigning now triumphantly in heaven and on earth through his church.

Amillennialist also take two other important theological positions to be aware of. Firstly, by spiritualising scripture, they do not believe in a literal restoration of the throne of David in Jerusalem. As Grant Jeffrey, a Canadian Bible teacher of Bible prophecy/eschatology points out, it 'denies the supernatural and visible return of Christ to establish His

---

[63] R. Ludwigson, *A Survey of Bible Prophecy* (Zondervan, Twelfth Printing, 1981), 103.

millennial rule'.[64] Therefore, there will be no earthly Jewish kingdom, thereby negating the words of the angel to Mary: 'He shall be great, and shall be called the Son of the Highest: and the Lord God shall give unto him the throne of his father David' (Luke 1:32). Amillennialism appropriates the promises given to Israel and applies them to the church. Secondly, they do not believe that the final seven years before the Second Advent, known as the Tribulation, have any evidence in the Bible.

After studying the prophecies of Daniel and Ezekiel, and their accuracy in terms of events that happen in time, it is difficult to grasp this total turnaround in interpretation taking hold, in which doctrine is produced based on generalities, and believers think God forgets his unconditional promises to Israel. God does not break his covenant.

Postmillennialist Position

Postmillennialism is a view that arose in the early 1800s. This view holds to a symbolic interpretation of scripture.[65] It maintains Jesus will come at the end of the millennial period as the church spreads throughout the world, bringing in the kingdom. As Raymond Ludwigson who was professor of Bible at Wheaton College notes, 'Post millenarians affirm that this growth will continue until the world is practically Christianised.'[66] It is the belief that the kingdom of God comes through development and progress, the influence of Christianity bringing change to social and political life.[67] This view of eschatology was very prominent in the nineteenth century, and its primary support came from Princeton Theological Seminary, headed by Charles Hodge who followed the orthodox Calvinist theological tradition in America at that time, followed by B. B. Warfield, who was the last principal of Princeton Theological Seminary.

Postmillennialism also sees Old Testament prophecies being spiritually realised and fulfilled in the church. The view was made all

---

[64] Grant R. Jeffrey, *Triumphant Return* (Toronto: Frontier Research Publications, 2001), 47.

[65] Ludwigson, *A Survey of Bible Prophecy*, 94.

[66] Ibid., 97.

[67] Sauer, *From Eternity to Eternity*, 154.

the more plausible as missionaries were going out in their droves to the nations of the world in the 1800s. As Sauer writes, 'This belief in progress stands in contradiction to experience and to the Scriptures.'[68] He goes on to quote the words of Jesus from Matthew 24: 'Lawlessness will take the upper hand, the love of many will wax cold and when the Son of Man comes He will find but little faith on earth.'[69]

This theological position holds to a symbolic millennium period which ends with the great Tribulation, then the Second Coming of Christ.

Post millenarians believe that the Jewish people will be converted sometime during this symbolic millennium. However, they do not hold to a literal restoration of Israel in fulfilment of Old Testament prophecies. Therefore, they see the establishment of Israel as a state only as an accident of history.[70]

One thing to be aware of: many postmillennialists and amillennialists have adopted the view that the book of Revelation is past history, having been fulfilled in AD 70. This is known as the preterist view. Jeffrey notes, 'Post-Millennialist and Amillennialist writers admit that their preterist system is false and will utterly fail if it can be proven that the book of Revelation was written at any time after A.D. 70 burning of Jerusalem.'[71]

Premillennialist Position

The premillennial system was the view of the early church. An example is Irenaeus's work *Against Heresies,* which gave a literal interpretation of these events. The teaching of premillennialism divides Jesus's Second Coming into two parts. In the first part, Christ will come for his saints, as described in the verses to the Corinthians and Thessalonians about the rapture of the church, also known as the Parousia. At this rapture, those who are alive are caught up to meet Jesus in the air.

---

[68] Ibid., 154.
[69] Ibid., 155.
[70] Ludwigson, *A Survey of Biblical Prophecy,* 98.
[71] Jeffrey, *Triumphant Return,* 43.

In the second part, after a seven-year tribulation, also known as Daniel's seventieth week, Jesus will come with his saints. This is the Second Coming of Christ, who will land on the Mount of Olives, subdue his enemies, and reign from Jerusalem for one thousand years. This will be a time of peace on earth.

During Jesus's reign, Satan will be cast into the bottomless pit. After the one thousand years, Satan will be loosed for a short time and allowed to stir up hatred towards Jesus, culminating in Satan being cast into the lake of fire.

This view lines up with the prophecies of Daniel, Ezekiel, and the early Christian theologians. So let us look at some of the writings of these theologians.

Early Christian Theologians

The early church taught the rapture of the believer. In addition to Irenaeus's work mentioned above, one of the most comprehensive works is that of Ephraem the Syrian (AD 306–373). He writes, 'For all the saints and the Elect of God are gathered, prior to the tribulation that is to come, and are taken to the Lord lest they see the confusion that is to overwhelm the world because of our sins.'[72] His work *On the Last Times, the Antichrist, and the End of the World* can be found quoted in a number of sources, including work by Grant Jeffrey. In his other book, *The Book of the Cave of Treasure*, Ephraem taught that the end of the age ends with Daniel's seventieth week, culminating in the battle of Armageddon at the Second Advent.

Ephraem the Syrian had a number of astute observations which we do not hear mentioned today. Therefore, it is worth our while to look a little further into his teachings. Jeffrey, who arranged the translation of Ephraem's writings by Dr. Cameron Rhoades of Tyndale Theological Seminary in 1995, expounds upon Ephraem's teaching after the rapture of the church: 'When therefore the end of the world comes, that abominable, lying and murderous one is born from the tribe of Dan. He

---

[72] Ibid., 174.

is conceived from the seed of a man and from a most vile virgin, mixed with an evil or worthless spirit.'[73] Then, talking about the Antichrist, he states, 'But when the time of the abomination of his desolation begins to approach, having been made legal, he takes the empire ... Therefore, when he receives the kingdom, he orders the temple of God to be rebuilt for himself, which is in Jerusalem; who, after coming into it he shall sit as God and order that he be adored by all nations.'[74]

Two important insights can be drawn from this. The first is that the Antichrist is from Dan, and the second is that it will be the Antichrist who will get the Temple at Jerusalem built. That would certainly solve a lot of problems with regard to a new Temple.

Other early Christian writers, such as Irenaeus and Hippolytus, also believed that the Antichrist will come from Dan. Looking back over the tribe of Dan from scripture, a number of things stand out. For example, when we arrive at Revelation chapter 7, Dan is not included in the tribes of Israel. Additionally, in various places throughout scripture, Dan can be seen as an outsider. In Genesis, we see that Dan doesn't actually settle in his inheritance in Israel. He appears in Sardinia. Some sources point to the tribe of Dan as mercenaries in the Aegean, possibly being at Troy.

Regardless of this, Jacob says, 'Dan shall judge his people, as one of the tribes of Israel' (Genesis 49:16). It is a strange prophecy, as it implies there is something unique or distinct about him. Jacob goes on to say, 'Dan shall be a serpent' (Genesis 49:17).[75] Deuteronomy tells us, 'Dan is a lion's whelp' (Deuteronomy 33:22). Leviticus says, 'A woman's son blasphemed the name of the Lord ... of the tribe of Dan.' This is the first time that we read of such a thing happening in scripture (Leviticus 24:11). In parallel to this, it is the Antichrist who lifts up his voice to blaspheme and curse the Lord during the Tribulation.

As we continue through Dan's history, we find in the book of Judges how the Danites came across a priest who was at the household of

---

[73] Jeffrey, *Triumphant Return*, 176.

[74] Ibid., 176

[75] The Wikipedia entry 'Dan, Son of Jacob' connects Dan (serpent) to Belial, a Hebrew term personifying the Devil.

Micah. Notice the continued resistance to serving the Lord. They come to Micah's house, and the Danites speak to the Levite priest who was there. They ask him to say what is better, to be a priest to one household or to be a priest to a tribe of Israel (Judges 18:19). This priest leaves the house of Micah. The Danites remove all the idols from Micah's house and take them. This results in those idols being worshipped by the tribe of Dan. The apostasy in Dan is complete.

From these events, we can understand Ephraem the Syrian's theology that the Antichrist will come from Dan. Dan went into idolatry, and we never read of any repentance.

We could easily add Hippolytus (AD 170–236), Lactantius (260–330), and other early theologians who maintained a literal view of end-time events. All of these reasons support the events Paul described to the church at Corinth as happening before the Tribulation and the actual Second Coming of Christ.

Before updating our time line John provides further insight to the timings of the resurrections given by Daniel and repeated by Jesus.

Apostle John's Insight

The apostle John elaborates on Jesus words where the Son of man has been given authority to execute judgement and they that are in the graves shall hear his voice (John 5:27, 28). Describing what is going to take place when the dead hear Jesus's voice: 'And I saw the dead, small and great, stand before God; and the books were opened: and another book was opened, which is the book of life: and the dead were judged out of those things which were written in the books, according to their works' (Revelation 20:12). This event is known as the Great White Throne Judgement, and John writes about the great white throne and the one who sits on the Throne (Revelation 20:11). It is at this time we have the resurrection *of* the dead.

Jesus taught there would be a resurrection *from* the dead (Luke 20:35) and the early church taught this same message (Acts 4:2). This is important for John is given revelation as to the timing of these two events and lets us know they are separated by one thousand years (Revelation 20:5).

Judgement Seat of Christ and the Great White Throne Judgement

In scripture, two judgements are highlighted which are relevant for this study. Until now in our timeline, the final judgement has been highlighted as taking place in the 'last days'. The context of this has been defined: when the Jewish Messiah comes – Second Coming of Jesus.

From the book of Revelation, we know also of another judgement: the Great White Throne judgement.

The Judgement Seat of Christ is not found in the Old Testament. It is from Paul's letter to the church at Corinth. He also brings it up in his epistle of Romans. In Romans, it is linked to how they judged brothers (Romans14:10). All those who follow Christ will appear at this judgement. Therefore, the followers of Christ will not appear at the Great White Throne Judgement. When the followers of Christ appear, it will be for judgement on how we have lived for Christ. It is a time when rewards will be given for our service to the Lord. Paul is letting us know the way we live after our conversion to Christ is important, for our works will be tried by fire. If our works are glorifying to Christ they will stand the fire and come forth as gold, silver, or precious stones. If our works do not glorify Christ they will not survive the fire and will be consumed like wood, hay, or stubble. We will be rewarded accordingly to that done in the body as a follower of Jesus (2 Corinthians 5:10).

As prophetic revelation, these two chief events are separated as to time.[76] The resurrection of the righteous will occur before the beginning of the kingdom of Messiah, and the general resurrection will occur thereafter, at the end of the world. Sauer gives the key from scripture:

> But the rest of the dead lived not again until the thousand years were finished. This is the first resurrection. Blessed and holy is he that hath part in the first resurrection: on

---

[76] Sauer, *From Eternity to Eternity*, 78.

such the second death hath no power, but they shall be priests of God and of Christ, and shall reign with him a thousand years (Revelation 20:5-6).

The Judgement Seat of Christ takes place after the rapture of the church, in the 'day of Jesus Christ'. This is before the setting up of the visible kingdom of heaven. This judgement covers the things believers have done since their conversion. Their works will be tried by fire. Sauer sums this up very graphically by saying, 'Paul even speaks of the heart stirring possibility that a believer, though saved personally, may suffer such damage to be compared to a man escaping out of a fire with his bare life.'[77]

The Great White Throne Judgement comes at the end of the world, after Jesus has put down all his enemies. All the wicked from the time of Adam are resurrected to appear at this judgement. This takes place after a one thousand year reign of Christ on the earth.

Final Timeline

We are now in a position to update our timeline with the apostle Paul's mystery of a resurrection and rapture included, as follows:

- There is a redeemer. God himself is the redeemer (Job 19:25–27).
- Jesus (God manifest in the flesh) provides his credentials, stating, 'I am the Resurrection' (John 11:25).
- Jesus demonstrates this truth by rising from the dead and bringing all the Old Testament saints with him (Matthew 27:52) and He led captivity (those in Paradise) captive. (Psalm 68:18, repeated in Ephesians 4:8).
- Many of these Old Testament saints walk through the streets of Jerusalem. It is a wild scene! (Matthew 27:53). Paul, referring to this resurrection, states, 'Christ the first fruits' (1 Corinthians 15:23).

---

[77] Ibid., 79.

- After the resurrection of Jesus the church came into being.
- Gentiles have the gospel preached to them. Paul is chosen to be the apostle to the Gentiles. Gentiles is the name given to all non-Jews.
- There is a resurrection and rapture of Church Age believers (1 Corinthians 15:51–53 and 1 Thessalonians 4:13–17). They are caught up to meet Christ in the air. Immediately after this is the Judgement Seat of Christ (2 Corinthians 5:10).
- There is an indeterminate time period from the rapture of the church to when a covenant is signed that starts the last seven years of Daniel's vision (Daniel 9:27).
- There is a rapture immediately before God brings in everlasting righteousness (Matthew 24:31; Psalm 50:3-5). This will be at the Second Coming of Jesus
- Jesus lands on the Mount of Olives (Zechariah 14:4).
- The time when this will take place is defined as 'at the latter day on the earth' or 'last day' (Job 19:25, repeated in John 11:24). Second Coming of Jesus.[78]
- Those raised to 'everlasting life' (Daniel 12:2) 'resurrection of life' (John 5:29) takes place at the Second Coming of Jesus.
- The one-thousand-year reign of Jesus on the earth begins. Satan is bound in the bottomless pit for one thousand years (Revelation 20:2–4).
- Those not resurrected when Jesus rose from the dead, those not resurrected at the rapture of the church, together with those not resurrected at Jesus Second Coming will be resurrected at a future time and will see God face to face. That will cover all the unrighteous from the time of Adam (Isaiah 26:19; Job 19:26).
- This will result in people being raised to 'shame and everlasting contempt' (Daniel 12:2) and also known as 'resurrection of damnation (John 5:29). This takes place after the one thousand

---

[78] Latter day on the earth is when everlasting righteousness is established (Daniel 9:24). Hence Second Coming of Jesus.

year reign of Christ on the earth at the Great White Throne judgement.

In conclusion, our journey has taken us back into the Old Testament, beginning in the days of the Babylonian captivity as the Word of the Lord came to Daniel and Ezekiel. These encounters laid out God's plans concerning the future of the Jewish people and the city of Jerusalem. This overview makes it possible to distinguish between the teachings of Jesus as he answered Jewish questions to Jewish believers on the Mount of Olives. He spoke about a rapture that will occur when he returns to this earth at his Second Advent.

We then looked at the mystery revealed to Paul on how the message of the gospel went to the Gentiles. From the letters to the churches at Corinth and Thessalonica we learn of the resurrection from the dead of believers when Christ comes in the air, along with those still alive, will be caught up to meet Jesus and in a twinkling of an eye receive an incorruptible body.

Jesus audience and teaching was to the Jewish people, Paul's audience and teaching was to non-Jewish people. Rightly dividing the word of truth gives us the sequence of events. It has enabled us to place in our timeline when these events take place. Paul's resurrection and rapture is pre-Tribulation, before the events of Daniel's vision of the final seven years. Jesus's rapture is a post-Tribulation rapture, happening at the end of Daniel's vision of seventy weeks immediately prior to landing on the Mount of Olives.

We have also seen how Jesus was sent to the house of Israel, whereas Paul is the apostle to the Gentiles. We have noted that those resurrected at the rapture of the church appear at the Judgement Seat of Christ and those whose names are not in the book of life since the time of Adam are raised to appear before God at the Great White Throne Judgement.

One thousand years pass from the Second Coming of Jesus to the Great White Throne Judgement.

CHAPTER 15

MYSTERY OF ISRAEL'S BLINDNESS

For I would not, brethren, that ye should be ignorant
of this mystery, lest ye be wise in your own conceits;
that blindness in part has happened to Israel,
until the fullness of the Gentiles be come in.

Romans 11:25

The Jewish people are unique in that they can trace their genealogy all the way back to Abraham, Isaac, and Jacob—that is, a period of four thousand years, give or take a few depending on whose chronology you take. It is an exceptionally long time within the framework of human history.

Abraham was called of God out of Ur of the Chaldees. His grandson Jacob had his name changed to Israel after he wrestled with an angel. Jacob had left his uncle Laban's house to return unto the land of his fathers, as per the Word of the Lord to him. He then had to face his brother Esau, whom he had tricked (along with his father) to gain the fatherly blessing, normally reserved for the first born. When he was alone, pondering the outcome of meeting his brother, Jacob wrestled with an angel during the night. Jacob refused to let this angel go until he received an answer to his prayer. Forever after this encounter, Jacob walked with a limp, but he also prevailed. His name was changed to Israel. He had power with God and man (Genesis 32:28). Since that day, the name Israel has been synonymous with the Jewish people.

The Jewish people can also trace their history to when God chose them as a nation in the wilderness: 'For thou art an holy people unto the LORD thy God: the LORD thy God hath chosen thee to be a special people unto himself, above all people that are upon the face of the earth' (Deuteronomy 7:6). It was during this time in the wilderness that Moses received the Ten Commandments, which were written by the finger of God on tablets of stone.

Also from this time, the Jewish people became custodians of all the writings found in the Law and the Prophets and the Writings. Their scribes were responsible for copying all of these writings. Their work was so precise that when ancient fragments of writings are found, they can be identified to the exact part of Old Testament scripture.

The Jews have been a people persecuted throughout their history. Yet they have remained as a distinct people even when dispersed among the nations. The culmination of their persecution was in the twentieth century, particularly the genocide carried out by the Nazis during the Second World War. It resulted in the fulfilment of God's promise to bring them back and establish them in their ancient homeland. Now in their ancient homeland, they are surrounded by nations who would welcome their destruction.

The persecution of the Jewish people through the centuries can be understood from the perspective of the promised Redeemer who would bruise the heel of Satan: 'And I will put enmity between thee and the woman, and between thy seed and her seed; it shall bruise thy head, and thou shalt bruise his heel' (Genesis 3:15). The Old Testament provided the lineage of the Messiah: Israel, then the tribe of Judah, followed by the House of David. At its core, the persecution has been satanically inspired in an attempt to thwart God's plans by destroying those involved in the lineage of the Messiah.

However, the nation of Israel underwent persecution also due to their own disobedience:

Even all nations shall say, Wherefore hath the LORD done thus unto this land? what meaneth the heat of this great anger? Then men shall say, Because they have forsaken the covenant of the LORD God of their fathers, which he made with them when he brought them forth out of the land of Egypt: For they went and served other gods, and worshipped them, gods whom they knew not, and whom he had not given unto them: And the anger of the LORD was kindled against this land, to bring upon it all the curses that are written in this book. (Deuteronomy 29: 24–27)

Israel was the nation God chose to fulfil his promise given in the Garden of Eden. As stated, they received the Law of God and became the custodians of all Old Testament writings that God gave through his prophets. However, their history also reveals their shortcomings and their inability to fulfil all the responsibilities placed upon them. There were generations that were faithful to God. Many priests and prophets stood for the cause of Jehovah. However, their history is also tarnished. They turned away from their God and ended up in captivity in Babylon, followed by dispersion under Rome. This dispersion under Rome resulted in Jewish people settling in countries all around the world. Their exile was long and arduous, lasting into the mid-twentieth century.

In the twentieth century, we begin to see the prophetic word spoken by the prophet Isaiah take shape, which continues to our day. Isaiah writes:

And it shall come to pass in that day, that the Lord shall set his hand again the second time to recover the remnant of his people, which shall be left, from Assyria, and from Egypt, and from Pathros, and from Cush, and from Elam, and from Shinar, and from Hamath, and from the islands of the sea. And he shall set up an ensign for the nations, and shall assemble the outcasts of Israel, and gather together the dispersed of Judah from the four corners of the earth. (Isaiah 11:11-12)

The children of Israel are returning from all over the globe to Israel. This is the second time God has brought his people back to their land just as he promised he would. The first time the Jewish people returned to their land, it was from only one place, and that was Persia—the return of the Babylonian captives.

To understand the places involved, Genesis chapter 10 provides a table of the nations. It shows the original names and allows us to trace people and nations throughout history as these names change.

Although Israel is established as a nation once more and Jewish people continue to arrive from the nations of the world, just as scripture states, they still remain in blindness. How did this blindness happen?

It is helpful to look at the history of Israel to understand how this has come about. Isaiah penned what must be one of the most tragic verses of scripture when he wrote, 'But they rebelled, and vexed his holy Spirit: therefore he was turned to be their enemy, and he fought against them' (Isaiah 63:10). Not only were they guilty of sinning against God, but they were charged with blasphemy. 'Your iniquities, and the iniquities of your fathers together, saith the LORD, which have burned incense upon the mountains, and blasphemed me upon the hills: therefore will I measure their former work into their bosom' (Isaiah 65:7). Their condition deteriorated to such an extent that Isaiah warned them about striving with their maker (Isaiah 45:9). These sins were like a cancer that has plagued Israel throughout its history.

In 2 Chronicles 36:14-19, the responsibility of turning away from God rested with the priests. The chief priests were the main culprits. Under their watch, the Temple at Jerusalem was polluted. They mocked those whom God sent with his Word, misused God's prophets, and despised God's words. They reached the place where there was no remedy for their sin. It was also in the days of the prophet Isaiah when the condition of Jerusalem, called the faithful city, was described as a harlot. It was once a place of righteousness, but it became a place of murderers (Isaiah 1:21).

How did this blindness happen?

There are pivotal moments in history which affect generations to come. One of those moments came when John the Baptist preached the message of repentance and baptised people at the River Jordan. A very diverse group of people came out to listen to John. It included priests sent from Jerusalem.

John was not a stranger to them. He was a priest, and his birth was a miracle known to the chief priest, priests, and Levites at the temple in Jerusalem. John was the son of Zacharias, 'of the course of Abia' (Luke 1:5). The whole religious hierarchy was not ignorant of the events that surrounded Zachariah as he carried out his duties in the Temple. Nor were they unaware of John's birth when his mother was well past the age of childbirth.

John the Baptist was not your typical priest. His appearance would have caused consternation within the religious hierarchy. He wore clothes of camel hair and a leather girdle around his waist. His main diet was locusts and wild honey (Matthew 3:4). To say he did not conform to the norm is stating it politely. There is a good probability he would have been looked upon as an eccentric. Some of the priests may have found John's appearance disgusting and inappropriate to their profession.

John's appearance aside, these priests were presented with the opportunity to proclaim the greatest event that each one lived for—the day of the appearance of their Messiah. However, rejection has only one outcome: catastrophe.

Also in the crowd that day were two disciples. We are given the name of one, Andrew, and we are told he was a fisherman. Everyone heard John the Baptist preach on repentance, but not everybody responded to his message.

When Jesus came to be baptised, John declared, 'Behold the lamb of God' (John 1:36). The duty of a priest was to examine a sacrifice before it was offered to God. If the sacrifice had a blemish, it was not accepted. John, in his priestly capacity, proclaimed God's sacrifice and told everyone it was acceptable, for it had no blemishes. It was pure.

A second thing of note was his declaration 'Behold the lamb of God' (John 1:36). That should have been a catalyst to draw the attention of all who heard John, particularly those Pharisees in attendance, to what was written in their own Holy Book. It should have reminded them of the first offering made which was accepted by God, when Abel gave a lamb out of his flock of sheep (Genesis 4:4). Then there was the Exodus from Egypt, when the blood of a lamb was put on the doorposts and across the lintels of the homes of the Israelites. So John's message of identifying God's lamb should have caught their attention. How could they have missed it?

In the gospels, when confrontations took place with Jesus, many times this same group of religious people proudly proclaimed in their arguments that they were of their father Abraham. Yet they appeared to be under a cloud that distorted their thinking. They did not connect what they were seeing to Abraham taking his son Isaac up the mountain. Abraham gave Isaac the assurance that God himself would provide the lamb for an offering (Genesis 22:8).

Scripture was before them as a guide. John pointed to Jesus as the promised Messiah. Yet they take John to task over his own identity: 'Art thou Elias? And he saith, I am not. Art thou that prophet? And he answered, No. Then said they unto him, Who art thou? (John 1:21-22). Finally, 'they asked him, and said unto him, Why baptizest thou then, if thou be not that Christ, nor Elias, neither that prophet?' (John 1:25).

In contrast, two disciples captured the truth of John's words and left following John the Baptist to follow Jesus (John 1:37). While the religious people interrogated John, Andrew immediately followed Jesus. The religious people were caught up with the messenger while the two ordinary fishermen followed the Son of God. They became famous, and their names are remembered today. Remarkable!

Jonathan Cahn notes that when the covenant changes, there must be a change of priesthood. When did this happen? He then notes that John the Baptist was 'the only priest in scripture whose birth was announced by an angel, in the sanctuary of the priests, the Temple, in the holy place, during the priestly ministry.'[79]

---

[79] Jonathon Cahn, *Book of Mysteries,* (Lake Mary: Charisma Media, 2016), 192.

When did the change of priesthood take place? The Bible tells us that Jesus was a priest after the order of Melchisedec. When he shows up at the Jordan River, we have the two priests of the two covenants standing together in the water. John declares the greater priesthood, and the transference takes place. This makes John's statement about decreasing all the more poignant (John 3:30). A pivotal moment in history occurs, and the Pharisees, Sadducees, and whole religious hierarchy are completely blind to its significance.

Yet the psalmist declares that the Lord has sworn that thou art a priest forever after the order of Melchisedec (Psalm 110:4). This is the Messiah who will take away sin. Abraham had an encounter with Melchisedec:

> Now consider how great this man was, unto whom even the patriarch Abraham gave the tenth of the spoils. And verily they that are of the sons of Levi, who receive the office of the priesthood, have a commandment to take tithes of the people according to the law, that is, of their brethren, though they come out of the loins of Abraham. But he whose descent is not counted from them received tithes of Abraham, and blessed him that had the promises. (Hebrews 7:4–6)

These verses in the book of Hebrews expand on the account in Genesis. They let us know that the Melchisedec priesthood is superior to the Levitical priesthood which came through Abraham. Jesus had to be of a higher priesthood, for he had to enter heaven and cleanse the temple in heaven by his own blood.

This transference of priesthoods passed undetected by the Pharisees. During the ensuing three and a half years of Jesus's ministry, he experienced constant conflict and attacks by the Pharisees, Sadducees, and lawyers. Many a time Jesus had to withdraw as others sought how to get rid of him, eventually culminating in Jesus's crucifixion on Mount Calvary.

When it comes to the resurrection of Jesus, scripture states, 'To whom also he shewed himself alive after his passion by many infallible proofs, being seen of them forty days, and speaking of the things pertaining to the kingdom of God' (Acts 1:3). In addition to scripture giving us infallible proofs of Jesus's resurrection, more events took place to confirm Jesus identity as the Jewish Messiah.

Going back to the birth of Jesus, the wise men came to Herod, seeking to find the baby born to be king of the Jews so they could worship him (Matthew 2:2). Herod in response had brought before him the chief priests and scribes. He demanded to know the place where this king would be born. They quoted the prophet who had stated Bethlehem of Judea (Matthew 2:4–5). After this encounter, we never read about those chief priests and scribes enquiring themselves to find out if this was really the birth of the promised Messiah or not. No record is given of any of them going to Bethlehem.

When John pointed to Jesus, the events of thirty years earlier must have been stirred in the priests' memories, for scripture goes on to tell us:

> Then Herod, when he saw that he was mocked of the wise men, was exceeding wroth, and sent forth, and slew all the children that were in Bethlehem, and in all the coasts thereof, from two years old and under, according to the time which he had diligently enquired of the wise men. (Matthew 2:16)

The prophet Jeremiah prophesied:

> Thus saith the LORD; A voice was heard in Ramah, lamentation, and bitter weeping, Rahel weeping for her children refused to be comforted for her children, because they were not. (Jeremiah 31:15)

In addition to those events, there was Daniel's encounter with the angel Gabriel.

Seventy weeks are determined upon thy people (literally seventy-sevens in the Hebrew text making it four hundred and ninety years) and upon thy holy city, to finish the transgression, and to make an end of sins, and to make reconciliation for iniquity, and to bring in everlasting righteousness, and to seal up the vision and prophecy, and to anoint the most Holy. (Daniel 9:24)

The following verses give events and timelines so that the date of Messiah's death could be calculated.

Know therefore and understand, that from the going forth of the commandments to restore and to build Jerusalem unto the Messiah the Prince shall be seven weeks, and threescore and two weeks: the street shall be built again, and the wall, even in troublous times. And after threescore and two weeks shall Messiah be cut off, but not for himself. (Daniel 9:25-26)

Using the prophecies in Daniel, it was possible to determine the year that the Messiah would be cut off. The decree was issued, according to the Hebrew calendar, in the month Nisan, in the twentieth year of the reign of Artaxerxes, in 445 BC (Nehemiah 2:1). From the command to restore and build Jerusalem to the Messiah being cut off would be 483 years.

The year of Jesus's birth could be calculated. Is that not how the wise men from the east, who had Daniel's prophecy in front of them, knew the time? Was it all that difficult to match the events surrounding Herod and the massacre of the children less than two years old in the place where the Messiah would be born to the one being proclaimed as the Lamb of God? After Herod summoned the chief priests to ask where the Messiah would be born, we never find anyone from the Sanhedrin sending someone to Bethlehem to enquire about this child. Bethlehem is the place of bread, the village of David's birth, the place where Micah states Messiah will be born, yet no one from Jerusalem showed any interest whatsoever. Unbelievable!

At the Jordan River, these same priests were given another opportunity to identify their Messiah. Daniel wrote, 'Know therefore and understand' (Daniel 9:25). Judging from their actions, the words of Daniel fell on deaf ears.

Throughout Jesus's ministry, people wanted to make him King. However, scripture tells us, 'Many believed in his name, when they saw the miracles which he did. But Jesus did not commit himself unto them, because he knew all men' (John 2:23–24). Yet there came a day in his life where Jesus fulfilled scripture and allowed himself to be called King. 'Rejoice greatly, O daughter of Zion; shout, O daughter of Jerusalem: behold, thy King cometh unto thee: he is just, and having salvation; lowly, and riding upon an ass, and upon a colt the foal of an ass' (Zechariah 9:9). The people, says Zechariah, shout! for 'Blessed be he that cometh in the name of the LORD' (Psalm 118:26). When the Pharisees approached Jesus, looking for him to rebuke the people, he responded, 'I tell you that, if these should hold their peace, the stones would immediately cry out' (Luke 19:40). These events happened in line with the decree of Artaxerxes.

How has blindness come to Israel?

The Jewish people are the custodians of the Old Testament. Their scribes have always been exceptionally scrupulous to ensure that each and every copy of scripture is written without error. If an error is discovered, the work is destroyed. Konstanty Gebert states, 'In Judaism there is no higher instance than that of Scripture with its commentaries, and there is nothing worse than a scholar who leads the faithful astray.'[80]

The same author tells us what these commentaries are and states that the Talmud is 'a gigantic collection of 64 volumes, containing an account of rabbinic debates, conducted by sages who were centuries, and hundreds of miles apart'.[81] Within the Talmud there is the 'Mishnaic

---

[80] Konstanty Gebert, *54 Commentaries on the Torah* (Krakow: Publishing House Austeria, 2005), 63.

[81] Ibid., 53.

Commentary to Scripture written down in the second century CE. It soon became clear the Mishnah itself also called for a commentary and thus the Gemara was created. Subsequently, the Gemara lent itself to interpretation, and started to be accompanied by supplementary remarks, commentaries, analyses and footnotes, which found their own place on the pages of the Mishnah and Gemara. The codification of the Talmud had been completed by the sixth century CE, but in the deeper sense the Talmud has never been finished'[82] The writer goes on to state, 'Outside the Torah there have remained various commentaries and treatises ... created over hundreds of years.'[83]

Moses Maimonides in 1185, at the age of 50, wrote a major work on the Mishnah Torah, *The Repetition of the Torah*, 'and modestly claimed that his work would render studying the Talmud unnecessary.'[84] He stated it was easier to find Jewish law on any given matter within his writings. The Torah includes the first five books of the Bible and takes pre-eminence in the Jewish faith. Maimonides, although a Jew, was influenced by Greek thinking, particularly that of Aristotle, so it is said his method was 'as any decent Aristotelian.'[85]

As stated above, the Jewish people trace their roots back to Abraham, Isaac, and Jacob. The name Israel was given to Jacob after he wrestled with an angel. The covenant given to Abraham was circumcision. Every male was required to be circumcised from generation to generation (Genesis 17:10). The German rabbi Samson Hirsch states, 'The physical removal of the foreskin means here the removal of a spiritual barrier to self-perfection (an "uncircumcised heart" is stigmatized in the Torah, Lev. 26:41, and by the prophets).' This is not because a circumcised man automatically becomes better, but through circumcision he is given the chance to never forget he can.'[86] Some Jewish rabbis believe that Adam was circumcised, and his skin grew back after being banished from

---

[82] Ibid., 53.

[83] Ibid., 53.

[84] Ibid., 61.

[85] Ibid., 62.

[86] Ibid., 32.

paradise. 'Thus, both metaphorically and literally, Abraham is given a chance to redeem Adam's sin.'[87]

Compare this to the writer of the book of Hebrews:

> But Christ being come an high priest of good things to come, by a greater and more perfect tabernacle, not made with hands, that is to say, not of this building; Neither by the blood of goats and calves, but by his own blood he entered in once into the holy place, having obtained eternal redemption for us. (Hebrews 9:11-12)

So how has blindness come to Israel?

Double application has caused Israel to stumble!

The Jewish rabbis, in refusing to believe that Jesus was their Messiah, do not recognise the New Testament. Yet the New Testament provides revelation and understanding of Old Testament scripture. The prophet Hosea writes about Israel as a child. God loved this child and called him his son, stating that he brought his son out of Egypt (Hosea 11:1). From this passage, Jewish Rabbis extrapolate the meaning of other verses of the Old Testament. For instance, Isaiah writes, 'Behold my servant, whom I uphold; mine elect, in whom my soul delighteth; I have put my spirit upon him: he shall bring forth judgment to the Gentiles' (Isaiah 42:1), then continuing 'A bruised reed shall he not break, and the smoking flax shall he not quench: he shall bring forth judgment unto truth' (Isaiah 42:3). Isaiah adds 'and give thee for a covenant of the people, for a light of the Gentiles' (Isaiah 42:6). The Jewish rabbis teach that they, as a nation, are a son, and that they are the light to the Gentiles.

In the New Testament, Christ was taken to Egypt until the death of Herod, to fulfil the Word of the Lord spoken by the prophet, that out of Egypt God called his son (Matthew 2:15). The Jewish Messiah has the identical calling as Israel, He is a son called out of Egypt. It is the Jewish Messiah that the words of Isaiah are spoken over in the gospels:

---

[87] Ibid., 32.

'A bruised reed shall he not break, and smoking flax shall he not quench, till he send forth judgment unto victory. And in his name shall the Gentiles trust' (Matthew 12:20-21).

When we turn to Luke's gospel, we read about Simeon. He had a wonderful testimony; the Holy Ghost was upon him. He was an old man, but he lived on, holding on to a great promise: before his death, he would see the Lord's Christ. Notice how the Holy Ghost brings about the promise. The Spirit leads Simeon to the Temple at the exact time the parents of Jesus bring the child into the Temple as per the requirements of the Law of Moses. Simeon lifts the baby. In front of all the priests and scribes, as well as Mary and Joseph, Simeon declares his eyes have seen God's salvation and he prophesies he is a light to the Gentiles and the glory of Israel (Luke 2:25–32).

The words of Simeon must have resonated throughout the Temple that day. All the people who knew him would have known about the promise given to him. It is impossible to imagine him keeping such a promise to himself.

This leads to the well-known passage of scripture in the book of Isaiah: 'But he was wounded for our transgressions, he was bruised for our iniquities: the chastisement of our peace was upon him; and with his stripes we are healed' (Isaiah 53:5). The rabbis' interpretation of this verse, and indeed this chapter in Isaiah, is that it is speaking of Israel. Rabbi Bentzion Kravitz, founder of Jews for Jesus, was interviewed by Rabbi Yosef Levin on the subject 'six reasons why Jews don't believe in Jesus' and his comments on the prophet Isaiah's words, which reads, 'Therefore, I will divide a portion to him with the great, and he shall divide the spoil with the mighty' (Isaiah 53:12). Kravitz brings up the question asked by Rabbi's: If Jesus is God, does the idea of reward have any meaning? Is it not rather the Jewish people—who righteously bore the sins of the world and yet remained faithful to God—who will be rewarded? Rabbi Kravitz draws our attention to Psalm 44 which is given for this reasoning.[88] The Psalm covers the sufferings of the Jewish people

---

[88] https//jewsforjudaism.org/Bentzion Kravitz, (June 2018).

and is expressed powerfully as follows: 'Yea, for thy sake are we killed all the day long; we are counted as sheep for the slaughter' (Psalm 44:22).

So how has blindness come to Israel?

Another amazing statement, from a Christian's point of view, is that of Rashi, the greatest Jewish commentator on the Old Testament and especially the Talmud. Gebert quotes his statement, 'Salvation, whatever it is, is the reward of all the righteous.'[89]

In Judaism, righteousness is not understood like it is in the New Testament sense, where we are told there is none righteous, no, not one (Romans 3:10). The Jewish concept of righteousness 'is the fulfilment of all legal and moral obligations'.[90] From a legal perspective, 'the righteous man is the innocent party, while the wicked man is the guilty one.'[91] In their deliberations, they have to come to terms with the judicial element as well as the paradox of divine justice. It is interesting how they take the individual: 'The just man suffers in consequence of his very righteousness' then relates this by stating 'this individual problem takes on a national character in Jewish history, throughout which an innocent nation is constantly being persecuted.'[92]

When this concept of righteousness is taken into the eschatological realm, we read, 'Righteous action within a righteous society will restore peace in the world and will re-establish Jerusalem as the citadel of righteousness.'[93] It is a far cry from the writings of scripture and the Christian perspective that no peace will come to earth until the prince of peace returns to Jerusalem.

A related subject in the New Testament is the stated condition of every person: 'all have sinned' (Romans 3:23). In Judaism the term 'sinner' is not recognised. They believe man can perfect himself, and the inclination to evil is not at all inherent in us.[94] This requires a person to pursue that which is right, for it is not an inherent characteristic but

---

[89] Gebert, *54 Commentaries to the Torah*, 233.
[90] https://jewishvirtuallibrary.org/righteousness
[91] https://jewishvirtuallibrary.org/righteousness
[92] Ibid
[93] Ibid.
[94] Ibid.

learned behaviour. Gebert states 'Judaism is not an orthodoxy, but an orthopraxy. It commands the faithful what they are supposed to do, not what they are supposed to believe.'[95] Therefore, the Christian teaching of a Jewish Messiah who laid down his life and became sin with the purpose of redeeming mankind is a difficult concept for a Jewish person to grasp.

In Judaism, the Day of Atonement is the holiest day, and yet for two thousand years the Jewish people have not been able to fulfil its requirements. There have been no sacrifices, for there has been no Temple at which to offer the sacrifice. The Jewish people do not believe in a Messiah who gave his life as a sacrifice for sin and bore their iniquities. Yet Jonathon Cahn lets us know the Jewish people read from a prayer book called the Makhzor at Yom Kippur, the Day of Atonement. There it states, 'our righteous Messiah has departed from us ... we have no one to justify us. He has carried the yoke of our iniquities and our transgression. And he is wounded because of our transgression. He bears our sins upon His shoulders, so that we might find forgiveness for our iniquities.'[96]

How did this blindness happen?

In Paul's letter to the Romans, he states two major truths that should never be ignored. Firstly, blindness has come to Israel, to the Jewish people, and this blindness is due to their 'unbelief' (Romans 11:20). We have only gleaned through a few examples in this chapter, looking at how the Rabbi's interpret scripture, and define subjects. However, these examples demonstrate the blindness that Paul wrote about.

Secondly, the day is coming when this blindness will be removed completely from Israel, when the fullness of the Gentiles comes in. The times of the Gentiles began with the seventy-year captivity in Babylon, when Jerusalem was captured by the Babylonians. The times of the Gentiles will end at the Second Advent of Jesus Christ.

At this time, another great promise will be fulfilled which was also written by the prophet Isaiah. Nobody in Israel will say they are sick and

---

[95] Gebert, *54 Commentaries to the Torah*, 62.
[96] Cahn, *The Book of Mysteries*, 192.

unwell, for the people shall have their iniquity forgiven (Isaiah 33:24). Notice how this matches with the writing of the psalmist, who declares that God forgives all their iniquity and heals all their diseases (Psalm 103:3).

Isaiah continues to elaborate about this future time:

> Say to them that are of a fearful heart, Be strong, fear not: behold, your God will come with vengeance, even God with a recompence; he will come and save you. Then the eyes of the blind shall be opened, and the ears of the deaf shall be unstopped. Then shall the lame man leap as an hart, and the tongue of the dumb sing: for in the wilderness shall waters break out, and streams in the desert. (Isaiah 35:4–6)

It was only in 1967 that Jerusalem came back under the control of Israel. The importance of this was stated by Daniel. When the Messiah returns, it is to Jerusalem, it is to his holy city, and it is to his holy temple. This passage provides the basis of our expectation for the Temple to be rebuilt in Jerusalem.

Israel is God's time clock. Therefore, the end of the time of the Gentiles is on the horizon. As this day draws ever nearer, we are seeing an increasing number of Jewish people recognising Jesus as their Messiah. In Jewish thought, how a dispensation begins is replicated at its end. The New Testament church began with Jewish believers; then Gentiles were added. As the day approaches for the return of the Jewish Messiah, we are seeing a greater reflection of the church once more comprising Jewish and Gentile believers.

So how has blindness come to Israel?

The history of the nation of Israel can be found in Deuteronomy chapter 28 and Leviticus chapter 26. It is the history of a nation which received the oracles of God. The nation began at the Exodus from Egypt. It began by spending forty years in the wilderness due to its disobedience. The wonders that the Israelites saw God do in Egypt were soon forgotten. From that point through to John the Baptist at the

River Jordan, the nation experienced great highs—with the glory of God filling Solomon's Temple—to great lows during the years of Jeremiah the prophet, which ended in the captivity of the nation to Babylon.

Throughout its history, God brought judgement on Israel for its unfaithfulness. Neither other nation nor any people need to raise their voices against Israel, for God himself deals with Israel. His righteousness and justice are above all others. Instead scripture encourages us to continually pray for the peace of Jerusalem.

When John showed up at the River Jordan, the expectation of who the scribes and Pharisees were looking to come can be seen in their questions. However, nowhere in the debates that took place with John is there any reference to what Daniel prophesied. The debates with John were pivotal, for they demonstrated a theology held at the highest level of the Sanhedrin. The Sanhedrin held to specific passages and expected certain individuals to show up. When John produced the scripture passage that revealed his identity, it was not on their radar. The outcome was their rejection of Jesus, their Messiah.

Having rejected Jesus and the New Testament, the rabbi's continue in blindness, awaiting the day their Messiah will show up. When that day comes, scripture states, 'And they shall look upon me whom they have pierced, and they shall mourn for him, as one mourneth for his only son, and shall be in bitterness for him, as one that is in bitterness for his firstborn' (Zechariah 12:10).

CHAPTER 16

MYSTERY OF INIQUITY

*Now we beseech you, brethren, by the coming our Lord
Jesus Christ, and by our gathering together unto him,
That ye be not soon shaken in mind, or be troubled,
neither by spirit, nor by word, nor by letter as from
us, as that day the day of Christ is at hand.
Let no man deceive you by any means: for that day shall
not come, except there come a falling away first, and
that man of sin be revealed, the son of perdition.*

2 Thessalonians 2:1–3

The apostle Paul, in writing the above passage, deals with false teaching being propagated at Thessalonica among the believers. To give proper context and to refute the heresy Paul links two things together: the coming of the Lord Jesus Christ, and our gathering together unto him. Paul, in his first letter to the Thessalonians commended them on their patience of hope, which is, waiting on the return of their Saviour (1 Thessalonians 1:3). Furthermore, they were given assurance their spirit, and soul, and body would be preserved blameless unto the coming of their Saviour (1 Thessalonians 5:23). Therefore, when there came those into their midst stating they had missed the coming of the Lord it greatly troubled these believers. This teaching was propagated by Hymenaeus, Alexander and Philetus who had rejected sound doctrine. To replace the literal coming of the Lord Jesus would then imply Paul's teaching to be in error and that it should be understood in a spiritual sense.

Hymenaeus and Alexander came from Ephesus[97] and we know the teaching of Paul written in his letter to the saints at Ephesus. There Paul talks about being made alive and raised up to sit in heavenly places with Christ Jesus to those who were formerly dead in sins (Ephesians2:5, 6). As the physical return of the Saviour has not taken place it appears that these men teach the first resurrection is past, for it was a spiritual resurrection from the dead.

When Paul writes to Timothy, he is very explicit about the errors committed by these two men. Paul lays out the steps he took and says he has delivered Hymenaeus and Alexander to Satan, so they will learn not to blaspheme (1 Timothy 1:20). Paul never tolerated the Word of God being corrupted. He goes on to write, 'And their word will eat as doth a canker: of whom is Hymenaeus and Philetus; Who concerning the truth have erred, saying that the resurrection is past already; and overthrow the faith of some' (2 Timothy 2:17-18). Paul reiterates his teaching to the Thessalonians about the rapture of the church and gives the sequence of the coming of our Lord Jesus Christ and our gathering together unto him.

In this context, Paul speaks of the Day of Christ, about a falling away from the truth of the Word of God and the subsequent unveiling of the man of sin. It is only in the writings of the apostle Paul that we come across the terminology 'the Day of Christ', and its message is directed solely to the church, the body of born-again believers. Paul, writing to Timothy, calls it our 'blessed hope' (Titus 2:13). It is the day when believer's bodies are raised from the grave and along with those who are alive put on incorruption and meet the Lord in the air.

In the Old Testament, two standard designations are found over and over again. These are 'thus saith the Lord' and 'Day of the Lord.' In

---

[97] https://www.gotquestions.org/Hymenaeus-and-Alexander.html

the New Testament, we do not find these designations. Instead, we find 'Day of Christ' and 'thus saith the Holy Ghost'.

The contrast between the Day of Christ and the Day of the Lord has been outlined as follows:-[98]

Day of Christ	Day of the Lord
For the Church (the Body of Christ)	For the rejectors of Christ
A day of blessing and reward	A day of judgement
A heavenly hope	An earthly despair
Eagerly anticipated	Feared and dreaded

The Day of Christ covers the period before the rapture of the church. It goes through events taking place in heaven, such as the Judgement Seat of Christ, while simultaneously on earth it will be the day of the Antichrist. This indicates that the Day of Christ is associated with the Day of the Lord, as it relates to the Second Advent of Jesus Christ. Jesus, talking of his Second Advent, asks whether there will be faith on earth when the Son of Man returns (Luke 18:8).

Therefore, when Paul writes about the coming of the Day of Christ, he is removing a veil and providing revelation of the conditions that will be in place for these events to happen. He is letting us know what must take place before the man of sin can be revealed to the world. It is similar to Jesus telling his disciples about the cross that is before him (John 14:27). The disciples are told up front, before the crucifixion, not to be afraid when it happens (John 14:29). Paul warns, 'for that day shall not come, except there come a falling away first, and that man of sin be revealed, the son of perdition' (2 Thessalonians 2:3).

The falling away talks about rebelling against truth; it is a defection from truth. The mystery of iniquity is a term covering sin and the sin nature in man. What causes man to commit wicked deeds and live in a condition opposed to the Word of God? At its core is the spirit of lawlessness, a lying spirit. There is a hatred for truth. People do not

---

[98] https://doctrine.org/the-day-of-christ

want truth, for truth exposes sin. It exposes deceit. It exposes lies. Truth can provoke anger when sin is revealed. So it is not strange to find good being called evil and evil being called good. 'Woe unto them that call evil good, and good evil; that put darkness for light, and light for darkness; that put bitter for sweet, and sweet for bitter!' (Isaiah 5:20).

As Paul elaborates on what will unfold before the son of perdition is revealed, he shares with the Thessalonians that this mystery of iniquity is already operating in the world (2 Thessalonians 2:7). The mystery of iniquity is the working of Satan. From the creation of man, Satan has been man's arch-enemy and has tried on numerous occasions to bring about man's total destruction. He continually hatches plans to deceive, to kill, and to destroy man, for his hatred towards man is absolute. He hates man, for the original man, Adam, was made in the image of God (people on earth today are in Adam's image – a fallen nature). However, there is a day coming when the manifestation of this mystery will be revealed in a person—the son of perdition.

From scripture, we discover that originality is the mark of the work of God, the Creator of all things. Satan's mark is his ability to copy, to imitate, and to deceive. Originality is not in his vocabulary, but corruption is.

Creator versus Imitator

The mystery of godliness centres on how God became flesh and dwelt among us, and how Jesus became our substitute for sin, offering himself on the cross at Calvary. Scripture puts it this way: 'Forasmuch then as the children are partakers of flesh and blood, he also himself likewise took part of the same; that through death he might destroy him that had the power of death, that is, the devil' (Hebrews 2:14). The mystery of iniquity is at the opposite end of this spectrum and encapsulates the work of Satan—in particular, the fulfilment of the passage 'And I will put enmity between thee and the woman, and between thy seed and her seed; it shall bruise thy head, and thou shalt bruise his heel' (Genesis 3:15).

Jesus was the promised seed of the woman, with the DNA of God in him. The mystery of iniquity is about the seed of the serpent, the seed of Satan' (Genesis 3:15). As Missler points out, it is about the one who will be 'the son of Satan.'[99] Larkin points out Christ is the 'Son of God', the Antichrist is the 'Son of Perdition,' Christ, the mystery of godliness, is God became flesh, and the Antichrist is the 'mystery of iniquity', when Satan is manifested in flesh.[100]

In the book of Daniel, another comparison is given to us: 'Messiah the Prince' (Daniel 9:25). This is in a prophecy of when the Jewish Messiah would show up. He is the Eternal Word, a sinless man, Jesus of Nazareth. His adversary is called 'the prince that shall come' (Daniel 9:26). This is the son of perdition.

The Prince to come walked in the Garden of Eden and is the 'anointed cherub' (Ezekiel 28:14). He watched over the throne of God. He was light bearer of the divine glory.[101] The charge against him was as follows:

> Thou hast sinned: therefore I will cast thee as profane out of the mountain of God: and I will destroy thee, O covering cherub, from the midst of the stones of fire. Thine heart was lifted up because of thy beauty, thou hast corrupted thy wisdom by reason of thy brightness: I will cast thee to the ground, I will lay thee before kings, that they may behold thee. (Ezekiel 28:16-17)

He is also called the 'Prince of this world' (John 14:30). He is a created being, and we are told he appears as 'an angel of light' (2 Corinthians 11:14). Pride is his great sin, so it is not surprising to find he is king over all the children of pride (Job 41:34). In the book of Revelation, he is described as a 'great red dragon, old serpent' (Revelation 12:9).

---

[99] Dr. Chuck Missler, *Prophecy 20/20* (Nashville: Thomas Nelson, 2006) 70.

[100] Clarence Larkin, *Dispensational Truth* (Santa Fe: Sun Books, 1998), 182.

[101] Erich Sauer, *Eternity to Eternity* (Carlisle: Paternoster Press and Erdman Publishing, 1994), 84.

Satan's end is foretold by Isaiah: 'They that see thee shall narrowly look upon thee, and consider thee, saying, Is this the man that made the earth to tremble, that did shake kingdoms' (Isaiah 14:16). His is a horrible end: 'And the devil that deceived them was cast into the lake of fire and brimstone' (Revelation 20:10). There he will spend the rest of eternity—no escape, no remission, forever in torment!

Many titles are given in scripture about this person, such as 'the son of perdition', 'the man of sin', and 'Antichrist'. His objective is not to save man but to destroy man. As Missler points out, the Antichrist is a pseudochrist—in place of Christ, a counterfeit, rather than simply an adversary against Christ. 'A pseudochrist who will perform miracles, signs, and wonders by the power of Satan and ultimately deceive the world.'[102] Larkin calls him 'Opposing Christ'.[103]

Scripture has a lot to say about him. It provides a description of him and identifies when to expect him to show up. Missler adds that he is 'intellectual genius, political genius, commercial genius, governmental genius, military genius, religious genius and an attractive and popular leader.'[104] He will enter the scene as a peacemaker. Antiochus the Great is an example of what to expect, a vile man who enters by flatteries.

Before the day of the revealing of the son of Satan, Jesus warned that there would be many false Christs. It is imperative to understand that Christ is not a name but a title. Jesus means 'Jehovah saves' and Christ means 'anointed'. Jesus is the anointed one from God. Jesus warned the disciples not to be deceived. He told the disciples that many would come using his name, and this would lead many astray (Matthew 24:4–5). This is particularly pertinent to the time when the son of perdition comes on the scene, accompanied with signs and wonders. He will be a pseudochrist who will do miracles, one who will be anointed, but he will not be the Son of God.

From scripture we can lay out and compare the differences between Jesus Christ and the son of perdition, the Antichrist. These are as follows:

---

[102] Missler, *Prophecy 20/20*, 69.

[103] Larkin, *Dispensational Truth*, 182.

[104] Missler, *Prophecy 20/20*, 70.

Jesus Christ		Antichrist	
John 9:35	Son of God	2 Thessalonians 2:3	Son of Perdition
Isaiah 53:3	Man of Sorrows	2 Thessalonians 2:3	Man of Sin
1 Timothy 3:16	Mystery of Godliness	2 Thessalonians 2:7	Mystery of Iniquity
John 15:1–3	True Vine	Revelation 14:18	Vine of the Earth
John 10:14	Good Shepherd	Zechariah 11:17	Idol Shepherd
John 5:43	Comes in His Father's Name	John 5:43	Comes in His Own Name

The imitations of Satan do not stop with the above. In the book of Revelation, we read about the beast: 'And he causeth all, both small and great, rich and poor, free and bond, to receive a mark in their right hand, or in their foreheads' (Revelation 13:16). When we go back to the Exodus of the Jewish people from Egypt, they were given instructions so that they would remember the great deliverance God wrought for them. 'And it shall be for a sign unto thee upon thine hand, and for a memorial between thine eyes, that the LORD'S law may be in thy mouth: for with a strong hand hath the LORD brought thee out of Egypt' (Exodus 13:9). Satan's mark is his law, and it is not about deliverance—it is the exact opposite. Satan's mark is designed to bring people into bondage!

The Mystery of Iniquity Is Already Working—How Does It Work?

From the beginning, Satan has challenged God's words 'hath God said' (Genesis 3:1). He is also adept at subtracting or adding words as the occasion arises. It has been two thousand years since Paul wrote on this subject, so we can look back over history and get insight into Satan's methods. Satan hates the scriptures and makes every attempt to disparage Christ and to turn the hearts of the people from Jesus. He will do anything to bring wrong doctrine and to blur the truth about Jesus Christ, our hope of salvation and the eternal destiny facing each of us between heaven and hell. Jesus defined what scripture is when he said, 'That upon you may come all the righteous blood shed upon the earth, from the blood of righteous Abel unto the blood of Zacharias son of Barachias, whom ye slew between the temple and the altar' (Matthew 23:35). Cain murdered Abel, as found in Genesis. Zacharias's murder is found in 2 Chronicles.

The Hebrew Scriptures lay out their books in a different order than that of our reformation Bibles. The reformation Bible has the exact same number of Hebrew books but in a different sequence, with the last book being the book of Malachi. The last book in the Hebrew Scriptures is 2 Chronicles.

Jesus encapsulates all of the Hebrew Scriptures as follows:

1. Genesis	2. Exodus	3. Leviticus	4. Numbers
5. Deuteronomy	6. Joshua	7. Judges	8. 1 Samuel
9. 2 Samuel	10. 1 Kings	11. 2 Kings	12. Isaiah
13. Jeremiah	14. Ezekiel	15. Hosea	16. Joel
17. Amos	18. Obadiah	19. Jonah	20. Micah
21. Nahum	22. Zephaniah	23. Haggai	24. Habakkuk
25. Zechariah	26. Malachi	27. Psalms	28. Proverbs
29. Job	30. Song of Solomon	31. Ruth	32. Lamentations
33. Ecclesiastes	34. Esther	35. Daniel	36. Ezra
37. Nehemiah	38. 1 Chronicles	39. 2 Chronicle	

These were the books of scripture in Jesus's day, and Jesus testified to their authenticity. He also gave us the three divisions of the Hebrew Scriptures when he said, 'These are the words which I spake unto you, while I was yet with you, that all things must be fulfilled, which were written in the law of Moses, and in the prophets, and in the psalms, concerning me' (Luke 24:44). In Hebrew, those divisions are known as the Law (Torah) which the rabbis hold supreme; the Prophets (Nabhim); and the Writings (Kethubim). The Writings begin with the Psalms. The Hebrew Scriptures have never been altered, so today they reflect what Jesus told his disciples.

A basic question that everyone needs to answer: Do you believe Jesus told the truth?

In Paul's day, not everyone believed what Jesus said. When Paul writes to the church at Corinth, he says, 'For we are not as many, which corrupt the word of God: but as of sincerity, but as of God, in the sight of God speak we in Christ' (2 Corinthians 2:17). Even Jesus warned about false prophets coming to him and saying, 'Lord, Lord, have we not prophesied in your name?' (Matthew 7:22). Jesus's response to those workers of iniquity is 'I never knew you: depart from me' (Matthew 7:23).

We know there is one who constantly challenges us and challenges Jesus as to what scripture is, and that is Satan. This brings individuals to a place of responsibility and decision: who to believe? If a person does not believe Jesus, then who are they going to believe?

In Jesus's day, the Pharisees had elevated their traditions not only to be on a par with the Holy Scripture, but actually to be above their scripture. The outward appearance of religious activities was held up as the standard to comply with the Law of Moses and the teaching of the prophets. When Jesus walked around the land of Israel, he was challenged as to why his disciples did not uphold the traditions of the elders (Matthew 15:2). Jesus in reply asked why the Pharisees were transgressing the commandments of God by their traditions (Matthew 15:3). Jesus accused them of the same thing in the gospel of Mark (7:9).

As we move on from Jesus's day and look at the Christian church, we find similar failings over the past two thousand years. We find not only traditions being elevated above the Word of God, but other writings being given prominent place such as the Apocrypha. This is where you find teachings about Purgatory or praying to the dead. We never find Jesus quoting from the Apocrypha nor any other writings, no matter their source. Jesus only stood on the Hebrew Scriptures. Yet there are those who would add the books of the Apocrypha, to interject them as part of the Old Testament. It is a fundamental attack on Jesus's position and his authority.

The mystery of iniquity further works, not only by adding or subtracting from God's words, but by making them allegorical instead of literal. Jeffrey states, 'It is significant that every one of the early Christian writers taught that the prophecies of Daniel, Revelation, and Matthew 24 would be fulfilled in the last days at the end of this age until the publications of Origen (A.D. 185–254).'[105] Hill notes that Origen is the great textual critic of antiquity.[106]

What did Origen come up with that deviated from the early Christian writers? The Internet Encyclopaedia of Philosophy, A Peer Reviewed Academic Resource provides an overview of the life and times of Origen including his Philosophical System and notes, 'He drew upon pagan philosophy in an effort to elucidate the Christian faith.'[107] Origen was influenced by Greek writers, and he interpreted scripture using an allegorical method.

In Athens, Paul stated, 'his spirit was stirred in him, when he saw the city wholly given to idolatry' (Acts 17:16). He also stated they were 'too superstitious' (Acts 17:22). Jeffrey notes, 'The Council of Nicea (325AD) and the Council of Constantinople (381AD) rejected the allegorical interpretation of Revelation 20.'[108] Revelation 20 speaks about the Millennial Kingdom, Jesus one-thousand-year reign on earth (see chapter 15).

What do we know about Origen? Jeffrey says, 'He was brilliant but rather unbalanced, he castrated himself, taught the reincarnation of men into animals, rejected a literal belief in the scriptural statements.'[109] Given that information and given the teaching of Jesus, one thing we can know for certain is that Jesus and Origen were not speaking from the same script. Jesus was filled with the Holy Spirit. Perhaps the kindest thing we could say about Origen is a comment Maloney makes about those following Christ, which is an insightful observation: 'Even if the vessel is sincere in his or her intentions to give you that word, whatever spiritual, emotional, or mental baggage they continue to leave unchecked can be attributed to their vanity, and eventually the vessel is ultimately

---

[105] Jeffrey, *Triumphant Return*, 59.

[106] Edward F. Hills, *Believing Bible Study* (Des Moines: The Christian Research Press, third ed.1991), 138.

[107] Origen of Alexandria, Internet Encyclopedia of Philosophy, https://www.iep.utm.edu/origen-of-alexandria/

[108] Jeffrey, *Triumphant Return*, 128.

[109] Ibid., 45.

lessened in Devine unction and left with tarnishing and corruption—an imitation of what was once Devine.'[110]

Origen's teaching produced doctrines that destroyed the revelation of scripture about the son of perdition, the man of sin, and the antichrist. Origen's writings influenced Augustine, who came up with what we now call amillennialism, rejecting a thousand-year reign of Christ on earth and all the events surrounding the Second Coming of Jesus.

Amillennialism has been a prominent theology right up to modern times. As Missler points out, 'Amillennialism would seem to make God guilty of not keeping His unconditional covenants to the physical descendants of Abraham, Isaac, and Jacob: the Jews.'[111] This would include the promise of the land, the promise of a kingdom, a greater Son of David (Messiah) as its King, a promise of the restoration of the land of Israel from a worldwide dispersion, the establishment of the Messiah's kingdom, and promises that a remnant of the Israelites will be saved.'[112] Amillennialism takes the promises given to Israel and appropriates them to the church. As Missler states, it 'laid the foundation for widespread anti-Semitism'.[113]

In comparatively recent times a major influence on Christianity has been Westcott and Hort, two Anglican clergymen. The reason for this is their Greek New Testament. It is the source text for many of today's modern Bible translations. The evidence provided for this comes from the James Begg Society, named after the Reverend James Begg, D.D. who was a minister in the Church of Scotland and minister in the Free Church of Scotland from its foundation. The Society publishes works of Scottish Presbyterians from the sixteenth century onwards, and modern authors with the same faith from around the world. The information is on the web site of Jesus is Lord. [114] What is the problem with taking their work at face value? First, it contains seven books that Jesus excluded from scripture. As Hill notes, 'One of the features of Westcott and Hort

---

[110] James Maloney, *Dancing Hand of God*, vol. 2 (Bloomington: WestBow Press, 2011), 24.
[111] Missler, *Prophecy 20/20*, 92.
[112] Ibid., 92.
[113] Ibid., 93.
[114] https://www.jesus-is-lord.com/hort.htm

Greek New Testament is the rejection of Christ's agony in Gethsemane and Christ's prayer for His murderers.'[115] Riplinger quotes Hort's own words when he states he has 'fundamental difference in the subject of the Atonement, if it existed.'[116]

These men also had trouble believing the miracles in the Bible. They were engaged with Darwin's book and believe evolution was a strong theory that was unanswerable. Therefore, they did not believe the first three chapters of Genesis were literal history. They were also captivated by the worship of Mary. The web site Bible Ready, Historical Christianity for Ex-JW's, under the heading of Bibles gives a critique of Westcott and Hort providing details about their involvement in the occult and how the beginning of the new age movement has been traced back to them[117] Riplinger gives 'a peek into the private thoughts of the men' in appendix A of her book.[118]

When she examines the theology and beliefs of Origen, Westcott, and Hort, Riplinger makes a very profound statement: 'The Bible is not difficult to understand—it is impossible—unless God's criteria are met.'[119] When that which is holy is mixed with profanity, it creates a mixture which results in defilement. Defilement, when propagated, works like a cancer, destroying the revelation of scripture. It is the mystery of iniquity at work.

Large parts of Christendom have found themselves shackled to a theology that equates social justice reforms to salvation. It is the pursuit of social reforms as the vehicle to bring change to society, rather than the individual being changed by the indwelling Christ. It is expecting external changes to the environment to produce the life of God as opposed to the life of God being outworked in a life by the work of the Holy Spirit to bring change to society. It is subtle, the mystery of iniquity at work deceiving people.

---

[115] Hill, *Believing Bible Study* 1991
[116] Gail Riplinger, *New Age Bible Versions* (Ararat: AV Publications), 629.
[117] https://bibleready.org/Westcott-and-Hort, August 2018
[118] Riplinger, *New Age Bible Versions*, 618.
[119] Ibid., 636.

It is astounding that men who challenged the authenticity of scripture and challenged Jesus himself have their work accepted and propagated. Truly, the mystery of iniquity is very subtle.

Traditions, corrupting the words of God, and relying on substitutes to the work of the Holy Spirit have been core strategies of the mystery of iniquity throughout church history. The impact of these influences can be seen in the ineffectiveness of the church in society in our own day, giving us insight into how a falling away from truth can easily happen.

When Will the Son of Perdition Be Revealed?

The mystery of iniquity and the outworking of lawlessness that is in the world will one day be revealed for the full horror that it is. The Bible's description of this time is sombre: 'For then shall be great tribulation, such as was not since the beginning of the world to this time, no, nor ever shall be' (Matthew 24:21). It will be a time unlike anything that has gone before.

The events describe the next stage of the fall of Satan. 'Woe to the inhabiters of the earth and of the sea! for the devil is come down unto you, having great wrath, because he knoweth that he hath but a short time' (Revelation 12:12). The one who is currently 'the prince of the power of the air, the spirit that now worketh in the children of disobedience' is going to be restricted to walking on this earth (Ephesians 2:2). He will spew out his hatred for God and open his mouth to blasphemy against God, to blaspheme his name (Revelation 13:6).

From scripture we recognise this to be a description of events that take place in the last week of Daniel's vision, which will last for a period of seven years. Halfway through this seven-year period, Satan will reincarnate himself, take on flesh, and rule for the same length of time that Jesus ministered while on the earth, declaring he is god. Satan is the great imitator!

Scripture also makes clear that this period is 'the time of Jacob's troubles' (Jeremiah 30:7). When the dragon is cast out of heaven, he will go after those Jews who are still alive, for the dragon will be mad with rage. He will go after the woman to destroy her offspring (Revelation

12:17). The woman is Israel, and we know this from Joseph's dream in Genesis 37.

Talking of Israel, Hosea says he will draw her, Israel, and bring her into the wilderness (Hosea 2:14-15). In Revelation 12, Israel is lured into the wilderness and receives supernatural protection. Although Satan goes after Israel, notice what scripture states:

> Alas! For that day is great, so that none is like it: it is even the time of Jacob's trouble; but he shall be saved out of it. (Jeremiah 30:7)

> And at that time shall Michael stand up, the great prince which standeth for the children of thy people: and there shall be a time of trouble, such as never was since there was a nation even to that same time: and at that time thy people shall be delivered, every one that shall be found written in the book. (Daniel 12:1)

These words are also uttered by Jesus in Matthew 24!

The prophet Zephaniah tells us who will be delivered of the children of Israel: 'Seek ye the LORD, all ye meek of the earth, which have wrought his judgement; seek righteousness, seek meekness' (Zephaniah 2:3).

Notice how these passages line up with the teaching of the Sermon on the Mount, the constitution given to Israel, where it states, 'Blessed are the meek.' They are the people who are going to inherit the earth when the Lord puts all his enemies under his foot. Those hungering and thirsting for righteousness will be satisfied with the goodness of God (Matthew 5:5, 6). This is directed to the children of Israel.

When these events take place, the wickedness on earth is going to be very great. Even Jerusalem, the Holy City, will be full of corruption and idolatry, for we read, 'And their dead bodies shall lie in the street of the great city, which spiritually is called Sodom and Egypt, where also our Lord was crucified' (Revelation 11:8). Jerusalem is likened to Egypt, which in scripture always represents the world and the things of the world and to Sodom, known for its immorality and perversion.

The period of the Tribulation will be like no other time on earth. The destruction that will follow is beyond anything that has taken place before and along with the heavenly phenomena described is unimaginable to comprehend: hail and fire mingled with blood will fall over all the earth, burning up a third of the trees plus all the grass (Revelation 8:7). This will be followed by a picture which can only be described in similes: 'as' of a huge mountain on fire, being cast into the sea, causing a third part of the sea to become blood. This catastrophe will kill a third of all animals in the sea, and a third of all the ships in the sea will be destroyed. That will be followed by what is described 'as' a great star from heaven which burns like a lamp. It will destroy a third of the rivers on the earth and fountains of water (Revelation 8:8–10). The star that falls from heaven is described as wormwood. It will bring devastation, and many men will die of the waters.

Many believe the catalyst for such a disaster will be an asteroid hitting the earth. Tom Horn highlights the possibility of the asteroid named Apophis (which is the name of an Egyptian god of snakes and war) that is heading towards the earth at this present time.[120] Scientist expect the asteroid to pass earth on 13 April 2029 at a distance of 19,000 miles, which is very close.

During his life, Tom Horn has had a number of remarkable God encounters, resulting in him receiving knowledge of events before they come to pass. One of these amazing encounters is described in a book he wrote, detailing the month and year of Pope Benedict's resignation in 2013 before it took place. When the news of the pope's resignation was made public, the spotlight of the media was on him as they sought to discover his Vatican sources!

Scripture describes what will take place in the solar system simultaneous with the events on earth. A third part of the sun, a third part of the moon, and a third part of the stars will be smitten so that a third part of them is darkened. The effect on earth will be for a third part of the day not to have the light from the sun and a third part of

---

[120] Thomas Horn, *The Wormwood Prophecy* (Lake Mary: Charisma House, 2019).

the night not to have light from the moon (Revelation 8:12). These conditions are unimaginable.

Jesus compared this period of time to the days of Noah (Matthew 24:37) and to the days of Lot (Luke 17:28). These days are given as a time of great wickedness on the earth. Everything imagined in the heart of men was evil (Genesis 6:5). In other words, they were wholly given over to evil. They removed God from their thoughts, from their lives, and from their society. The consequence was that their imaginations were taken over by vanity (Roman 1:21). Violence filled the earth.

If that were not enough, the Nephilim (giants) were there. It begs the question: Will giants be seen once more? The giants were the offspring of fallen angels whom we read of in Genesis 6. The sons of God are mentioned as being present when God laid the foundations of the earth (Job 38). Every indication from scripture points to the probability that the third of the sons of God, who rebelled with Satan, will be on the earth at this time.

The flood of Noah was a consequence of the corruption of the DNA of man. Currently, scientists are experimenting with our DNA. It has been stated that only 1 per cent of man's DNA has to be changed before he is no longer human. The Bible is clear that Christ died for man, not for any hybrid or other configuration that may present itself in the days ahead. We are looking at a complete disintegration of society—no law, no order, no morality—and the corruption of the DNA of man. The disruption will cover the whole earth. Perhaps this is why Jesus speaks of the need for those days to be shortened. When the flood came, Noah and his family were rescued – no one else! When Sodom and Gomorrah were destroyed only Lot and his family were rescued – no one else!

Brent Miller's observations about Jesus's statement 'as in the days of Noah' states his belief that all aspects will be replicated in the future. He notes that part of what happened was a pole shift.[121] Pointing to the conditions on the earth before the time of Noah, Miller states that the earth was watered by a mist, and this mist watered all the ground

---

[121] Prophecy Watchers, https://prophecywatchers.com/videos/brent-miller-the-coming-pole-shift YouTube, February 2019.

(Genesis 2:6). Miller states this indicates that the axis of the earth was parallel to the axis of the sun. In the days of Noah, a geographic pole shift occurred, resulting in the earth being tilted by 23.5 degrees.

Miller then talks about another kind of event: the effects of a crustal pole shift. In this scenario, the earth continues to spin. But as the crust shifts around the spinning axis at the equator, it literally rips apart and collapses, releasing lateral forces that cause buildings to collapse, tsunamis to rise, and earthquakes to multiply. The orbit of the earth would be altered.[122]

The passage in the Bible that indicates such a thing occurring is very descriptive. It talks of the heavens fleeing, just as if the sky were a scroll rolled up. Mountains and islands in the sea are moved out of their place (Revelation 6:14).

The prophet Isaiah, describing the time preceding the Second Coming, states the heavens will be shaken and the earth will move out of its place, as the wrath of the LORD of hosts is released in the day of his fierce anger (Isaiah 13:13). This cataclysmic event is likened to a drunken man staggering from side to side (Isaiah 24:20). It will be impossible to tell what day it is or what time it is, literally fulfilling Jesus's words about not knowing the day nor the hour of his return. It is only God the Father who knows the exact time; even the angels do not know (Matthew 24:36). This may explain why Daniel talks about times and laws being changed in the last days, when the Antichrist comes speaking great words against the Most High. He is the one who wants to change times and laws (Daniel 7:25).

Who Is the Son of Perdition?

Jesus spoke to his disciples about this time period: 'While I was with them in the world, I kept them in thy name: those that thou gavest me I have kept, and none of them is lost, but the son of perdition; that the scripture might be fulfilled' (John 17:12). Jesus identified Judas as the son of perdition.

---

[122] Ibid.

Earlier in his ministry, Jesus made another remarkable statement when he spoke to the disciples, identifying one of them as a devil (John 6:70). This brings up the following strange verse of scripture. The apostles looked for a replacement for Judas, 'That he may take part of this ministry and apostleship, from which Judas by transgression fell, that he might go to his own place' (Act 1:25). The phrase 'his own place' is a strange thing to say; therefore, it catches our attention. What is his own place?

There are a number of places in scripture where we find this phrase, and we can easily get the meaning by looking at them. For instance, Jacob, speaking to Laban, says he wants to return to his own place (Genesis 30:25). That is back to the land promised to Abraham and from which Jacob had to flee after deceiving his father to get the birth right.

When the Philistines found their god Dagon lying broken, face down on the floor of their temple in pieces, their response was to get rid of the ark of the God of Israel. They wanted to send it back to its own place, where it belonged (1 Samuel 5:11). After Saul ceased following the Philistines, they returned to their own place (1 Samuel 14:46). When tragedy hit Job, his friends came from their own place (Job 2:11). The prophet Zechariah tells us the day is coming when Jerusalem will be inhabited again in her own place, her proper place (Zechariah 12:6). These verses tell us Judas's own place is very specific location—it is the abyss, the bottomless pit.

We know from scripture that the abyss, the bottomless pit, is not the place where human spirits go. Scripture tells us that this is the place where demonic spirits are held in prison. Therefore, what comes out of the abyss is demonic. This indicates the end time will be permeated by supernatural phenomena, the likes of which man has never known.

When Jesus was in prayer to his Father, he prayed, 'While I was with them in the world, I kept them in thy name: those that thou gavest me I have kept, and none of them is lost, but the son of perdition; that the scripture might be fulfilled' (John 17:12). In the book of Revelation, we read of a king who is an angel of the bottomless pit. His name in Hebrew is Abaddon, and in Greek his name is Apollyon (Revelation 9:11). Apollyon is the Greek word for perdition, as in son of perdition!

John in the book of Revelation tells us further information about the beast of the bottomless pit. 'The beast that thou sawest was, and is not; and shall ascend out of the bottomless pit, and go into perdition: and they that dwell on the earth shall wonder, whose names were not written in the book of life from the foundation of the world, when they behold the beast that was, and is not, and yet is' (Revelation 17:8). This last verse gives a conundrum: the beast was, is not, and yet is.

The important thing for us to notice is Daniel defines for us the beast and equates the beast with a man. He gives details of great beasts, four in number, who are four kings, and they arise out of the earth (Daniel 7:17). There are contrasting views among theologians as to whether we are dealing with an individual, with a kingdom, or with both. Larkin would point to a duality—both a king and a kingdom.

We have the 'son of perdition' and we have the 'beast' who is a king, and they are both connected to the bottomless pit. If the son of perdition is Judas—and he was, according to Jesus—then Judas was. At the time of John's writing in AD 90, he is not, and yet is, for he is going to come out of the bottomless pit at a future time.

Will You Be Able to Recognise the Son of Perdition When He Shows Up?

Scripture gives us the physical description of the Antichrist, the son of perdition: 'Woe to the idol shepherd that leaveth the flock! the sword shall be upon his arm, and upon his right eye: his arm shall be clean dried up, and his right eye shall be utterly darkened' (Zechariah 11:17).

Notice that this description of the idol shepherd is given in the context of Judas Iscariot's betrayal of Jesus Christ for thirty pieces of silver. 'And I said unto them, If ye think good, give me my price; and if not, forbear. So they weighed for my price thirty pieces of silver. And the LORD said unto me, Cast it unto the potter, a goodly price that I was prised at of them. And I took the thirty pieces of silver, and cast them to the potter in the house of the LORD' (Zechariah 11:12-13).

The verse states the idol shepherd will leave his flock. That indicates he is Jewish or has some Jewish connection, for Daniel states, 'But in his estate shall he honour the God of forces: and a god whom his fathers knew not shall he honour with gold, and silver, and with precious stones, and pleasant things' (Daniel 11:38). 'His fathers' would normally indicate Abraham, Isaac, and Jacob.

Furthermore, we know where the man of sin will come from: 'the people of the prince' (Daniel 9:26). This means the old Roman Empire, and more specifically the Syrian part of the Greek empire, which Rome conquered.[123] When Alexander died, the Greek empire was divided into four by his generals. Daniel 11 indicates he comes from the northern part of the Greek empire—that is, from Syria.

One further thing to note about Judas is his name, Judas Iscariot. Judas is a Greek name which means Judah. Our Lord Jesus Christ came from the tribe of Judah. Iscariot comes from the Hebrew word *ishkerioth*, or a man from Kerioth.[124] It was located ten miles south of Hebron in the land of Moab (Amos 2:2). His description fits Daniel as the one who 'shall also stand up against the Prince of princes' (Daniel 8:25).

Much has been written about this time period, including a great amount of speculation. Daniel lets us know that it cannot happen until the Jewish people are back in their homeland and Israel is once more a nation with Jerusalem at the centre of their daily lives. Only then can the prophecies be fulfilled. The trigger will be the signing of a peace treaty with the Antichrist, which he shall subsequently break.

Summary

At the church in Thessalonica, false teachers began spreading the word that the rapture of the church, as taught by Paul, should not be taken literally. Paul was asked if they had missed the rapture or if he meant it was a spiritual experience. In reply, Paul assured them that the rapture would take place. He explained to them how wickedness was working in the world. There would come a time that wickedness would so invade the church that a great falling away from truth would occur. He further

---

[123] See appendix 1.
[124] https://dictionary.com/browse/iscariot

explained that this was necessary before the son of perdition could be revealed and the mystery of iniquity could be made manifest in a person.

Iniquity is perversion of all that God has set up, and it will be embodied in an individual in the end times. This person has many names attributed to him, the most common being the Antichrist or man of sin. He is a great imitator. Paul talks about what happens before he can be revealed. Scripture identifies him and gives a description of his appearance so he can be recognised.

Unfortunately, the church has found itself engrossed in traditions, challenging the words of Jesus and attempting to bring change without the work of the Holy Spirit. The Word of God in many respects has been watered down so as not to offend anyone.

The falling away has been gaining momentum, and an unsuspecting humanity, failed by the church, is heading for a doomsday scenario. This work results in ignorance of the event coming upon the earth.

Israel is God's time clock. God has kept his promises to bring them back from the four corners of the earth and to establish them as an independent nation once again. We are living in a time period when unnatural events are on the horizon. The eyes of the people are blinded to the work of iniquity.

CHAPTER 17

MYSTERY BABYLON

And upon her forehead was a name written, MYSTERY,
BABYLON THE GREAT, THE MOTHER OF HARLOTS
AND ABOMINATIONS OF THE EARTH.

Revelation 17:5

The amount of literature written on this verse of scripture is so substantial that it could easily fill a library. Therefore, by necessity, this exposé only covers salient features about the origins of mystery Babylon, the impact on the world, the history up to our time, and the final destruction in the end times, the period known as the Tribulation. It is near impossible to come up with anything that has not been critiqued and dissected. The doctrinal and historical views are well defined.

From the outset, I want to make clear that I am tracing a system originating at the time of Nimrod, known as the Babylonian system, through to the current day, and is found in the Roman Catholic Church. In that system there are many who have known the Lord Jesus Christ in an intimate way, like Madame Guyon.[125] However, at the time of the

---

[125] Madame Guyon, https://womenofchristianity.com/biography-of-madame-guyon
https://www.ukbiblestudents.co.uk/servants/guyon.htm.

reformation in Europe opinions differed on how to bring reform and bring the Roman Church back to the Word of God. Erasmus never advocated any changes in the doctrines of the church. He believed that a disciplinary reform was all that the church required. Luther, on the other hand, differed from Erasmus about the kind of reform that was required.[126]The first Scottish martyr of the Scottish Reformation, Patrick Hamilton, found the corruption and disorder in the Roman Catholic Church to be such that the only solution: a radical and urgent transformation.[127]

Nimrod, who was the thirteenth generation from Adam, is at the centre of a mystical system in opposition to the God of creation. His name means 'rebel', and we are told he was a mighty hunter (Genesis 10:9). The first empire or kingdom is attributed to him, and his victims were men whom he brought into slavery.

The prophet Micah associates the Assyrian, who is identified with the Antichrist coming into the Promised Land, with Nimrod in the last days. 'And they shall waste the land of Assyria with the sword, and the land of Nimrod in the entrances thereof: thus shall he deliver us from the Assyrian, when he cometh into our land, and when he treadeth within our borders' (Micah 5:6). Cross references take us to Daniel: 'And out of one of them came forth a little horn, which waxed exceeding great, toward the south, and toward the east, and toward the pleasant land' (Daniel 8:9). This thread runs through history of the one who will emerge in the last days to come against Israel. It is highlighted with references to Babylon, the Assyrian, Nineveh, and the land of Nimrod.

The description given in Revelation about mystery Babylon immediately tells us a number of things, beginning with the obvious: there is a mystery, it is associated with Babylon, and Babylon is the mother of harlots and abominations that have polluted the whole earth. History is the outworking of only two seeds: the seed of the woman and the seed of Satan. The seed of God comes through the nation of Israel,

[126] Joe Carvalho, *Patrick Hamilton, The Stephen of Scotland* (Dundee: ADpublications, 2009), 75.
[127] Ibid., 69.

while Babylon is Satan's counterfeit. Satan's counterfeit weaves its way in and out of history.

The Reverend Alexander Hislop, in his classic work *The Two Babylons*, identifies Babylon as the origin of a mystical religious system. He traces its many facets as it evolved through time. Those participating in the system went through initiation rites. The rites were kept secret from outsiders. The system operated just like a secret society: it was a religious abomination!

At the centre of this worship at Babylon is the Goddess Mother and her son, represented as a mother with an infant in her arms. This goddess also has the designation of Queen of Heaven. This son's birth was 'boldly proclaimed to be miraculous'.[128] Hislop points out this worship spread from Babylon so that in Egypt, 'the Mother and the Child were worshipped under the names of Isis and Osiris'; in India it was 'Isi and Iswara'; in Asia it was 'Cybele and Deoius'; in pagan Rome it was 'Fortuna and Jupiter, the boy'; in Greece it was 'Ceres, the Great Mother, with the babe at her breast or as Irene, the goddess of Peace, with the boy Plutus in her arms'. The Madonna was also found in Tibet, Japan, and China as Shing Moo with the glory around her.[129]

As Hislop notes, 'It was from the son, that she derived all her glory and claims to deification.' All the stories at their centre were the worship of one who had a violent death.[130] Hyslop further notes, 'Thus the whole system of the secret Mysteries of Babylon was intended to glorify a dead man.'[131] As time passed, 'the mother became the favourite object of worship. To justify this worship, the mother was raised to divinity as well as her son'.[132] In Ancient Babylon, their temples depicted the woman as the one to bruise the head of the serpent, an idea also found in Catholicism.[133]

---

[128] Alexander Hislop, *The Two Babylons* (Glasgow: Century Reprographic and Print Services, 1998), 76.

[129] Ibid., 9, 10, 56, 73.

[130] Ibid., 21.

[131] Ibid., 69.

[132] Ibid., 75.

[133] Ibid., 75.

The tentacles of Babylon are also seen in the history of Israel. God sent prophets when the people turned to the worship of the idols of surrounding nations, breaking their covenant with Jehovah. Jeremiah spoke against them, declaring, 'Babylon hath been a golden cup in the LORD'S hand, that made all the earth drunken: the nations hath drunken of her wine; therefore the nations are mad' (Jeremiah 51:7). In Revelation we continue to find the influence of Babylon with the golden cup in her hand: 'And the woman was arrayed in purple and scarlet colour, and decked with gold and precious stones and pearls, having a golden cup in her hand full of abominations and filthiness of her fornication' (Revelation 17:4).

The prophet Nahum prophesied a similar message against Nineveh during the days of Hezekiah. 'Woe to the bloody city! It is full of lies and robbery (Nahum 3:1), 'Because of the multitude of the whoredoms of the well favoured harlot, the mistress of witchcrafts, that selleth nations through her whoredoms, and families through her witchcrafts' (Nahum 3:4).

In Jeremiah's day, we see the religious abominations—first in the worship of the Queen of Heaven, and second in the worship of her son. Notice the blindness of the people: 'Since we left off to burn incense to the queen of heaven, and to pour out drink offerings unto her, we have wanted all things, and have been consumed by the sword and by the famine' (Jeremiah 44:18). This spiritual fornication was seen in the worship of the child Tammuz, which Ezekiel saw when he was taken in the Spirit to Jerusalem and came to the door of the gate of the Lord's house. It was facing north. There he beheld women weeping for Tammuz (Ezekiel 8:14). Similarly, Phoenician and Assyrian women had wept for Tammuz.

Jeremiah paints a vivid picture of the condition of Judah, pointing out that on every high hill and under every green tree, the nation was playing the harlot (Jeremiah 2:20). There was also the call for them to turn away from their harlotry and from their many lovers and to return to the Lord (Jeremiah 3:1). That call fell on deaf ears. God laid bare their sin and pointed out their backsliding (Jeremiah 3:6). These messages would be reiterated by other prophets in one form or another.

John states he was in the Spirit and taken into the wilderness, where he saw a woman sitting upon a scarlet beast which had names that were full of blasphemy (Revelation 17:3). Scripture goes on to give an interpretation of what John saw: 'And the woman which thou sawest is that great city, which reigneth over the kings of the earth' (Revelation 17:18). It is the city whose colours are purple and scarlet, and her symbol is a golden cup.

Dake states, 'It is simple to trace in the archives of history the relation of Babylon to Rome and of Rome to the Roman Church.'[134] Furthermore, Dake notes that the 'Babylonian Cult was a system claiming the highest wisdom and ability to reveal the most divine secrets' and that this 'cult was characterised by the word "Mystery" because of its system of mysteries'.[135]

Notice what else scripture says about this city: 'And I saw the woman drunken with the blood of the saints, and with the blood of the martyrs of Jesus: and when I saw her, I wondered with great admiration' (Revelation 17:6).

There is overwhelming agreement that the city is Rome. The question that arises is this: Is it pagan Rome of old, or is it Rome today? The answer boils down to when John wrote the book of Revelation: before AD 70 or around AD 94? The evidence points to John writing in AD 94 and is supported by many different arguments.

Notice John's reaction. He knows all about Rome's persecutions. He is imprisoned by Rome, but he 'wondered with great admiration' (Revelation 17:6). He describes a religious system holding to the birth, death, and resurrection of Jesus, yet it is a religious system that has opposed both the Jewish people and the followers of Christ. 'And I saw the woman drunken with the blood of the saints, and with the blood of the martyrs of Jesus' (Revelation 17:6).

This takes us back to the parable Jesus gave to his disciples:

---

[134] Finis Jennings Dake, *Revelation Expounded*, enlarged ed. (Lawrenceville: Dake Bible Sales, 1950), 195.
[135] Ibid., 196.

> Another parable put he forth unto them, saying, The
> kingdom of heaven is like to a grain of mustard seed,
> which a man took, and sowed in his field: Which indeed
> is the least of all seeds: but when it is grown, it is the
> greatest among herbs, and becometh a tree, so that the
> birds of the air come and lodge in the branches thereof.
> (Matthew 13:31-32)

The mustard seed talks about faith, but the birds of the air Jesus defined as demons. No wonder John greatly wondered!

This woman is drunk with the blood of the saints. Tyndale was strangled and burned at the stake for translating the Bible. Wickliff was persecuted and, forty-one years after his death, his body dug up and burned. *Foxe's Book of Martyrs* provides details of the religious persecutions from Rome. Jewish communities also suffered at the hands of Rome, all told countless millions have been persecuted and killed by Rome.[136] As Dake notes, Rome has slain 'people in the past because they would not conform to her system of religion and yield to the supremacy of the pope over their wills'.[137] It was Rome that crucified Christ.

Also, one must never forget that in the Old Testament the Jewish people have the designation of saint, they are the saints of the most High who shall possess the kingdom for evermore (Daniel 7:18). This is the kingdom of which the angel spoke to Mary 'He shall be great, and shall be called the Son of the Highest: and the Lord God shall give unto him the throne of his father David' (Luke 1:32).

The events of Revelation 17 takes place in the Tribulation, it is the time of Jacob's troubles. It is the time Jesus spoke about 'For then shall be great tribulation, such as was not since the beginning of the world to this time, no, nor ever shall be' (Matthew 24:21). The church at this point has been raptured, we are now in the last week of Daniel's vision of seventy weeks that are 'determined upon thy people and upon thy holy city, to finish the transgression, and to make an end of sins, and to make

---

[136] http://webwitness.org.au/estimates.html
[137] Dake, *Revelation Expounded*, 209.

reconciliation for iniquity, and to bring in everlasting righteousness' (Daniel 9:24). It is the psalmist David who is said to have a heart after God's own heart; so we are not surprised when we read 'Keep back thy servant also from presumptuous sins; let them not have dominion over me: then shall I be upright, and I shall be innocent from the great transgression' (Psalm 19:13). The great transgression: the crucifixion of the Messiah. It is only when Jesus returns that the people of Israel 'shall look upon me whom they have pierced' (Zechariah 12:10).

Larkin states, 'Babylon continued to be the seat of Satan until the fall of the Babylonians and Medo-Persian Empires, when he shifted his capital to Pergamos, where it was in John's day.'[138] Larkin continues, 'When Attalus (Attalus 111), the Pontiff and King of Pergamos, died in B.C. 133, he bequeathed the Headship of the "Babylonian Priesthood" to Rome. When the Etruscans came to Italy from Lydia (the region of Pergamos), they brought with them the Babylonian religion and rites.'

Dake notes this pontiff was eventually accepted by Rome as their civil ruler. Julius Caesar became the Supreme Pontiff of the Babylonian Order in 63 BC, and the title was passed on to each Roman emperor.[139] In AD 378, the head of the Babylonian Order became the ruler of the Roman church. According to Wikipedia, in 205 BC, Rome turned to Attalus to have the Mother Goddess brought to Rome, where she became known as the Magna Mater.

The church at Pergamos gave position to those who held the doctrine of the Nicolaitans, which was an abomination before God (Revelation 2:15). There are two Greek words that make up the term Nicolaitans: *nikan*, which means 'to conquer', and *laos*, which means 'people'.[140] In other words, a system was set up according to which the clergy ruled over the people and claimed apostolic succession. The Ephesian church was commended for not just accepting a person because they gave the title of apostle, but tried them first, and found they were liars (Revelation 2:2).

---

[138] Clarence Larkin, *Dispensational Truth* (Santa Fe: Sun Books, 1998), 214.

[139] Dake, *Revelation Expounded*, 197.

[140] https://www.biblegateway.com/resources/encyclopedia-of-the-bible/Nicolaitans

The lineage of this mystical system can be traced through the seven empires in scripture, represented by the seven heads of the dragon. 'And there appeared another wonder in heaven; and behold a great red dragon, having seven heads and ten horns, and seven crowns upon his heads' (Revelation 12:3). This dragon is identified in scripture as 'the Devil, and Satan, which deceiveth the whole world' (Revelation 12:9). Satan deceives the whole world: he is the 'anointed cherub' (Ezekiel 28:14) who becomes a 'red dragon'. He appears as 'an angel of light' (2 Corinthians 11:14). His end is given by Isaiah: 'In that day the LORD with his sore and great and strong sword shall punish leviathan the piercing serpent, even leviathan that crooked serpent; and he shall slay the dragon that is in the sea' (Isaiah 27:1). The psalmist unveils revelation when he informs us that God breaks the heads of leviathan (Psalm 74:14).

We have Satan's kingdoms (which he offered to Jesus on the condition Jesus would bow down to him), represented by seven heads and seven crowns that cover Israel's history and go into the future. They were not only the political enemies of Israel but the empires that embraced the Babylonian cult in one form or another. The seven kingdoms are:

Babylon	Nimrod	Details in Genesis 10.
Egypt	Pharaoh:	

'Speak, and say, Thus saith the Lord GOD; Behold, I am against thee, Pharaoh king of Egypt, the great dragon that lieth in the midst of his rivers, which hath said, My river is mine own, and I have made it for myself' (Ezekiel 29:3).

Assyrian	Sennacherib, who came against Jerusalem in the days of Hezekiah. The Antichrist is called the Assyrian.
Babylon	Nebuchadnezzar:

'Nebuchadnezzar the king of Babylon hath devoured me, he hath crushed me, he hath made me an empty vessel, he hath swallowed me up like a dragon, he hath filled his belly with my delicates, he hath cast me out' (Jeremiah 51:34).

Media Persia	Darius
	He conquered Babylon and the last king of the Chaldeans, Belshazzar, was slain (Daniel 5:30, 31).
Greece	Alexander
	Description of the fight in the heavenly realm, firstly, with the prince of Persia and the revelation the prince of Greecia was about to come (Daniel 10:20).
Rome	Caesar
	Jesus was born in the days of Caesar Augustus, when all the world was taxed (Luke 2:1).

Rome is the seventh head, which goes into a mystery form: 'MYSTERY, BABYLON THE GREAT, THE MOTHER OF HARLOTS AND ABOMINATIONS OF THE EARTH' (Revelation 17:5). The Holy Roman Empire, the Holy Roman Church, and the Vatican are political and religious entities. Notice the first and fourth kingdoms are Babylon. One of the strangest things you will hear from Rome itself is that Babylon is another word for Rome. Their proof text is 'the church that is at Babylon' (1 Peter 5:13). It is given as Peter's connection with Rome.

This Babylonian mystery set up a priesthood to oversee a religious system in which people were initiated into divine secrets. This system required confessing to the priest, who was under a high priest, before becoming a member of a 'mystical priesthood'. According to Prescott, 'One is astonished to find so close a resemblance between the institutions of the American Indian, the ancient Roman, and the modern Catholic.'[141]

The literature written about Rome, its history, and its religious system is very extensive. Comparisons with religious Babylon have been debated for what seems like an eternity. Catholic theologians look to give the book of Revelation an early date of authorship. That would put what is written there into the past, thereby having no relevance to future events—the unveiling of what is to come.

---

[141] Quoted in Hislop, *Two Babylons*, 224.

Although there are Catholics who read the Bible, historically Rome is not known for encouraging people to read the Word of God for themselves. Knowing the Word of God and how to use the Word of God defeated Satan in the story of Jesus's temptation. Notice that Jesus himself said the words he spoke were both spirit and life for us (John 6:63). The psalmist states, 'thou hast magnified thy word above all thy name' (Psalm 138:2). Church history reveals the lengths to which the Roman Church has gone to prevent the Word of God being available for people to read for themselves. It is the doctrine of the Nicolaitans at work.

Jeremiah asked a question about the possibility of a leopard changing its spots and applied it to the Ethiopian (Jeremiah 13:23). If we ask the same question and apply it to Babylon/Rome, what would we expect the answer to be?

A well-known writer in the twentieth century was Baron Avro Manhattan (1914–1990), an Italian by birth. He was prolific writer who numbered H. G. Wells, Pablo Picasso, and George Bernard Shaw among his friends. He spent his life right up to his death detailing the intrigues of the Church of Rome. Wikipedia lists the works of Manhattan and provides an excerpt from his book *Vatican Imperialism in the Twentieth Century* (1965). Clicking this link brings up a page headed The Vatican against the Orthodox Church where he writes:

> The Catholic Church, the greatest surviving giant in the world, is a colossus with no peer in antiquity, experience and above all, in her determination to dominate the human race. To reach such a goal, she will suffer no rivals, tolerate no competitors, put up with no enemies.[142]

Manhattan's work on the Church of Rome is probably one of the most extensive and consistent projects of anyone's life. The sources from which he obtained his information are vast, including archives from

---

[142] Avro Manhattan, *Vatican Imperialism in the Twentieth Century*, Excerpts from Wikipedia, June 2020.

various governments around the world. The Wikipedia entry under his name provides the following works that can be downloaded to read, plus many more:

- *The Catholic Church Against the Twentieth Century* (1947; 2nd ed. 1950)
- *The Vatican in Asia* (1948)
- *The Vatican in World Politics* (1949)
- *Catholic Imperialism and World Freedom* (1952; 2nd ed. 1959)
- *Terror Over Yugoslavia: The Threat to Europe* (1953)
- *The Dollar and the Vatican* (1956)
- *Vatican Imperialism in the Twentieth Century* (1965)
- *Catholic Power Today* (1987)
- *The Vatican-Moscow-Washington Alliance* (1982)
- *The Vatican Billions* (1983)
- *Vietnam ... Why Did We Go? The Shocking Story of the Catholic "Church's" Role in Starting the Vietnam War* (1984)
- *Murder in the Vatican: American, Russian, and Papal Plots* (1985)
- *The Vatican's Holocaust* (1986)
- *The Dollar and the Vatican* (1988)

When we come to the twenty-first century, the inner workings of the Vatican are still being exposed by whistle-blowers. This comes down to a conflict with traditionalists and Pope Francis.

A second, more important controversy has in recent years come to the surface. It has major ramifications for the doctrines held by the Roman Catholic Church. Senior Vatican theologians now believe in the existence of extraterrestrial beings and that these beings once visited planet Earth. This is not implausible, for in Genesis chapter 6 we read of the sons of God, fallen angels, marrying the daughters of men producing a race of giants that went on to produce a race of hybrids. However, the outcome of this position has these theologians working on positional papers to change the narrative of the biblical text and the status of Jesus as the Son of God.

Vatican theologians are now working in conjunction with scientists at the Mount Graham Observatory, using their large binocular telescope named Lucifer to search for the return of alien entities. Dr. Tom Horn, the author of *Petrus Romanus: The Final Pope*, in a video published 24 March 2019, talks about the Vatican theologians, saying they believe that Jesus Christ, the Son of the Most High God, is a star child or an alien. Horn cites the names of the theologians.[143] No ordinary Roman Catholic has any idea about this expectation or the view now held by Vatican theologians awaiting visitors from outer space!

From a strict biblical stance, we know demonic entities are coming. We know that in Genesis 6, an attempt was made to corrupt the DNA of man when the 'Sons of God' came and had relationships with the 'daughters of men', which produced giants as offspring.[144] It was also done to a lesser extent after Noah's flood. David slew Goliath. 'And there went out a champion out of the camp of the Philistines, named Goliath, of Gath, whose height was six cubits and a span' (1 Samuel 17:4).

Bear in mind that the day is coming when Satan and the fallen angels will be cast down to our physical earth. 'And his tail drew the third part of the stars of heaven, and did cast them to the earth' (Revelation 12:4). This is the passage that is used to support the claim that a third of the angels rebelled with Lucifer (Satan). Revelation 1:20 defines for us what stars represent: they are angels. However, in this passage, they are described as messengers. The question arises, will we have a replay of Genesis 6?

It is surprising the subject of extra-terrestrials is now being discussed at the Vatican with scientists. What information do they have in their possession that is so overwhelming that they are prepared to put the biblical narrative aside and no longer believe Jesus is the Son of God?

In scripture, it is possible to get confused with definitions. For instance, the 'Sons of God' are the divine beings mentioned in Job 38. Some of these angels left their first estate; hence the accounts in Genesis

---

[143] https://www.youtube.com/watch?v=gf2RzH-cnTA
[144] 'Sons of God' is a term found in Job 38:7, from the Hebrew term *ben elohim*. The generic term 'angels' usually gets applied to different ranks/types of divine beings.

6. However, never confuse them with the 'sons of God' whom we read of in the New Testament. 'Beloved, now are we the sons of God, and it doth not yet appear what we shall be: but we know that, when he shall appear, we shall be like him; for we shall see him as he is' (1 John 3:2). These are two separate categories, one which we broadly designate as angels, and the other the saved men and women born again by the Spirit of God.

From scripture, we know Jesus is the image of God. God's image could not be restored to man until after Jesus's death and resurrection. Before Christ's resurrection, men had the image of Adam—a fallen image! Jesus is the 'image of the invisible God' which he restores in us (Colossians 1:15). Furthermore, when we look at Jesus, we see the goodness of God. Jesus heals the sick. He cleanses the leper. He raises the dead. He brings peace and restoration to the troubled heart. No wickedness nor evil is found in him. Perfect love exudes from him. What a Saviour!

Returning to the battle between the traditionalists and the present pope, one of the major schisms in 2020 surrounds Archbishop Vigano, a Vatican whistle-blower. He does not mince his words: in the June 2020 Catholic publication *Church Militant*, in an article titled 'Catholic-News Report-Vigano,' Archbishop Vigano made the following accusation: 'What is being created is a single world religion without dogmas or morals, according to the wishes of Freemasonry. It is obvious that Bergoglio (Pope Francis) along with those who are behind him, aspire to preside over this infernal parody of the Church of Christ.'[145] Dr. Taylor Marshall, a Catholic You Tube commentator also discusses these issues.[146]

Who is Archbishop Vigano? Archbishop Vigano was once third in the Vatican hierarchy from the Pope. He discovered financial impropriety at the Vatican from which a banking scandal ensued. He found hidden accounts—that is, they were off the record. So what was an initial $10 million deficit was turned around to $44-45 million surplus

---

[145] Militant Church – Serving Catholics, https://churchmilitant.com/news/article/pope-francis-knew-about-mccarrick-in-2013
[146] Taylor Marshall, https://www.youtube.com/watch?v=bZEGv6HkC-w

when these accounts came to light. According to news reports, the bank scandal was behind the resignation of Pope Benedict XVI. Archbishop Vigano subsequently became the nuncio at Washington, DC. Here he encountered political and church corruption. Exposing the scandals resulted in the archbishop having to go into hiding.

This whole affair became very public when, in June 2020, he wrote to President Donald Trump about the infiltration of the church and the role of the deep state, highlighting the corruption that was taking place in both the religious and political realm. Dr. Taylor Marshall covers the story in detail[147] President Trump in turn tweeted this on his Twitter account.

Vatican impropriety did not stop with the revelations that came from Archbishop Vigano. Once again the Vatican was in the news in 2020, this time with regard to the vindication scandal of Cardinal Pell. A writer at thearticle.com, which comprises a team of independent journalists based in London, wrote, 'The unholiest of scandals has erupted inside the Holy See—yet again. Vatican finances have always been unsavoury, but in recent years Europe's smallest state has acquired a reputation as the most corrupt on the Continent.'[148]

Cardinal Pell, like Archbishop Vigano before him, found financial improprieties in the Vatican's accounts. Brian Shanahan, political editor of Sky News Australia, discovered $2.3 billion had been transferred from the Vatican to Australia between 2014 and 2020. The greater percentage of this transfer took place after Cardinal Pell had been arrested. Following up his investigations with senior Roman Catholic authorities in Australia, Shanahan discovered they were unaware of these transfers. Incredibly, no person knew of these transactions, nor who authorised them or who the final recipients were. Surrounding this sad saga, there are allegations that the funds were used to pay off people who were involved in setting up Cardinal Pell to have him removed, so

---

[147] Taylor Marshall, https://youtube.com/watch?v=_4upHPYKtqE
[148] The Article, https://www.thearticle.com/a-new-vatican-scandal-vindicates-cardinal-pell-but-frustrates-pope-francis.

he could not follow through on his investigation of Vatican financial accounts.[149]

Scripture exposes the Babylon religious system for what it is—an abomination.

> The merchandise of gold, and silver, and precious stones, and of pearls, and fine linen, and purple, and silk, and scarlet, and all thyine wood, and all manner vessels of ivory, and all manner vessels of most precious wood, and of brass, and iron, and marble. And cinnamon, and odours, and ointments, and frankincense, and wine, and oil, and fine flour, and wheat, and beasts, and sheep, and horses, and chariots, and slaves, and souls of men. (Revelation 18:12-13).

They are more interested in riches and political influence than in the souls of men: slaves are rated higher.

Horn points out how this corrupt theology will feed into the great deception that aliens are our space brothers and creators. A much fuller discussion, giving all the sources to follow up, can be found in 'The Vatican and Alien Connections'.[150] They discuss why the Vatican has some of the most powerful telescopes. The Vatican is expecting someone to show up.

Tim Alberino has been involved in producing *The True Legends Trilogy,* and the second documentary is of particular relevance: 'True Legends, The Unholy See: The Vatican Knows All The Secrets'.[151] The documentaries highlight information the Vatican has known and kept secret for centuries. Those of you who have watched the film *Noah* and know your Bible would have been surprised to find in that film that the giants were the good guys. Where do you think that came from?

---

[149] Sky News Australia, https://www.skynews.com.au/australia-news/vatican-transfers-to-australia-amount-to-2.3b

[150] https://youtube.com/watch?v/=n6eCmSVAyTA

[151] GenSix Productions, https://www.gensix.com.

The Bible is clear that the last days will be like the days of Noah and the days of Lot. The outstanding event was the incursion of the Sons of God who married the daughters of men, corrupting the DNA of man. Then it was a limited number of fallen angels who left their first estate. Who knows how many will turn up this time?

In expounding the details of the image that Nebuchadnezzar had in his dream, we are left with a strange verse concerning the end times: 'And whereas thou sawest iron mixed with clay, they shall mingle themselves with the seed of men' (Daniel 2:43). In Genesis 6, the 'they' were the angels who left their first estate. Their prodigy were hybrid beings.

In Revelation 17, judgement is being poured out upon this religious system that originated at Babylon and permeated the ancient world and beyond. The priesthood that originated at Babylon moved to Pergamos, 'even where Satan's seat is' (Revelation 2:13). They eventually ended up at Rome.

Rome is the church that claims apostolic succession. They believe in Jesus Christ, his death, and his resurrection (at least until now). But it is the church that adopted the Babylonian worship of Mary, designating Mary as the 'Mother of God' at the Council of Ephesus in AD 431. They passed the inquisition of heretics instituted by the Council of Verona in AD 1184.[152] It is the system above all that keeps the souls of men in darkness.

In scripture, the church's position is laid out by the apostle Paul, who tells us we are the body of Christ. We are all individual members (1 Corinthians 12:27). Paul also talks about how the church functions: 'And he gave some, apostles; and some, prophets; and some, evangelists; and some, pastors and teachers; For the perfecting of the saints, for the work of the ministry, for the edifying of the body of Christ' (Ephesians 4:11-12).

We can compare this with a woman who is a harlot and an abomination. This is important, for the church is never called a woman but a chaste virgin: 'For I am jealous over you with godly jealousy: for I have espoused you to one husband, that I may present you as a chaste

---

[152] Dake, *Revelation Expounded*, 203.

virgin to Christ' (2 Corinthians 11:2). Satan's work is always one of counterfeit and imitation, with the express purpose to deceive mankind.

A further major position of extreme importance is in Paul's letter to the Ephesians: 'by grace are ye saved through faith; and that not of yourselves: it is the gift of God' (Ephesian 2:8). Paul is telling us about how salvation starts and ends with God and no flesh is involved. Compare that with Vatican II, which stated, 'From the most ancient times in the church good works were also offered to God for salvation of sinners. All men may attain to salvation through faith, baptism and the observing of the commandments.' In other words, the sacrifice of Jesus on the cross was insufficient in itself, and man has to do something additional to attain salvation.

The end times are described as a time of great wickedness and falling away from all that is righteous, true, and good. It will see the breaking of every cord that ties people and nations to the Word of God. This will result in an end-time judgement hidden in the writings of a major prophet. 'The earth also is defiled under the inhabitants thereof; because they have transgressed the laws, changed the ordinance, broken the everlasting covenant. Therefore hath the curse devoured the earth, and they that dwell therein are desolate: therefore the inhabitants of the earth are burned, and few men left' (Isaiah 24:5-6).

Jeremiah was also told about 'the curse that goeth forth over the face of the whole earth' (Zechariah 5:3). This curse affects two categories of people: those who steal (thieves) and those who swear (blasphemers). We read about this curse in the last book of the Old Testament, where there is the possibility stated of God coming and striking the earth with a curse (Malachi 4:6). The context of this verse is the Second Advent of Jesus Christ, and here we have Elijah showing up. We read about an imposter portraying himself as a shepherd, but scripture calls him 'an idol shepherd' (Jeremiah 11:17). He is not a true shepherd. He can be compared to a thief or a robber (John 10:1). In the Tribulation, we read of the Antichrist having a mouth full of blasphemy and speaking great things against the Lord (Revelation 13:5).

The result of this curse on thieves and blasphemers is described as follows, 'it shall enter the house of the thief, and into the house of him that sweareth falsely by my name: and it shall remain in the midst of his house, and shall consume it with the timber thereof and the stones thereof' (Zechariah 5:4). The one disease that we read of in the Bible that fits this description is leprosy. In biblical times the only cure for leprosy is to burn everything contaminated by it with fire and completely remove all the rubble of burned-down buildings. At this time people have taken the mark of the beast and are worshipping the image that has been set up. Upon these people falls a noisome and grievous sore (Revelation 16:2).

Particular attention also has to be given to the supernatural element in the destruction of the Babylonian cult. 'The beast that thou sawest was, and is not; and shall ascend out of the bottomless pit, and go into perdition: and they that dwell on the earth shall wonder, whose names were not written in the book of life from the foundation of the world, when they behold the beast that was, and is not, and yet is' (Revelation 17:8).

The first thing to be aware of is the beast foremost is a man before being identified with a kingdom. In Daniel, we read of the beast being slain and his body burned (Daniel 7:11). The second thing to note is that the beast was here before, and at the time of John's writing he is no longer living. The answer is found in the book of Acts: 'Judas by transgression fell, that he might go to his own place' (Acts 1:25): his own place being the bottomless pit.

What began in Babylon will have its final demise at Babylon. This is the place that will become the habitation of devils and every foul spirit (Revelation 18:2).

We also know this to be true from the information given to Zechariah. The prophet was told about an ephah, a measuring container like a basket. 'And, behold, there was lifted up a talent of lead: and this is a woman that sitteth in the midst of the ephah. And he said, This is wickedness. And he cast it into the midst of the ephah; and he cast the weight of lead upon the mouth thereof' (Zechariah 5:7-8). Then we are told two women with wings like a stork carried her to the land of Shinar, the location of Babylon, where she is set down 'upon her base'(Zechariah 5:11) like an image.

Isaiah prophetically declares the fall of Babylon and how all her images and all her gods are broken in pieces on the ground (Isaiah 21:9).

When Satan and his angels are cast to the ground in the Tribulation, this religious system will be destroyed. Larkin has it happening in the middle of the Tribulation, for it will no longer be required to deceive the nations. Satan incarnate, the mystery of iniquity, will be walking on the earth. The Antichrist will be setting himself up to be worshipped as God in the Holiest of Holies in the future third temple at Jerusalem. He will be destroyed by the brightness of the coming of the Lord Jesus Christ at the Second Advent.

In summary, after the flood of Noah, Nimrod set up a kingdom in opposition to the God of heaven. This kingdom, as well as being a political entity, set up a religious system that infiltrated all subsequent kingdoms. Hislop, bringing together three hundred sources, details its workings down through the centuries. Larkin and Dake show how this Babylonian cult moved from Babylon to Pergamos and eventually to Rome.

The seven kingdoms of Satan are enemies of Israel. The seventh kingdom metamorphoses into a mystery system that continues throughout the centuries in the form of the Holy Roman Empire, the Holy Roman Church, and the Vatican. Mystery Babylon is found at Rome, which killed God's people. It is full of political intrigue and corruption. Today, at the highest level, it is working on preparing to teach its adherents that Jesus was really just a star child or an alien, and that his progenitors are coming back to earth. It's going to be a crazy ride with wild days to come!

CHAPTER 18

GREAT MYSTERY: CHRIST AND THE CHURCH

This is a great mystery: but I speak concerning Christ and the church.

Ephesians 5:32

In the Holy Bible, there are three distinct groups of people identified. The first is Israel, comprising the Jewish people who are the descendants of Abraham, Isaac, and Jacob. The second group is known as Gentiles, those who are non-Jewish. The third group is the church, which can comprise both Jews and Gentiles who follow the Lord Jesus Christ.

It is to this last group that the apostle Paul unfolds the marvellous revelation of the church as the bride of Christ, referring to it as 'a great mystery'. No writer in the Old Testament received any insight into this plan of God. We are aware of the prophecy of Isaiah that is quoted in Matthew's gospel in relation to Christ, which records how God's Spirit will be upon him and that Christ will be the one to show judgement to the Gentiles (Matthew 12:18). 'In his name shall the Gentiles trust' (Matthew 12:21). But no one hearing these words would have any inkling of how this will be accomplished nor any understanding of what we now know. Nobody in the Old Testament, for example, knew anything about the body of Christ, the church.

In Ephesians chapter 5, there is a comparison of the relationship between a husband and a wife. It is applied to the Lord Jesus Christ and his bride. Even as a husband loves his wife, we are told Christ loves the church that he gave his life for (Ephesians 5:25). Paul continues this comparison and talks about how people do not hate their own flesh; they look after it and take care of it. Likewise, the Lord sustains and takes care of the church (Ephesians 5:29).

Up to this point, we can understand the meaning through personal experience. However, Paul gives further insight into this relationship, describing the church as part of his body, part of his flesh, and part of his bones (Ephesians 5:30). When Jesus rose from the dead and appeared to his disciples, notice the words he spoke to his disciples: 'Behold my hands and my feet, that it is I myself: handle me, and see; for a spirit hath not flesh and bones, as ye see me have' (Luke 24:39). Look what is not mentioned. Jesus's resurrected body did not have blood.

When Paul wrote to the Corinthians, he repeated the same message as that given to the church at Ephesus. He told them their bodies were now members of Christ's body, and they were part of his body (1 Corinthians 6:15). As a man and woman become one flesh, so two become one flesh (1 Corinthians 6:16). 'One flesh' reminds us of Adam's words when Eve was created from one of his bones. He tells Eve she is bone of his bone and is also part of his flesh (Genesis 2:23). Again, it is noticeable what is left out: blood. When sin entered the world, man inherited blood, and the life of the flesh is in the blood. Paul gives the reasons a man leaves the house of his father and mother: he cleaves to his wife, and they become one flesh (Genesis 2:24).

When Paul says it is a great mystery, we start to get a glimpse at what he is talking about. Multitudes of people are members of Christ's body, his flesh, and his bones, yet they are his bride. We can understand many members making up the church, but multitudes being part of his flesh and his bones? That is a great mystery.

When we turn back to Corinthians, Paul says, 'For I am jealous over you with godly jealousy: for I have espoused you to one husband, that I may present you as a chaste virgin to Christ' (2 Corinthians 11:2). In

Corinthians the bride is as yet not married. Notice also that 'bride' is singular, a chaste virgin.

To the Corinthians, the church is described as a virgin bride. To the Ephesians, it is compared to a wife. How can this be?

Paul had previously written to the church at Ephesus, explaining how they all had been raised up as a group to sit together with Christ Jesus in heavenly places (Ephesians 2:6). This allows us to come before the throne of grace with great boldness (Hebrews 4:16). How can we be here on earth, yet we are seated in heavenly places?

Remember, Paul has been telling the Corinthian church that while they are living on earth in their mortal bodies, they are absent from the Lord (2 Corinthians 2:5:6). 'We are confident, I say, and willing rather to be absent from the body, and to be present with the Lord' (2 Corinthians 5:8).

It is the limitations of our understanding and experience that makes this such a mystery. To recap: to the Corinthians, Paul expounds upon the virgin bride; to the Ephesians, Paul talks of marriage between a man and his wife, but adds that we are already seated in heavenly places. The writer to the Hebrews says we come boldly before God's throne. We may not know the ins and outs of this mystery, but Paul does add a caveat for us, stating that when we are joined to the Lord, we are joined together as one spirit (1 Corinthians 6:17). So in the spirit this joining together has already taken place, but the church is still here on the earth. We know from scripture that the marriage of the Lamb has yet to take place.

This mystery which Paul expounds is not something easily grasped or understood, but nevertheless it is a mystery that we have a responsibility to declare. The greater understanding for us awaits in glory. In the meantime, we can look at other events in scripture that reveal similar patterns for us to be aware of.

It is not a strange thing to have an encounter with a supernatural God and not to fully comprehend everything, for God seeks those who will trust him implicitly. However, how will you know if this mystery has an impact upon you like it did upon Paul? The answer is straightforward. When you grasp a revelation, it changes everything in your life—how you live, how you walk, and the company you keep. A true revelation forever leaves an indelible mark upon you.

The supernatural ways of God transcend our environment and experience of living on earth. This supernatural environment is what God has called his people into. Looking at the day of Pentecost, theologians consider it as the day the church came into being. But what happened on that specific day? The people gathered together were the disciples and followers of Jesus. They were Jewish men and women who believed that Jesus Christ was the Son of David, the promised Messiah to Israel. They were waiting in Jerusalem at the instruction of Jesus for the promised outpouring of the Holy Spirit: 'And, being assembled together with them, commanded them that they should not depart from Jerusalem, but wait for the promise of the Father, which, saith he, ye have heard of me' (Acts 1:4). They wait in obedience to Christ's command, expecting the coming of the Holy Spirit. But did they have any idea what it would look like?

The Reverend Henry Wotherspoon points out 'the consequences of the Incarnation as they emerge in the Third person of the Trinity and His relation to humanity, these are purely in the region of the unseen—the eye cannot discern them, as it can the flesh of the Son of Man'.[153] Reverend Wotherspoon highlights for us another challenge that we face—only when the Son of God became flesh could our natural eyes see him. It is impossible to understand the spiritual through natural abilities. Therefore, he goes on to say, 'What is new is that which is not natural but supernatural.'[154] It is an entrance of new power, not as the increase of a power formerly operating, 'a new gift, a new presence, a coming to balance a going, a Descent to balance an Ascension, a personality to confirm, to take the place of that personal 'Comforter' (Paraclete) on Whom in the days of His flesh, they had leant.'[155]

---

[153] H. J. Wotherspoon, *What Happened at Pentecost* (Edinburgh: T & T Clark, 1937), 4.

[154] Ibid., 9

[155] Ibid., 8

On the Day of Pentecost, the Holy Spirit filled everyone in the upper room. Throughout the book of Acts (see 2:24; 4:8; 4:31; 9:17; 13:19) we find they were filled with the Holy Ghost.

Scripture asks if we are aware that our bodies are now temples of God, that the Spirit of God has come to reside in us (1 Corinthians 3:16). We can see in these verses similar patterns of the supernatural working of God that give us confidence to hold on to Paul's revelations of the bride of Christ and the details of the union of the bride to the bridegroom. We are in Christ; the Holy Spirit is in us.

The apostle Paul stretches us with his mysteries, but in reality he is only building on that which has gone before in terms of the stretching of our faith. Scripture states our confidence in God should not be cast aside, for there is great reward when we hold on to the things God has spoken to us (Hebrews 10:35).

Larkin points out, 'The first Adam had his bride, and the Second or Last Adam must have His bride.' Larkin uses the illustration of Eliezer as a type of the Holy Spirit. Even as Eliezer was sent to get a bride for Isaac, 'so God has sent the Holy Spirit into this world in this dispensation to get a wife for His Son Jesus, and when the full number of the church is complete, the Holy Spirit will take her back with him to the Father's house, and Jesus, whose bride she is to be, will come out into mid-air at the "Eventide" of this dispensation to meet her.' The marriage of the bride to the bridegroom is called the marriage supper of the Lamb (Revelation 19:9). 'Let us be glad and rejoice, and give honour to him: for the marriage of the Lamb is come and his wife hath made herself ready' (Revelation 19:7).

Returning to Paul's letter to the Ephesians, he states, 'That he might present it to himself a glorious church, not having spot, or wrinkle, or any such thing; but that it should be holy and without blemish' (Ephesians 5:27). This is the church Jesus has 'purchased with his own blood' (Acts 20:28). Jesus cleanses, he heals, he restores, and he makes all things new. His is a glorious church!

Before this glorious church is presented for all to see, the church will be brought to stand before the judgement seat of Christ. In the Lord's presence, each individual will receive things done in their bodies according to what they have done, both good and bad (2 Corinthians 5:10).

Paul writes a similar message to the church at Rome and warns them about their infighting and judging of a fellow believer. He tells them they shall give an account to God for their behaviour (Romans 14:12). This will occur at the judgement seat of Christ.

What happens at the Judgement seat of Christ?

Paul, when he writes to the Corinthian church, talks about life after being converted to Christ Jesus. Basically, it is how we live our lives as Christians. Our lives as disciples, following Jesus, are going to be 'scrutinised and examined' to see if we have built upon the foundation Jesus Christ has provided (1 Corinthians 3:11). Every work as a Christian is going to be purified by fire. Paul uses an analogy we can understand by looking at the natural earthly realm. He takes gold, silver, and precious stones, things which endure, and compares them to wood, hay, and stubble, which do not last (1 Corinthians 3:12). Gold, silver and precious stones are refined in the fire, but wood, hay and stubble are burned—they go up in the smoke. Gold, silver, precious stones represent those people we win for Christ, for we are turning them away from wickedness and destruction to righteousness. Wood, hay and stubble are lifeless and dead.

Scripture exhorts us to turn from selfishness to live unto the Lord Jesus Christ, who died and rose again for us (2 Corinthians 5:15). As a Christian lives unto Christ and builds upon the foundation Christ has laid with gold, silver, and precious stones, it is work that lasts forever, and God in his goodness gives a reward (1 Corinthians 3:14). Likewise, if the work is built on dead things, upon another foundation than that of Christ, then that person will suffer loss.

After this purifying and giving of rewards, the Lord Jesus presents 'his glorious church without spot or wrinkle' (Ephesians 5:27). It is good always to have before us the apostle John's exhortation when he writes to remind everyone that when Jesus shall appear, we do not want to be ashamed; therefore, stand confident in the Lord (1 John 2:28).

It is appropriate at this juncture to remind ourselves what scripture teaches us about Israel. Paul in the book of Romans tells us plainly that

God has not forgotten them and has not cast them aside. They are still his people (Romans 11:1). Paul continues with a dissertation on Israel that covers three chapters.

Larkin highlights that we read about two brides in scripture.[156] In the Old Testament there is the bride of Jehovah.

> For thy Maker is thine husband; the LORD of hosts is his name; and thy Redeemer the Holy One of Israel; The God of the whole earth shall he be called. For the LORD hath called thee as a woman forsaken and grieved in spirit, and a wife of youth, when thou wast refused, saith thy God. For a small moment have I forsaken thee; but with great mercies will I gather thee. In a little wrath I hid my face from thee for a moment; but with everlasting kindness will I have mercy on thee, saith the LORD thy redeemer. (Isaiah 54:5–8)

The prophets Jeremiah, Ezekiel, and Hosea talk of Israel as being the cast-off wife who will be taken back. In the New Testament, the church is never called a wife. The church is always referred to as a chaste virgin, the bride of Christ.

One further distinction made by Larkin is that during the millennium, Israel the bride will reside in the earthly Jerusalem, while the bride of Christ will reside in the New Jerusalem.

When Paul talks about the church as the bride of Christ, he himself is overwhelmed by the revelation. He finds it not only a mystery, but a great mystery. The nearest example he provides to help us get some understanding of what is going to take place is Adam and Eve when they were in the garden, before sin came in. The parallel he uses is the process of how Eve came from the body of Adam before she became his bride.

Although it is a mystery to us, the church had an earlier experience in which we have become the temple of God, the Holy Spirit dwelling within all believers. Paul's mystery stretches our faith to another level.

---

[156] Clarence Larkin, *Dispensational Truth* (Santa Fe: Sun Books, 1998), 116.

When Jesus stated that the Gentiles would trust in him, no one could have imagined the extraordinary processes that would be put into place to achieve this, and in particular, how the church would come into being and thereby become members of Christ's body, his bones, and his flesh. We can truly say no eye has seen, nor any ear has heard, nor even entered into the heart of men the surprises God has for all those who love him (1 Corinthians 2:9).

CHAPTER 19

MYSTERY OF HIS WILL

Having made known unto us the mystery of his will, according
to his good pleasure which he hath purposed in himself:
That in the dispensation of the fullness of times he might
gather together in one all things in Christ, both which are
in heaven, and which are on earth; even unto him.

Ephesians 1:9-10

This is one of those passages of scripture that we do not always give the attention it is due. It is easily glossed over without realising its full significance. In the biblical usage, a 'dispensation' is a period of time that operates under specific conditions. Examples of this would be the dispensation when men do that which was right in their own eyes. Then there is the dispensation of the Law. Today we talk about the dispensation of grace, which will continue until the rapture of the church.

In this passage, Paul, writing to the church at Ephesus, speaks to them of the dispensation that will be the culmination of all previous dispensations that this world has gone through. This dispensation will occur when everything on earth and in heaven is brought together in

Christ. It is the revelation of the plans and purposes of God, which covers the outworking of God's kingdom in eternity.[157]

In literature, this dispensation to come has been labelled the Perfect Dispensation, for it will restore order out of the chaos that resulted from Lucifer's insurrection. Many things have to be restored, and the process of restoration will cover an extended time period. Of great significance on a personal level for a Christian is the transformation from living in a body of clay to having a body like the Lord Jesus Christ.

When we study the Bible, we become aware of two different realms that the Lord Jesus Christ rules over. The book of Job, which is believed to be the oldest book in the Old Testament, right at the very beginning reveals to us a realm outside our own dimension. Some call it the heavenly realm or the invisible realm, while others call it the realm of the supernatural. In this realm, there are a plethora of heavenly beings. Two-thirds of them give allegiance to God the Creator, and one-third rebelled under Lucifer.

The book of Job opens with the sons of God presenting themselves before the Lord. They come before Jehovah and find Satan, God's adversary, coming among them (Job 1:6). Everything in this invisible realm, just like in our earthly realm, has been created by God. God dwells in eternity. 'Before the mountains were brought forth, or ever thou hadst formed the earth and the world, even from everlasting to everlasting, thou art God' (Psalm 90:2). God sets over his creation a structure whereby the administration of his kingdom functions. Within these two different realms, the will and purposes of God are at work.

We can see this in scripture. Israel was warned not to go down to Egypt for help, and the reason given is quite stark: 'Now the Egyptians are men, and not God; and their horses flesh and not spirit' (Isaiah 31:3). Notice how the men of Egypt and their horses are described as flesh and not spirit: two realms together, one of flesh and one of spirit, with the spirit realm always dictating to the earthly realm. When the king of Assyria threatens Jerusalem, it is worded 'With him is an arm

---

[157] For a more in-depth study, see Clarence Larkin, *Dispensational Truth* (Sun Books, 1998).

of flesh; but with us is the LORD our God to help us, and to fight our battles' (2 Chronicles 32:8).

Those two realms do not operate independently of each other. We can see in the story of Job the influence of the spiritual realm and the impact it had on his life. Because we do not see the invisible realm, we tend to view all events through filtered glasses as natural occurrences. We live in the natural realm, and it dominates our way of thinking.

In Isaiah, we find insight into this spiritual realm and into an event that took place and affects us on earth. It highlights the ambitions of Lucifer, the son of the morning. He is a created being, yet he thought to exalt himself above God. His downfall is pride. Job describes Satan in detail. Satan is king over all the children of pride (Job 41:34).

Paul describes Satan's present position and activities when he writes to the Corinthians. Satan is the god of this world. He covers men's minds with darkness to keep them coming to the light. He uses all his power to prevent men from finding out about the glorious gospel of Christ, for Christ is the image of God, and the light that exudes from him lights up the path that men should walk in (2 Corinthians 4:4). We are also told, 'Satan himself is transformed into an angel of light' (2 Corinthians 11:14). Hence we hear people talking about Satan as an angel. However, a cherub is of a much greater rank! Paul provides further information to the Ephesians, stating that Satan is 'the prince of the power of the air, the spirit that now worketh in the children of disobedience' (Ephesians 2:2).

There are a number of things we know about Satan. Firstly, he was 'the anointed Cherub' who watched over the throne of God, full of wisdom and perfect in beauty (Ezekiel 28:14). A lot of our information about him is found in chapter 28 of Ezekiel and chapter 14 of Isaiah, which describe the cause of his fall. 'For thou hast said in thine heart, I will ascend into heaven, I will exalt my throne above the stars of God: I will sit also upon the mount of the congregation, in the sides of the north: I will ascend above the heights of the clouds; I will be like the most High' (Isaiah 14:13-14). Five times we have the personal pronoun 'I'—the anointed cherub is very self-centred. There are points in scripture where five does not represent grace, and here we have an example of that.

All of the fallout from this rebellion has to be cleaned up—restoration.

As stated, it is natural for us to explain circumstances purely from our human perspective. Job, when he went through the mill, does not appear to have any inclination to credit another realm with determining his destiny. This view is reflected in a verse in Paul's letter to the church at Corinth, elaborating on the inability of the eye, ear, and heart of man to conceive the things God has prepared for those who love him (1 Corinthians 2:9).

Many stop at this verse rather than pressing on to know more of the heavenly realm. When we stop here, we are essentially in the place and position of Job when everything appeared to turn against him with no explanation.

We go on to read about the operation of the Spirit of God. It is through the Spirit that those things that cannot be known or comprehended naturally are revealed unto us. God's Spirit searches all things, including the deep things of God (1 Corinthians 2:10). Even those who grasp the significance of these words tend to categorise it within a narrow framework, such as the work of salvation for mankind. However, God has revealed unto us by the Holy Spirit the deep things of God, the things he has prepared for us in eternity. In this passage, Paul provides the key for knowing and understanding these deep things of God: it is only possible through the Holy Spirit. The natural man, utilising natural methods, cannot know nor fathom the things of the Spirit. Our natural ability of sight or hearing only operates in the earthly realm.

The important thing to note is that both of these realms are sustained by God. Watch how Paul brings this out when he visits Athens. In that great portion of scripture where Paul visits the city of Athens, we read, 'his spirit was stirred in him, when he saw the city wholly given to idolatry' (Acts 17:16). Notice his observation: 'I perceive that in all things ye are too superstitious' (Acts 17:22).

In his deliberations with the philosophers at Mars Hill, Paul spoke the words of one of their own poets to state a biblical truth applicable to all who live on this earth. It is God who gives us the breath to live and to move. He is the one sustaining all life, and it is in him we have our being (Acts 17:28). It is in Christ that we live. He is the giver of life to all on earth. All things on earth are upheld by the Word of his power.

Paul took this revelation further when he wrote to the church at Colosse, and expanded it to cover the spiritual realm: 'For by him were all things created, that are in heaven, and that are in earth, visible and invisible, whether they be thrones, or dominions, or principalities, or powers: all things were created by him, and for him. And he is before all things, and by him all things consist' (Colossians 1:16-17). Paul writes to the believers at Ephesus to unveil the intentions of God to unify all of his creation, the natural, earthly realm with the heavenly, spiritual realm.

When the apostle John wrote to the church at Laodicea, talking about the Lord Jesus Christ, he summed it up in a few words: Christ is faithful and his witness is true (Revelation 3:14). This creation has been marred by sin, resulting in the greatest sacrifice that ever took place in time and eternity: the crucifixion of the Son of God.

This plan of God to restore all things was hinted at in the Old Testament. Isaiah wrote about the intention of God to create new heavens and a new earth. This earth and the universe we see will be forgotten, never to be remembered (Isaiah 65:17). The apostle Peter picks up on this. He writes and speaks of the promises of God, and how all will dwell in righteousness in the new heavens and earth (2 Peter 3:13).

Isaiah also wrote something directly for the Jewish people in connection with the final restoration: 'For as the new heavens and the new earth, which I will make, shall remain before me, saith the LORD, so shall your seed and your name remain' (Isaiah 66:22). This promise has never been rescinded. Satan throughout history has tried to destroy the Jewish people. At times they have been reduced to a remnant, but they have never been annihilated. Even when the time of Jacob's troubles come, which will take place in Daniel's seventieth week, a remnant will be rescued. God has his plans for Israel in eternity.

Paul writes about the gathering of 'all things in Christ' (Ephesian 1:10). The same message is found written to the church at Colosse: 'And, having made peace through the blood of his cross, by him to reconcile all things unto himself; by him, I say, whether they be things in earth, or things in heaven' (Colossians 1:20). It is important to be aware that an event has taken place that requires reconciliation of things on earth as well as in heaven. This reconciliation is made possible through the blood of his cross.

At Christ's first coming, we are well aware of his destiny as the Lamb of God who takes away the sin of the world. However, there is something much deeper revealed in this verse. Heaven itself needs to be cleansed by the blood of the Lord Jesus Christ. In our preoccupation with Christ dying for us at Calvary, we neglect an important truth: sin originated in heaven. Heaven and the heavens have been contaminated. Therefore, we read in Hebrews that Jesus 'by his own blood ... entered in once into the holy place' (Hebrews 9:12). That is, he entered the holy place in heaven, not made by hands, and cleansed it.

In all this work to bring about reconciliation of earth and heaven and to bring these realms together, Christ is the one who is going to have pre-eminence. 'And he is the head of the body, the church: who is the beginning, the firstborn from the dead; that in all things he might have the pre-eminence' (Colossians 1:18).

The Bible makes it plain that the Gentiles were 'without Christ, being aliens from the commonwealth of Israel, and strangers from the covenants of promise, having no hope, and without God in the world' (Ephesians 2:12). Through the death and resurrection of Jesus, Gentiles can come to God by the blood of Christ (Ephesians 2:13). We are a purchased possession, waiting to be redeemed unto the praise of his glory (Ephesians 1:14). We are adopted into God's family, made heirs and joint heirs with Christ. We are called sons and daughters (Ephesians 1:5). The will of God is for us to be like Christ, who is the image of God (Romans 8:29).

Picture the Lord Jesus Christ, after his resurrection, walking through the walls into the room where the disciples are hiding. This is a picture of the resurrected, glorified body which awaits every believer in Christ. Then we will know and experience the truth of scripture in a way hitherto only seen through a shadow. Christ is all and in all (Colossians 3:11).

In addition to a reconciliation taking place, the Bible also talks about restitution of all things. Restitution is returning to the rightful owner that which has been lost or stolen. 'And he shall send Jesus Christ, which before was preached unto you: Whom the heaven must receive until the times of restitution of all things, which God hath spoken by the mouth of all his holy prophets since the world began' (Acts 3:20-21). The context of this verse of scripture is Peter preaching to the people after the healing of the lame man at the Temple in Jerusalem. Peter speaks of God blotting out the sins of Israel when God from his presence pours out times of blessing (Acts 3:19).

The Old Testament speaks of this in many places. For example:

> In those days, and in that time, saith the LORD, the iniquity of Israel shall be sought for, and there shall be none; and the sins of Judah, and they shall not be found: for I will pardon them whom I reserve. (Jeremiah 50:20)

> And I will plant them upon their land, and they shall no more be pulled up out of their land which I have given them, saith the LORD thy God. (Amos 9:15)

The writer of the book of Hebrews speaks of Israel's sins being blotted and the fulfilment of the Old Testament prophets. 'For this is the covenant that I will make with the house of Israel after those days, saith the Lord; I will put my laws into their mind, and write them in their hearts: and I will be to them a God, and they shall be to me a people' (Hebrews 8:10).

Jesus also spoke to his disciples of Israel's future: 'in the regeneration when the Son of man shall sit in the throne of his glory, ye also shall sit upon twelve thrones, judging the twelve tribes of Israel' (Matthew 19:28). The 'Son of Man' is a particularly Jewish designation, and so is the 'throne of his glory'. Jeremiah pleaded, 'Do not abhor us, for thy name's sake, do not disgrace the throne of thy glory: remember, break not thy covenant with us' (Jeremiah 14:21). The angel spoke to Mary about the birth of Jesus and told her, 'He shall be great, and shall be called the Son of the Highest: and the Lord God shall give him the throne of his father David' (Luke 1:32).

The perfect dispensation, the subject of Paul's words to the Ephesians, will come together in a new heaven and a new earth. The Bible opens: 'In the beginning God created the heaven and the earth' (Genesis 1:1). As we draw near to the end of the Bible, we read, 'And I saw a new heaven and a new earth: for the first heaven and the first earth were passed away; and there was no more sea' (Revelation 21:1).

The process by which this happens is explained by the apostle Peter. 'Looking for and hasting unto the coming of the day of God, wherein the heavens being on fire shall be dissolved, and the elements shall melt with fervent heat' (2 Peter 3:12). We are also told, 'new Jerusalem coming down from God out of heaven' (Revelation 21:2). All the host of heaven, along with the redeemed of the ages, are going to be brought together in Christ. It will be said God's tabernacle is now with men, and God will dwell with men. He will be their God, and they will be his people (Revelation 21:3). Ezekiel prophesied this same message to Israel (Ezekiel 37:27). An old hymn written by Carrie Ellis Breck[158] captures the moment:

> Face to face with Christ, my Saviour,
> Face to face—what will it be,
> When with rapture I behold Him,
> Jesus Christ who died for me?
>
> Face to face I shall behold Him,
> Far beyond the starry sky,
> Face to face in all His glory,
> I shall see Him by and by!

This time period is also known as the day of God, wherein 'the heavens and the earth, which are now, by the same word are kept in store, reserved unto fire against the day of judgement and perdition of ungodly men' (2 Peter 3:7). Peter talks about past events that happened to the earth when it was dry, then submerged in water. Peter also throws

---

[158] Carrie E Breck, https://www.hymnal.net/en/hymn/h/963

in a revelation of the age of the heavens, declaring the heavens are old (2 Peter 3:5). The earth goes in and out of the water, reminding us of Genesis, when the water covered the earth. The next renovation will be with fire. It is a complete remodelling of the heavens and the earth.

Everything is going to be restored, reversing the chaos that followed the rebellion of Lucifer (Satan) and all the consequences of the fall of man. Our text says, 'That in the dispensation of the fullness of times he might gather together in one all things in Christ, both which are in heaven, and which are on earth; even unto him' (Ephesians 1:10).

However, 'all things' does not cover Satan, the angels who rebelled, the hybrids from the incursions of the sons of God mentioned in Genesis chapter 6, or any unclean spirit. Nor does it offer any hope if a person dies in their sins. 'The wicked shall be turned into hell, and all the nations that forget God' (Psalm 9:17). If a person is wise, they will grab hold of the promises of God. 'The way of life is above to the wise, that he may depart from hell beneath' (Proverbs 15:24). Remember, it is the goodness of God that we should be saved from such a fate. 'For great is thy mercy toward me: and thou hast delivered my soul from the lowest hell' (Psalm 86:13).

Genesis chapter 6 reveals to us an incursion that took place on the earth in the days of Noah, which we have alluded to in earlier chapters. A number of the sons of God left their first estate and intermingled with the daughters of men. The result was to change the DNA of man, corrupting and marring man's original DNA. The intermingling produced offspring called giants. They in their turn mingled with other creatures to produce hybrids. Descriptions of these hybrids are found in different cultures. Ultimately, this led to Noah's flood and the rescue of Noah and his family. 'There were giants in the earth in those days; and also after that, when the sons of God came into the daughters of men, and they bare children to them, the same became mighty men which were of old, men of renoun' (Genesis 6:4).

After the flood in the days of Noah, a lessor incursion took place. We know how David slew Goliath, who was one of the giants. 'Giants' is a translation of the Hebrew word *Nephilim*. We read of the Nephilim again when Israel is about to enter the Promised Land. The spies sent ahead report, 'And there we saw the giants, the sons of Anak, which come of the giants: and we were in our own sight as grasshoppers, and so we were in their sight' (Numbers 13:33). Then we have over twenty mentions of the Rephaim and the Rapha, all connected with the giants.

The sons of God involved in these incursions are still to be judged. Peter makes reference to Jesus preaching to them when he descended into hell: 'By which also he went and preached unto the spirits in prison' (1 Peter 3:19). Sardinia is a known place to find the tombs and skeletons of these giants. True Legends the Documentary Film Series, episode three, Holocaust of Giants, explored the island of Sardinia where skeletal remains of giants are still being extracted.[159]

The pivotal point in the process to redeem all of creation and bring all things together in Christ was the crucifixion of the Lord Jesus Christ. Its impact is so unfathomable and its consequences so far-reaching that man cannot plumb its depth. In ignorance they crucified the Son of God; therefore, we are told if the princes that rule over this world had any idea of the consequences to themselves, they would not have crucified the Lord of glory (1 Corinthians 2:8).

The Jewish religious hierarchy never believed Jesus was their promised Messiah. Pilate asked Jesus about truth but did not wait to get an answer. However, Pilate knew Jesus was not guilty of the crimes laid against him, and we find his judgement on Christ that he could find no wrong in him (John 18:38). He still went ahead and authorised the crucifixion. The testimony of the centurion standing at the cross also declared Jesus's innocence and that he was a righteous man (Luke 23:47).

The demonic realm, on the other hand, was not ignorant of who Jesus was. 'What have we to do with thee, Jesus, thou Son of God? art thou come hither to torment us before the time?' (Matthew 8:29). Therefore, they knew at Calvary that they were killing the Son of God. They actually had the audacity, being created beings, to imagine they could overcome the living God and defeat him.

---

[159] Steve Quayle, Timothy Alberino, and Tom Horn, https://www.gensix.com/true-legends-films

We have mentioned that the process of bringing in the perfect dispensation covers an extended period of time. I give an outline not only to show the grace and mercy of God, but to make aware that all will give an account to God. It covers individuals and it covers nations. These accounts take place at different times under different judgements.

After Christ rose from the dead, having the keys of death and hell, the church came into being. The gospel since that time has been preached throughout the earth. All who come to faith in this time, which culminates in Christ coming for his church, must appear before the judgement seat of Christ. 'For we must all appear before the judgement seat of Christ; that every one may receive the things done in his body, according to that he hath done, whether it be good or bad' (2 Corinthians 5:10). This takes place in heaven immediately after the church is raptured, and is centred on how a Christian has lived for the Lord Jesus Christ since the day of their salvation. People at this judgement already have obtained eternal life.

A second judgement we read of is the judgement of the nations, described in Matthew's gospel. This takes place when Jesus returns to earth at his Second Advent. Jesus returns in glory along with the angels of heaven. At this time, Jesus sits on the throne of his glory (Matthew 25:31). Matthew tells us who is being judged—all nations. The nations will be brought before the Lord, and a separation will then take place, just like a shepherd dividing sheep from goats (Matthew 25:32). This judgement of the nations is based upon how each nation has treated God's people, the Jews.

The third judgement is the one most familiar to people, the Great White Throne Judgement at the throne of God at the end of the millennium.

> And I saw a great white throne, and him that sat on it, from whose face the earth and the heaven fled away; and there was found no place for them. And I saw the dead, small and great, stand before God; and the books were opened: and another book was opened, which is the book of life: and the dead were judged out of those

things which were written in the books, according to their works. (Revelation 20:11-12).

It is also at the end of the millennium that Lucifer, after being set free for a short time with the fallen angels and all of the demonic realm, has the sentence of judgement enforced. Their fate is sealed for eternity. It is described thus: 'And the devil that deceived them was cast into the lake of fire and brimstone, where the beast and the false prophet are, and shall be tormented day and night for ever and ever' (Revelation 20:10). Jesus, talking about this lake of fire, stated it is a fire that never goes out. It is an everlasting fire, and it is prepared for the devil and all the fallen angels (Matthew 25:41).

Hell was never prepared for man. However, due to man's rebellion against the living God, the prophet writes the sad words that hell had to be made larger to accommodate the wicked (Isaiah 5:14). In the gospel of John it is revealed how man can escape eternal damnation and be delivered from spending eternity in the same place as Satan, with the same torment. The price to secure the redemption of mankind was bought by the precious blood of the Son of God, hence we read 'God so loved the world, that he gave his only begotten Son, that whosoever believeth on him should not perish, but have everlasting life' (John 3:16).

At this point, when all have been judged and their sentences carried out, and before the creation of the new heavens and the new earth, we find another level of revelation: 'And when all things shall be subdued unto him, then shall the Son also himself be subject unto him that put all things under him, that God may be all in all' (1 Corinthians 15:28). In eternity the Godhead comes back into focus. Jesus Christ, the Son of Man, God in the flesh, takes his rightful place once again in the Godhead as the Word of God, as found in John: 'In the beginning was the Word, and the Word was with God, and the Word was God' (John 1:1). The question arises about Jesus's human nature and whether Jesus lays it aside when God is all in all. Views on this vary.

Larkin has a slightly different take as to the exact time God becomes all in all. He defines the perfect kingdom as that of the new heavens and new earth. Returning to Ephesians 1:10, when all things are brought together in Christ, he ties it in with Isaiah describing how the nation of Israel and their seed remain before the Lord as long as the new heavens and new earth remain (Isaiah 66:22). Going to Deuteronomy, he brings up God's covenant, which lasts for a thousand generations (Deuteronomy 7:9). He then calculates the age of Jesus at his death, 33 years old, and multiplies this by the thousand generations, thus deducing that the perfect kingdom lasts for 33,000 years. After this, Christ, the Son of Man, returns to take his place within the Godhead.

Jesus returning to take his place and submitting to his Father is not surprising, for Jesus made constant reference to the Father in his earthly ministry. Examples include:

> Jesus answered and said, I thank thee, O Father, Lord of heaven and earth. (Matthew 11:25)

> In that hour Jesus rejoiced in spirit, and said, I thank thee, O Father, Lord of heaven and earth, that thou hast hid these things from the wise and prudent, and hast revealed them unto babes: even so, Father; for so it seemed good in thy sight. (Luke 10:21)

> Then answered Jesus and said unto them, Verily, verily, I say unto you, The Son can do nothing of himself, but what he seeth the Father do: for what things soever he doeth, these also doeth the Son likewise. (John 5:19)

> Jesus answered and said unto him, If a man love me, he will keep my words: and my Father will love him, and we will come unto him, and make our abode with him. (John 14:23)

> And when Jesus had cried with a loud voice, he said, Father, into thy hands I commend my spirit: and having said thus, he gave up the ghost. (Luke 23:46)

Following on from God being all in all, we have the implementation of great changes to the universe. 'And I saw a new heaven and a new earth: for the first heaven and the first earth were passed away; and there was no more sea' (Revelation 21:1). The curse that came upon the earth because of sin, as recorded in Genesis chapter 3, will be removed. It will be extinguished. In the midst will be the throne of God and of the Lamb, and we will serve our God (Revelation 22:3).

The holy city, which is New Jerusalem, comes 'down from God out of heaven, prepared as a bride adorned for her husband' (Revelation 21:2). The apostle Paul, in writing to the Galatian church, provided the relationship of New Jerusalem to the church, stating that the Jerusalem which comes down from above is the mother of us all (Galatians 4:26). It is the dwelling place for the body of Christ. In this new environment:

> God shall wipe away all tears from their eyes; and there shall be no more death, neither sorrow, nor crying, neither shall there be any more pain: for the former things are passed away. And he that sat upon the throne said, Behold, I make all things new. And he said unto me, Write: for these words are true and faithful. (Revelation 21:4-5)

This life was spoken of by Jesus when he ministered in person. An example is the conversation with the woman of Samaria, in which Jesus turned the subject of discussion from the water that was in the well to himself. He tells her that if she drinks from this well, she will have to return again, but if she drinks the water he will give her, she will never thirst, for it springs up from her innermost being to produce everlasting life (John 4:14).

Summing up the will of God, we have seen how comprehensive the work of God is to remove all vestiges of the insurrection that began in heaven and its subsequent impact on earth, when Adam surrendered the sovereignty he had over the earth to Lucifer. The one at the centre of this restoration is Christ. It is the Lord Jesus Christ who will bring together the two realms over which he is both Lord and God. 'That at the name Jesus every knee should bow, of things in heaven, and things in earth, and things under the earth' (Philippians 2:10).

The prophet Isaiah reveals to us in no uncertain terms the one who is above all in power and authority: 'I have sworn by myself, the word is gone out of my mouth in righteousness, and shall not return, That unto me every knee shall bow, every tongue shall swear' (Isaiah 45:23). The apostle John brings these words back to our remembrance by quoting this passage (Revelation 14:11). Jesus is the head of all principalities and powers. Having done the will of his Father in heaven, he will once more take up his position within the Godhead as the Word of God, and God shall be all in all.

APPENDIX 1

Further Notes on the Introduction

Subjects:
Four Hundred Silent Years
The Seleucid Empire
Statue of Zeus in Jerusalem
Altar of Zeus in Pergamon
Replica of the Altar of Zeus in Nuremberg
The Book of Malachi

God works through the generations. He is a generational God. This is a foundational principle of scripture. It is demonstrated in history, though we do not always see it. For instance, take Malachi, who wrote the last book of the Old Testament. A general consensus of when Malachi wrote is between 434 and 397 BC, with some theologians proposing slightly different dates. From this time till the birth of John the Baptist, there is no record of God sending any prophets to Israel. Hence it is very common for commentators to talk about 'four hundred years of silence'. It is also given this designation because it appears God is not doing anything. It appears that God has forsaken his people. This is a bit simplistic and can also be a bit misleading, for though we read of no prophets being sent by God to his people, prophecy continues to unfold before the eyes of the Jewish people.

The vision given to Daniel, interpreted by the angel Gabriel, of the Greek empire overcoming the Medes and Persians, and its subsequent demise and break-up into four divisions, takes place during these silent years. There is no prophet, no Word from the Lord, yet the Jewish people witnessed God's Word being performed. This unveils one of the great truths of scripture. There are times when God's people are called to remain steadfast and faithful to the calling and purposes of God, knowing that behind the scenes, God's plans continue unabated.

Consider the twentieth century through today. Western Christianity has mainly been in decline. However, the re-establishment of Israel as a nation is in alignment with the promises God gave through the prophets of restoring the nation. Today we see a constant flow of Jewish people returning to the land of their forefathers. In this time of silence, the vision given to Daniel while in Babylon is being outworked.

In the book of Daniel chapter 8, we read of this vision given to Daniel. The details are explained to Daniel by the angel Gabriel. In the vision, Daniel saw a ram with two horns, which represented the kings of Media and Persia. He saw a he-goat with a horn between its eyes, coming swiftly from the west against these two kings and overcoming them. From history we know this to be Alexander the Great (356–323 BC), who rose to prominence in 331 BC and is regarded as being among the greatest military strategists of all time. Taught by Aristotle, Alexander became ruler at age 20 after the death of his father, Phillip II of Macedon. In a few short years, he created one of the greatest empires, spanning all the way from Greece to India.

Gabriel continued to open up the vision to Daniel, letting him know that out of one of the divisions of Alexander the Great's empire, a little horn would arise in the last days, the time when transgression would come to its full extent. The little horn will be great; he will exalt himself and turn to invade the pleasant land, the land of Israel.

Daniel chapter 11 foretells Alexander's horn being broken, which speaks of his death and his empire broken up. We are informed in Daniel 11:4 that Alexander the Great will not be the head of a new dynasty, for no descendant is going to succeed him.

The four kingdoms that arose after Alexander the Great's death were Egypt, Syria, Macedonia, and Asia Minor. Today we recognise them as Egypt, Syria, Greece, and Turkey. Four of Alexander's generals split the empire among themselves. They were Cassander (358–297 BC) who became king of Macedonia, Lysimachus (360–281 BC) who became king of Asia Minor, Ptolemy 1 Soter (367–282 BC) who became the ruler of Egypt, and Seleucus 1 Nicator (358–281 BC) who took over Syria.

Daniel chapter 11 gives an in-depth view of two particular divisions: the Ptolemaic dynasty, represented by the designation 'king of the south', and the Seleucid Empire, represented by the designation 'king of the north'. It is a remarkable portion of scripture, detailing the battles, the intrigue, the lying, and the deceit of each king towards the other. The accuracy is so astonishing that critics of scripture have postulated it had to be written after the events. Any priest who studied the words of Daniel and was in a place to observe events could literally give a running commentary on this feud and also be able to declare who would ultimately prevail without any fear of contradiction. The only problem is the requirement of successive rabbinical priests specialising in Daniel's visions. We know that when Jesus walked the city of Jerusalem, people like Simeon and Anna were looking for the fulfilment of Daniel's visions. There is no mention of any priest following events and linking them to prophecy.

In Daniel chapter 8, Gabriel told Daniel that out of one of the divisions of the Greek empire, after the death of Alexander the Great, a little horn would arise in the last days. In Daniel chapter 11, we find a vile person, identified as the Antichrist to come, and he is from the land represented by the king of the north, the Syrian part of the Greek Empire. If you have ever come across a teaching that the Antichrist will come from Syria, this is the source. It is also believed that the Antichrist must be part Jewish—otherwise the Jewish people would not initially accept him as their Messiah.

The Syrian division of the empire subsequently became the Seleucid Empire (312–63 BC). The major event, from a Jewish perspective, during this four-hundred-year period came with the rise of a leader named Antiochus IV. (He used the title Epiphanes which means 'God

Manifest'.) He had a devastating effect on Israel. It was Antiochus IV who tried to bring the Jewish people into alignment with the Hellenistic culture which held sway at that time over the land of Israel.

The tipping point of Antiochus IV's actions took place in 167 BC, when he polluted the Temple at Jerusalem. In place of the worship of Jehovah, he set up an idol of Zeus and sacrificed pigs in the holy place. He stopped the evening and morning sacrifices, replacing them with an image of himself and demanding that sacrifices be offered at the feet of his image. Hence he is seen as a type of the Antichrist who is still to come.

This action of Antiochus IV led to the Maccabean revolt, which is celebrated today in the feast of Hanukkah. Hanukkah is also known as the Feast of Dedication, and it is held in the winter. It is not a feast listed in the Old Testament. Instead, this feast was initiated to celebrate the cleansing of the Temple after it had been recaptured from the Seleucids, who had polluted it with their sacrifices to idols. In John's gospel we read of Jesus being in the Temple at Jerusalem on the Feast of Dedication, where he asserted his deity in response to the questions asked by the crowd (John 10:22).

With regard to the period when Antiochus IV came in and set up the abominations in Jerusalem, we find in Daniel's prophecy a reference to the people who knew their God would do exploits. This was literally fulfilled by the Maccabean revolt. They did exploits, they subdued the intruder, and they expelled him from their land. No prophet speaks, there is silence, but people lived who knew their God and demonstrated it by fulfilling prophecy (Daniel 11:32).

The king of the north, from Syria, eventually prevailed over the king of the south. Syria is also connected with the Assyrian who is mentioned throughout the Bible. When we go back to the prophet Isaiah, another connection with the Assyrian appears (Isaiah 52:4). Isaiah informs us that when Israel was in the land of Egypt, a king arose who never knew the history of the Jewish people in Egypt. As a result, this king persecuted the children of Israel without cause. The king who persecuted Israel came from Syria.

Following on from the Maccabean revolt, for a period lasting the better part of a century, Israel was not subjugated by any other nation. They ruled themselves. This all changed around 63 BC, when the Romans arrived. By 65 BC, the Romans had made Syria a province within their empire, and the era of the Seleucid Empire was confined to history. When Jesus was born, the Roman Empire reigned supreme over the greater part of the then-known world. Jerusalem and Judea were only a small corner of this vast new empire.

In Israel's history, we find them in Egypt persecuted by an Assyrian. It was an Assyrian who erected the statue of the god Zeus in the Temple at Jerusalem during the time of the Maccabees. It is an Assyrian who will come into the land of Israel in the latter days to set himself up as God in the Temple at Jerusalem.

After the Maccabean revolt, we hear nothing of the worship of Zeus till John writes his letter to the seven churches. The worship of Zeus turns up at a place called Pergamon. Scripture tells us that this is where Satan is operating from, the place of Satan's seat. It already sounds ominous! Zeus, known as the king of the gods, had the largest altar of all the Greek deities, and it was located at Pergamon. In the letter to the church at Pergamon, we find there are those who are bold for their faith and stand firm in the midst of persecution. We see Antipas being murdered.

Pergamon is a good place to study the work of Satan and the influence he exerts. In his realm, the doctrine of Balaam is encouraged. In this instance it is greed, the love of money (see chapter 12, which covers the sin and error of Balaam). His realm also encourages the rise of the Nicolaitans, those in the religious sphere who take responsibility away from the ordinary man in the street. They exercise their power and control in order to rule over the laity. The worship of idols is encouraged, and the food offered to those idols is given to idol worshippers. Paul, in his letter to the believers at Corinth, warns them against taking food that has been offered to idols, for behind those idols lie demonic entities (1 Corinthians 8). Satan's kingdom is one of selfishness, greed, lust, corruption, power, immorality, and all sorts of perverse wickedness. Also at Pergamon, political correctness is prominent, for Satan's hatred is on display towards the servants of the living God who will not bow their knee to him.

Contrast the kingdom of darkness with the kingdom of God, where righteousness and truth are proclaimed. The love of God is manifest in people's lives, breaking immorality, self-importance, greed, love of self, and love of money, which the Bible states is at the root of all evil. In God's kingdom, people are not manipulated nor controlled, for God's kingdom is built on relationship and the love of God.

Nearly two thousand years later, in the latter part of the nineteenth century, a German archaeologist, Carl Humann (AD 1839–1896), uncovered the ruins of Pergamon. The site was excavated and an altar, along with various artefacts, was taken back to Germany and reassembled. A museum in Berlin was named after this altar. When Hitler came to power, his architect, Albert Speer, built a massive replica of this altar to Zeus at Nuremberg. It was from the podium of this altar that Hitler looked out over his troops, delivering his speeches. These rallies were mainly held at night so that the effects of the lighting around the grounds would set the atmosphere. We are well aware of the horrendous atrocities committed by the Nazi regime, including the Holocaust, in which the lives of six million Jews were exterminated along with members of many other sections of society deemed unfit to live. It was one of the twentieth-century's darkest moments.

Much has been written about the link between the Nazis and the occult. Some have identified the birth of anti-Semitism in Germany with the arrival and erection of the altar of Zeus.

The same spirit was behind the persecution of the children of Israel in Egypt, the days of Antiochus IV, Pergamon, and the Holocaust. It is demonic. As surely as night follows day, this demonic spirit will raise its ugly head again before the Second Advent of the Lord Jesus Christ. This demonic spirit has a hatred towards the Jewish people and towards all who follow Christ. It has no compassion for humanity. Those who are beguiled and seek after the power and influence of this demonic realm should be aware that their final end will be destruction and torment in the lake of fire.

To conclude this appendix, let's look once more at Malachi. We have mentioned that Malachi was the last Old Testament book to be written. However, in the layout of the Hebrew Scriptures, it is not given as the last book. The Hebrew Scriptures finish with Second Chronicles (see chapter 16). What is most remarkable in the last chapter of Second Chronicles is a command for Jewish people to return to Israel. Wherever in the world a Jewish person is found, as they read their sacred scripture, they are constantly reminded to return to the land promised to Abraham, Isaac, and Jacob.

Contrast this with the last book of the Old Testament found in a Christian's Bible, the book of Malachi. It is Malachi who writes about the Messiah coming to set up his kingdom. We understand this to be the Second Advent of the Lord Jesus Christ. Look closely at who shows up just before Christ's return: Elijah the prophet. It is awe-inspiring and very impressive to stop and consider how scripture is laid out to capture both Jew and Gentile.

When Jesus returns at the Second Advent, he is going to set up his kingdom on earth and fulfil scripture by sitting on the throne of David, also known as the throne of his glory. Therefore, it is not surprising that the Jewish people are constantly reminded to return to Israel, to the land God has given them.

The command to return is given because their Messiah, when he returns, is going to come to Jerusalem, and more specifically to the Mount of Olives. Malachi who informs them that, preceding the coming of the Messiah, Elijah the prophet will be sent to herald that great day. Until that day arrives, the demonic powers behind the idol of Zeus, led by Satan himself, will do their utmost to kill, to steal, and to destroy the hopes of Israel and the promises God gave Israel. But God is a generational God, a covenant-keeping God, who is always working to accomplish his purposes. Never forget that and remain faithful!

APPENDIX 2

Further Notes on Chapter 1

Subject:
The Postponement Theory

Ludwigson highlights what has become to be known as the postponement theory. This view states that the Second Advent of the Lord Jesus Christ could have occurred at any time from the preaching of Peter in Acts chapter 2 to the death of Stephen in Acts chapter 7. His theory is based on a number of premises, the major one being that all the Old Testament prophecies concerning Christ's birth, death, and resurrection have come to pass.

At the time of the resurrection of Jesus and Peter's sermon on the day of Pentecost, no book of the New Testament was in existence. The disciples had in their hands the Hebrew Scriptures of the Old Testament. These scriptures were the only source of information regarding the plans and purposes of God that anyone had access to. There were no conflicting manuscripts to argue over.

Matthew recorded the words of Jesus when he shares with his disciples the environment they are going to find themselves in when he is not with them in bodily form (Matthew 10:16–23). He talks to them about being brought before councils, governors, and kings. The purpose will be for a testimony against those in the synagogues who will stand up and oppose them. It will also be a testimony to the Gentiles.

Jesus goes further to explain what will take place within a family unit: brother will put to death brother, father will put to death son, and parents will be put to death by the actions of their children. Jesus caps the conversation off by telling them they will be hated by everyone for his name's sake. Notice the instructions they are given, along with the expected outcome: when persecuted in one city, they are to flee to the next city, and before they have covered all the cities in Israel, the Son of Man will come.

We are confronted with the words in Matthew not being fulfilled (Matthew 10:23). We have Christ fulfilling all scripture concerning himself with regard to his birth, his death, and his resurrection. There is no outstanding prophecy left to be fulfilled. Everything is in place for the Second Advent to take place. Therefore, the question arises why the Second Advent failed to materialise. We are in a situation similar to what we find mentioned in Hosea, as we will see below.

When Peter preached on the day of Pentecost, he brought up the prophecies contained in the book of the prophet Joel. It is worth the time and effort to read through Acts chapter 2, then look at the context of the verses Peter quotes from Joel. Joel describes events that take place on the day of the Lord. 'The day of the Lord' is a common expression throughout the Old Testament, and although it can allude to various events, the day of the Lord is mostly associated with the return of the Jewish Messiah—what Christians call the Second Advent.

When Jesus returns to reign on earth, the Bible describes phenomena in the heavens. This is what we find Peter preaching: wonders in the heavens and then signs on the earth, events that include blood, fire, and a vapour of smoke. The day of the Lord is also described by Zephaniah as a day of wrath, trouble, distress, waste, and desolation. The prophet Amos warns the people not to desire the day of the Lord, for it will be horrific. It will be a day of extreme darkness. These are not events that took place on the day of Pentecost nor immediately afterwards, but we do expect these things to take place at the Second Advent.

When we come to the death of Stephen, who was killed by stoning, he saw heaven opened and he saw the glory of God (Acts 7). Jesus was standing at the right hand of God. In Revelation chapter 4, a similar picture is given. A door is open and the voice like a trumpet says to come up hither. As this is recognised as corresponding with the rapture of the church, it would appear to indicate that the call to come up was near at hand. But the act that followed brought it to a halt: the martyrdom of Stephen.

Three things stand out that happen immediately after Stephen's death. The first one is the absence of any more miracles being recorded at the church in Jerusalem, even though there are apostles still among them, including Peter. The second thing of note is how short a time period the church operated out of Jerusalem in the scheme of things: forty years at the most. The days of the Jerusalem church come to an end with the destruction of Jerusalem by Titus in AD 70. The third observation is the immediate calling out of Saul of Tarsus, who becomes the apostle Paul, the apostle to the Gentiles, and a prolific writer to the churches in the New Testament. It is the apostle Paul who receives revelations and visions, which he elucidates under the heading of mysteries in his epistles.

The postponement theory is not a well-known view among Christians, and it is not found in many writings. There are those who dismiss it as a worthless theory, and that is quite all right. However, it is worth pondering the rationale behind the evidence given in support of the theory—namely, the words of Jesus given in Matthew, Jesus's words on the cross indicating all prophecies have been fulfilled, and the cessation of the signs and wonders reserved for the Jewish people. The apostle to the Gentiles is called out. From this point, the church in Jerusalem continued to exist for a relatively short time before it too went into oblivion.

The circumstantial evidence surrounding the view of postponement theorists is not limited to this one example in scripture. The prophet Hosea gives us insight into God's plans to heal Israel, but that too never came to pass (Hosea 7:1). We know from scripture that King Jehoahaz sought the Lord, and the Lord heard his prayer (2 Kings

13:4–5). However, Israel was not healed. King Jehoahaz did not take away the grove in Samaria, and he continued to follow in the footsteps of Jeroboam. Therefore, when God would have healed the nation of Israel, the actions of the people spoke louder than words. They preferred their idols to Jehovah. The opportunity slipped away from Israel, and they were overthrown by the Assyrians, a cruel enemy.

Many years ago, I read a book on the Bible code when that subject seemed to be all the rage. A plethora of work was churned out by many different authors. The author of the work I read wrote two books, one in 1997 and the other in 2002. The first one ended up as a *New York Times* bestseller.

The writer, who was not a Christian, made what I thought at the time was a very astute observation that gave a remarkable insight into what he discovered. The writer, Michael Drosnin, who wrote two books on the Bible Code, noted how codes could be used to find information, such as the name of a person and the year of their birth or events in the past. He also wrote about his astonishment at finding DNA hidden in a code within the book of Genesis. He also found the destruction of the Twin Towers on 9/11. The code gave an accurate count of the number of people who lost their lives.

The writer noted that the codes did not tell the future. What he did observe was that the codes appeared to give a choice of possible options that could come to pass without detailing results or consequences. This observation was completely unexpected. And yet the one thing we know from scripture is that God is full of surprises. Think of the promise given to King David that the Messiah would sit on the throne through his lineage. All looked impossible when the son of Jehoiakim, Coniah, pronounced on him captivity and no children to sit on the throne. However, the Messiah's lineage to sit on the throne of David came through the lineage of Nathan, David's son. Ah! God has all things worked out. Mary was of that line and Jesus step father Joseph was of the lineage of Solomon.

When we consider scripture, God always talks about choosing life. Choose life, not death. But many times Israel did not make the correct choice. Israel's history is one of learning lessons the hard way. It is a stark warning to those who follow Christ to always choose life.

If the concept of choice is applied to the events after the resurrection of Jesus Christ, then those things which were spoken of as being near at hand in the gospels, such as the physical kingdom of heaven, could have become a reality instead of two thousand years of wandering throughout the nations of the earth by the Jewish people. Why would we say this? In the early part of the book of Acts, the offer of forgiveness is preached by Peter. It is couched in terms that the act of Jesus's crucifixion was carried out by the Jews' religious hierarchy in ignorance (Acts 3:17). As we stop to dwell on this offer of forgiveness, the level of grace and mercy God extends to those who crucified Christ is astounding and incomprehensible to the natural man. Yet this is the same level of grace and mercy God extends to every one of us.

The immediate future of Israel is placed in the hands of the leaders of the Jewish nation—the Sanhedrin, which comprised Pharisees, Sadducees, and lawyers. They hounded Jesus throughout his three and a half years of teaching. Would they now repent of their great transgression and acknowledge their sin, the crucifixion of their own Messiah (Psalm 19:13)? History records their steadfastness against the preaching of the apostles. It records the authorisation of persecution against the followers of Jesus.

We have Jesus's words, found in Matthew's gospel, about the imminent return of the Son of Man. Jesus has fulfilled all necessary prophecies, and Peter, on the day of Pentecost, is preaching Second Advent passages from scripture. The religious rulers of Israel are given the opportunity to repent for committing the great transgression. Like Israel in the days of Hosea, they let slip the opportunity extended to them to repent and turn from their sin, consequently, they missed what is Israel's greatest expectation - to experience the return of their Messiah. And like their forefathers, they were forcefully removed from their land.

It is a strange thing when we consider the Pharisees were looking for a prophet like unto Moses. When Jesus showed up, there never had been anyone like him since the days of Moses. He had all the signs and wonders to identify him as the one prophesied in scripture. This is important because the Jewish people looked for signs. Jesus even replicated the feeding of the multitude: to push the point home, he did it on more than one occasion.

Perhaps the events that had befallen Israel—the captivity in Babylon, followed by being brought under the Greek influence of the Seleucids, and then Roman culture—warped their perspective of interpreting scripture. They became consumed by looking for a deliverer, to the point of excluding everything that did not meet that narrative. They looked for a deliverer to establish Israel as a nation free from subjugation. We do not know all their motives, but we do know both John the Baptist and Jesus spoke stern words to them. Jesus came to fulfil what was written in scripture concerning himself, and that led to his crucifixion on Mount Calvary.

Jesus laid down his life willingly. On the cross, he cried, 'It is finished.' Jesus died not only for the Jewish people, Israel, but for people of all nationalities, so that everyone who trusts in his redemptive work will know forgiveness of sins and the victory over death, hell, and the grave.

When we pay close attention to Old Testament prophecies concerning the coming of the Jewish Messiah, we find the first and second comings of Christ are so closely knit together in many places that in Jesus's day, it appears the Pharisees could not distinguish them.

At the beginning of Jesus's ministry, after the temptation in the wilderness, Jesus came to Nazareth. In the synagogue, scripture was opened at the book of Isaiah. Jesus began to read from chapter 60, stating the Spirit of the Lord God was upon him and that he brought good news: He had come to heal the broken-hearted. He had come to set free those who were bound and open the prison doors that had kept people in bondage.

Notice where Jesus stopped. It was in the middle of a sentence, for the text goes on to speak of what will happen at the Second Advent. Jesus was declaring what he had come to do in his first coming. Jesus never completed all of verse 2, which speaks of the vengeance of God that takes place at the Second Advent. The two comings are so intertwined, yet so clearly separated. One brings deliverance, the other judgement.

The two comings of the Lord are found intertwined in this fashion throughout the Bible, and some examples are very familiar to us. Take Genesis 49:10–11. In verse 11, it is intimated that the Lord will ride a donkey into Jerusalem. However, the verses immediately before and immediately after this are second coming references. What we discover here is the order of the two comings given in scripture is not necessarily laid out in chronological order.

Again, look at Zechariah 9:8–10, where a similar situation is given. Verse 8 is clearly a second coming passage, but look at verse 9. It is about Jesus riding into Jerusalem. Verse 10 gives us the extent of the Lord's dominion when he comes: the kingdom of Messiah will extend from sea to sea and to the ends of the earth. When we turn to the Psalms, we find Psalm 21 covers the reign of Messiah when he comes, but Psalm 22 is known as the crucifixion psalm.

In many ways this brings us to the crux of the view that the Second Advent could have happened by the latest at Acts chapter 7. The only way to distinguish the two comings, which were tied so closely together in the Old Testament, was to have a heart right with God and thereby open to receive revelation, knowledge, and instruction from the Holy Spirit. A heart must be open to repent from the great transgression of crucifying Christ, the Lord of Glory. Two separate comings may have gone undetected by the custodians of scripture. It is frightening to believe how they could have been so blind.

When we bring all of this down to a personal level, often in our Christian journey, choices are set before us. We do not always know the full outcome of a choice we make. However, the importance of having a repentant attitude and being willing to be led by the Holy Spirit must be paramount in a Christian's life if we wish to fulfil the destiny God has planned for us.

APPENDIX 3

Further Notes on Chapter 3

Subjects:
Spiritual entities
Biblical definitions
Origin of disembodied spirits (unclean spirits/devils/demons)
Kingdom of God and Kingdom of Darkness
Psalm 82

The Bible is very clear in its teaching that man is not alone in the universe. The Bible goes further in letting us know there are 'other entities' in the universe. Their make-up and ability is at a higher level than man, for man is made lower than the angels. The Bible reveals two realms, a heavenly realm and an earthly realm, with the heavenly realm being able to manifest itself in the earthly realm.

The unseen realm of the spirit is sometimes described as the area of the supernatural. In this context I am specifically referencing the angelic beings and entities we find mentioned in scripture. They include the cherubim, seraphim, archangels, angels, fallen angels, unclean spirits (disembodied spirits/demons/devils), and Satan. As this information is scattered throughout the Word of God, it has to be pieced together to gain knowledge and understanding.

It is not that the information is not in scripture. It is more a challenge to recognise who is being addressed at times, as we will see later on. Even in the area of prophecy, the challenge is to decipher those words spoken in the past tense: do they describe what is still a future event? The best-known example of that is Isaiah 53, detailing the crucifixion of Jesus. The words are laid out in the past tense, although the event was still in the future at the time it was written. Until areas like this are pointed out to us, we seem to live with blinkers over our eyes.

We have descriptions from scripture of different heavenly beings. For instance, seraphim, known as the burning ones, have six wings. The prophet Isaiah informs us that two wings are used to cover their faces, two wings are used to cover their feet, and two wings are used to fly (Isaiah 2). Ezekiel talks of a heavenly creature, and his description of wheels within wheels as it moved stretches our imagination. There are other beings that come under the generic category of angels. However, even here the Bible reveals the existence of a hierarchical structure of angels with different purposes and functions, including councils, for the administration of God's kingdom.

We are also told that some people have come into contact with angels without recognising them as such. The humans were completely oblivious to their presence, for angels have the ability to appear as normal men. There are also instances in scripture of angels appearing as such to people. Abraham had such an experience and so did Gideon. In these cases, the angels did not have wings as commonly believed. Other people in scripture had their eyes opened to see mighty angels. Some descriptions are given of an angel having a flaming sword.

The universe is populated by spirit beings, and they are divided into two camps: those who are on the Lord's side, and those who rebelled under the leadership of one of the anointed cherubs—Lucifer, son of the morning. Those who rebelled operate at this time above the earth, but in the future they will be cast down and confined to working only on the earth.

The earliest writing giving insight into what is taking place in the unseen realm is the book of Job. It is probably the oldest book in the Bible. You find in it references to pre-flood men of renown. What is so significant about this book is that it opens up immediately, telling us up front that there is a conflict raging in the universe and man is caught unwittingly in this conflict.

When searching through the Bible, we are able to piece together the causes of this conflict, where man fits into it, how to recognise it, how to choose the correct side, and how to have victory, for no one is immune from it. In this realm of the unseen (although there are those with a seer gifting who see into this realm), we are told there is a war, and the combatants are not flesh and blood like the human race. This realm has principalities and powers. We are told about rulers of darkness, spiritual wickedness, and spirit beings. The book of Daniel gives insight into those who have great authority over nations—for example, the princes of Persia and Grecia.

There are provided details of a rebellion that originated in heaven. Heaven is not a vague, woolly concept that is intangible. The psalmist tells us heaven is in the north direction of the universe, and it is beyond a huge empty space. The Bible tell us there is a sea of glass that is frozen.

Like all subjects that one studies at university, the Bible has its own definitions. This is important to grasp. For example, the word 'sleep' is used to describe death, informing us that death is not the end. There is something else beyond.

When it comes to the spiritual realm, this is important as well. If we take the sons of God as an example, we find this phrase used both in the Old Testament and in the New Testament. In the book of Job chapter 38, the sons of God watched as God laid the foundations of the earth. The word for god, *elohim*, is given to them. Similarly, in Genesis 6, these sons of God turn up. In the New Testament, we read believers are called the sons of God, from the Greek word *Theos*, but believers are not the same as the angels who have been given this designation. The word *elohim* is found in many places in scripture. We also find God calling Israel his son, but that is not compatible with Jesus, God's Son.

The Bible opens with God, Elohim, the Creator of the heavens and the earth. When we come into the second chapter of Genesis, we are given deeper revelation of the Creator: he is the Lord God. He is Jehovah God, the self-existing and eternal One, as opposed to lesser entities with the title of 'god'. This is why in modern scholarship, when *elohim* on its own appears in relation to 'god' or 'gods', it can be understood as talking of a 'divine being'. But, importantly, these divine beings are not to be worshipped. Therefore, when 'god' is used, it is not because there is more than one true God, Creator of all things. The word describes a particular divine being.

The God of creation has many attributes tied to his name that separate him from the rest of his creation. These divine beings, or 'gods', are among his creation. When we read of the Lord God, revelation is revealed about how God creates and administers his kingdom.

Throughout the Bible, the term 'god' or 'gods' appear in connection with the unseen realm of the spirit world. This can be confusing to us. However, these entities with this title are differentiated from the Creator, the God of Israel.

Before continuing along this line of thought, let us take a step back to examine the origin of what have been termed 'disembodied spirits'. They are the ones we find Jesus casting out of people. They are devils, sometimes called demons or unclean spirits. They do not have bodies of their own; therefore they are on the lookout to find bodies to live in. This should not be understood in the sense of demon possession—that is, total control by a demonic entity. However, they are afflicting spirits that can torment, cause illness, and oppress people. Many times Jesus cast out a spirit before the person received healing. In effect they are squatters.

In one instance, during an outreach event, I was among the participants in a number of different teams providing ministry to individuals. One person directed to our small team for prayer was very cast down, like they were carrying the world on their shoulders. As we prayed, nothing seemed to make a difference. So we changed tactics and commanded the spirit of affliction to leave the person. I can still picture the reaction today as the person screamed out. Everyone in the building looked at us. The demeanour of the person instantly changed. Then we could minister healing. The person described a sharp pain in their chest, like something being torn out and gone from them.

What are these spirits and where do they come from? Some have postulated they are angels, but this is very unlikely. We know the fallen angels, the sons of God from Genesis 6, are already chained up in prison. There are two main areas that have been looked at to discover where these disembodied spirits come from. One is known as the gap theory. The other is that they are the spirits of the giants and hybrids that came about due to the incursion of fallen angels which we read of in Genesis 6. Let's look at these two alternatives.

Gap theory suggests, as its name implies, that there is an intermediate period between two events, specifically between Genesis 1:1 and Genesis 1:2. Genesis opens with the creation of the heavens and earth, the word for 'earth' meaning dry ground. The second verse relays how the earth was without form, a bleak place, and water covered its surface. Darkness permeated the whole earth.

This scene is viewed as a picture of judgement occurring upon some pre-Adamic civilisation. To bolster this view, evidence is supplied to show that God never creates anything void and without form. A cross reference is usually provided to the judgements found in Jeremiah chapter 4, particularly verse 23, which describes the earth in a similar fashion to Genesis 1:2. The main premise can be summarised in this way: a pre-Adamic world existed, and Genesis 1:2 is a reflection of judgement occurring. Hence the disembodied spirits are from a pre-flood creation. As a side issue, this view has been articulated to demonstrate the earth can be millions, if not billions, of years old.

The challenge that we face with Jeremiah 4:23 and other references in support of this view is to distinguish whether this describes a past event or an event that is still in the future. For example, is Jeremiah prophesying events to take place at the day of the Lord?

The alternative view links the origin of disembodied spirits to the incursion of fallen angels found in Genesis chapter 6. It is probably the prevailing view due to the amount of evidence now collated. The giants who were the offspring of this incursion, known as the sons of God, are found in literature from many cultures. We know why this event took place—to corrupt man's DNA and prevent the promised seed of the Messiah being born on earth. Noah was declared to be perfect in his generation. That is, he was complete, without blemish, whole, without spot—all descriptions of a man who did not have his original make-up corrupted by the sons of God, who were trying to thwart the plans of God.

As mentioned, plenty of evidence has been found throughout the world of species different from man. An example is beings with elongated heads that have been examined using various scientific tests, proving their DNA is different from that of man. Bodies of giants have been found and attempts have been made to extract their DNA, especially by the military. There have been findings of what looks like a complete, formed body of a miniscule creature believed to be about eight years old, still awaiting identification.

Let us return to the term *elohim* and to the importance of the flood in the days of Noah. The importance of Noah's flood is found in Psalm 82. The striking thing about this psalm is that it takes us back to the *elohim*, the gods we covered above.

Psalm 82 opens with a description of a great gathering of the mighty. God stands in their midst. This scene is from heaven, and it is the type of thing that is easy to overlook in other parts of the Bible. Notice what is taking place. There is a judgement, but no man is involved in this judgement. It is the gods, the *elohim*, who are being spoken about.

In Isaiah 13:3, we read of God commanding his sanctified ones and his mighty ones. Our first instinct is to bring these references down to the natural realm. Yet scripture unveils to us that different principalities and powers can rule over nations.

The Hebrew word for God, *elohim*, is used in Psalm 82. The comparison is between a heavenly being, sons of the most high, and ordinary men. They are gods but they will die as men. The gods, the fallen sons of God who walked the earth in the days of Noah, died like men when the flood came. The Bible lets us know that the angels who came to earth to be the instigators of this plan to destroy man are held in chains of darkness, awaiting their final punishment that is to come. This information is found in the book of Jude in the New Testament.

In the Old Testament, when we read of judges, they were men with titles reflecting their different standing within Israel, such as a chief from one of the tribes. This psalm is not speaking of those types of judges, as some have characterised it, but another category of judge, called gods. They have rebelled against God. They are the *elohim*, and they are going to die just like men. When these *elohim* appeared, they were in the likeness of men.

The fallen angels who left their first estate took to themselves the daughters of men, and their offspring were a race of giants. In secular history, there are records of hideous-looking creatures that different people have recorded seeing. These hideous creatures are most likely the result of bestiality performed between the giants and other forms of life. We know bestiality took place in the Promised Land, for Moses was given instructions that the offspring from such relationships were to be destroyed. The Bible talks about 'all flesh' being corrupted. That goes beyond man. Everything demonic goes to the lowest common denominator. The mythology found in the Greek legends did not come from a person's imagination! Experiments by scientists today replicate this process by transferring DNA from one animal to another, producing hybrid creatures. When the sons of God came, the corruption not only produced hybrid creatures, but creatures with their own distinct DNA.

When we recognise that gods were on earth in the days of Noah and died, and their death was caused by drowning, then we acknowledge that they died in the same way as all who lived in the pre-flood world, just as Psalm 82 says. These gods left their first estate and suffered the same fate as unrepentant man when judgement came. In the book of Revelation, we read of the sea giving up the dead. It is more than just mariners who were drowned and are resurrected. These gods have already been judged, and they are going to be brought up before God to have the sentence carried out as a result of their rebellion against God.

Psalm 82 also points to a future period when the gods will once again walk on this earth as they did in the days of Noah. The psalm provides prophecy given in the past tense. Why would we say this? From the time the psalm was written to our present day, there has not been any time that we can state unequivocally that the foundations of the earth have been out of place. We find hidden in this psalm a future event when a great shaking will occur. This is supported by the prophet Isaiah, who describes the earth to a staggering drunken man.

We must always remember that Christians have been given all power and authority over all the powers of darkness. Christians have power to cast out devils. They have been given instructions on how to even resist Satan himself. Scripture is there for us to use as a sword and be more than overcomers. We are truly in a spiritual warfare, and the weapons we use are not carnal ones. The weapons of our warfare have been supplied by God himself.

APPENDIX 4

Further Notes on Chapter 7

Subjects:
Jewish Feasts
Feast of Tabernacles

The Jewish feasts and what they represent is not a subject that is well known in many Christian circles. Sure, if we mention Passover, there is a strong recognition of its origins and purpose. To a Christian, it is associated with the crucifixion of the Lord Jesus Christ as God's Lamb who takes away the sin of the world. Of course, to a Jewish person, the understanding is very different.

If we turned to the Feast of Unleavened Bread and asked an ordinary churchgoer to tell us what it is all about, probably the person would stare back with a blank look on their face. It is also probably true that among many of us in Christendom, Jewish feasts are relegated and seen as less important. We wrongly think everything in the Old Testament has been superseded by the writings in the New Testament.

Another thing to consider when looking at the feasts is the instructions the Lord gave as to when they should be held. Dates and times in scripture always hold some significance. Therefore, let us look at the feasts Israel was commanded to observe and the place of the Feast of Tabernacles among them.

The book of Leviticus lists seven main feasts given to the children of Israel. From a Jewish perspective, it can be viewed as an overarching plan of God that contains the plans of God that go into eternity. Furthermore, the number seven speaks of completion. Also it is a reminder of God's signature, which can be found throughout scripture.

We have already mentioned the Feast of Passover. This is the first feast that is listed for the people of Israel to remember. The feast is to be held on the first month of the Jewish religious calendar, the month Nisan, the month Israel left Egypt. Like all feasts, this feast requires an offering to be made. The feast celebrates the great deliverance the Jewish people experienced when they were in slavery in Egypt. A lamb was slain for each Jewish household, and the blood was put on the doorposts and lintel. When the Angel of Death went through the land of Egypt, it passed over all houses covered by the blood.

The month Nisan is found in our Gregorian calendar in springtime. Jesus kept the Passover, broke the bread with his disciples, and gave them the cup to drink before he was taken, tried, and crucified on Mount Calvary. When we pay close attention to the instructions given to Moses, we find something quite startling. The people were commanded to take a lamb on the tenth of Nisan and slay it on the fourteenth of Nisan. You never find in scripture where the children of Israel kept to this exact formula. However, in the New Testament, we find Jesus presenting himself on the tenth of Nisan and being crucified on the fourteenth of Nisan.

Immediately after Passover is the Feast of Unleavened Bread. This feast was to last seven days. Leaven in scripture speaks of sin, so here the children of Israel were to eat unleavened bread which, being the exact opposite of leaven, speaks of holiness. The Jewish bread known as matzo usually is displayed with stripes, which reminds us how the Romans' cruelty left Jesus's back looking like a ploughed field. Jesus in his ministry told his audience, 'I am the bread of life' (John 6:35). He could have easily added, 'My place of birth, Bethlehem, was known as the house of bread.'

We continue with the Feast of Firstfruits. That follows on from the Feast of Unleavened Bread. These are three feasts which really just run into each other. Firstfruits talks of the land yielding its produce it is the early harvest. To celebrate this feast, the people were to come before the Lord and wave a sheaf. To a Christian, it speaks of Jesus, who rose from the dead, bringing out those Old Testament saints who were confined to Abraham's bosom.

A break of fifty days occurs before the next feast arrives on the Jewish calendar, and that is Pentecost. This feast is held at the start of summer. This is the time when the people looked forward to gathering in the main harvest. When the Holy Spirit was poured out on the day of Pentecost, we can see how it was on God's heart that a harvest should be brought into his kingdom.

The remaining three feasts all take place in the autumn, the first of which is the Feast of Trumpets. Notice also these feasts take place in the seventh month, which usually straddles September and October in the Gregorian calendar. The sounding of the trumpets would be a joyous time, for it speaks of proclaiming liberty. Liberty to the captives is a theme throughout scripture. It was regarded as a memorial to Israel. Blowing the trumpet was at the centre of Joshua's great victory at Jericho, and the people of Israel are told to blow the trumpet in Zion. For Christians, we are drawn to the book of Thessalonians, where Paul talks of a trumpet being heard. The graves open, and we who are alive are caught up in the air to meet Christ.

The Feast of Trumpets takes place on the first day of the seventh month. On the tenth day is the Feast of the Day of Atonement. This is the time when the people humble themselves and afflict their souls before God. On the Day of Atonement, the high priest would sprinkle blood seven times in front of the veil in the Temple. This reminds us of the seven occasions when the blood of Jesus was shed:

- when Jesus sweated great drops of blood at Gethsemane
- when a crown of thorns was placed on Jesus's head
- when his face was smitten and his beard plucked
- when the Roman soldiers whipped his back
- when his hands were nailed to the cross

- when his feet were nailed to the cross
- when his side was pierced by a Roman spear

Above all else which the blood of Jesus accomplished, it allowed sinful man a way to enter into the presence of God. Man comes by the 'Blood of Sprinkling'.

Finally, we reach the Feast of Tabernacles, which takes place on the fifteenth day of the month, five days after the Day of Atonement. This feast celebrates how God provided shelter for Israel during their wilderness wanderings. However, like all things in scripture, we are left to ponder the significance of tabernacles. In the Old Testament, the Jewish people had to appear three times a year in Jerusalem: at Passover, at Pentecost, and at Tabernacles. Passover stands out, for that is when the Messiah was crucified. Pentecost stands out, for that is when the church came into existence. What about Tabernacles?

Tabernacles falls on the seventh month, as we have seen with the Feast of Trumpets and the Day of Atonement. When we look at all of the feasts, the number seven is very prominent. In scripture, seven stands out in various time elements: seven days, seven weeks, seven months, and seven years. It has long been recognised that the feasts in the spring are connected with the first coming of the Lord Jesus Christ, and the feasts in the autumn foreshadow the time of the Second Coming of the Lord Jesus Christ. It may have a dual application, covering both the rapture of the church and the time of the Second Advent, or only the Second Advent. Some writers put the rapture of the church around Passover or Pentecost. As Tabernacles indicates the presence of God with man, it stands out as the last feast.

The Old Testament book of Malachi pictures this presence of God with man in the natural realm with the rising of the sun. The book of Genesis tells us God created the sun on the fourth day, and according to Peter, a thousand years are as a day. Prophetically, Christ appears on the fourth day, based on this method of interpretation known as the Ussher chronology. An interesting observation is that the shortest distance between the sun and the earth for a four-day period occurs at the Feast of Tabernacles. There are also those who are persuaded that the birth of 'the Sun of Righteousness' was at this same time period. We certainly know it was not December.

When Jesus shows up, scripture calls it the mystery of godliness. God in the flesh walked and dwelled with man. When Peter, James, and John were taken up the Mount of Transfiguration, Peter wanted to build three tabernacles. Of course, we know of the rashness of Peter to speak before thinking at times. However, these three disciples were privileged to get a glimpse of what will take place when Jesus returns at the Second Advent. When he comes, he will dwell with man—that is, he will tabernacle with us. It is a glorious hope!

There are those who have put forward their belief that the Feast of Tabernacles dates the time of creation. A strange anomaly takes place on the seventh month, the beginning of the Jewish New Year, which is called Rosh Hashanah. It is followed by a ten-day period known as the Days of Awe. This is when Jewish people are required to reflect on their faith. It ends on the Day of Atonement. Traders on Wall Street, the New York stock exchange, have an old adage which basically says, 'Sell on Rosh Hashanah and buy on Yom Kippur.' The time between two Jewish feasts tends to highlight a regular weakness in the financial markets. Who would have believed it?

The Jewish New Year begins in the seventh month, called Tishri. This signals the start of the civil calendar. The feasts that we have just covered are attached to the religious calendar beginning in the month Nisan, sometimes called Abib, in the spring. These two calendars make Israel unique among the nations.

APPENDIX 5

Further Notes on Chapter 14

Subject:
End Times and Persecution

In chapter 14, we looked at three theological positions: premillennialism, amillennialism, and postmillennialism. One of the criticisms given against those who hold a premillennial position is that they are advocating a view that tries to avoid persecution. As we shall see, this is disingenuous. Church history, from the earliest of times, is one of recurring persecution of believers in Christ. Let us look at what scripture teaches us.

The Bible goes into a lot of detail with regard to the events of the end times. In Western Christianity, when talking about the return of the Lord Jesus Christ and the conditions that will prevail leading up to Christ's return, the things people immediately think of are a great falling away from the church and the message of the gospel being widely rejected. Simultaneously, there is the expectation of a rise in suppression of the gospel by the introduction of laws that contradict biblical teaching, classifying followers of Christ as criminals if they do not conform to man's laws. Some people may look at today's environment and start imagining that the end times are upon us. Of course this is a very negative view and does not really give an accurate picture. For instance, when the Communist Party took control in China, it was estimated that the number of Chinese Christians was in the region of one million believers. After seventy years of intense levels of persecution, the Chinese church is now at one hundred million believers.

As noted in an earlier appendix, Jesus spelled out to his followers the level of persecution they could expect as they preached the message that the Messiah had come, had been crucified, and had been raised from the dead. When we read through the book of Acts, we read of the persecutions that arose. The gospel spread due to persecution. John the beloved disciple spent time as a prisoner on the isle of Patmos due to persecution during the rule of Domitian. When people joined the early church, it was not a light decision. They were fully aware that they were taking a momentous step that carried with it major consequences for themselves and for their family.

Persecution has followed the church throughout history. In many places in the world today, Christians are suffering greatly under regimes which are antagonistic to the gospel. In the Western world, the church by and large has not known any serious persecution for a number of centuries. We are not the first generation to think we are living in the last days due to the decline in our civilisation's moral conditions and an ever-increasing voice of opposition to all things related to the standards of righteousness set out in God's Word. There have been generations that witnessed the decline of Christianity and saw the influence of the church wane. Those who stood for Christ were subjected to great persecution.

The other side of the coin is that when Christ does return, it will be for a glorious church which he is going to present to his Father, without spot and without blemish. At the present time, this is not what we see in the Western world. In the Western world, churches have been in decline for decades. Many of the clergy have compromised the gospel. Many have lost faith. Yet when Christ comes, it will not be for a church that is weak, that has lost its way in the world, and that has no power. When Christ comes, it will be for an overcoming church. We are looking at two conditions, one negative and the other positive. When only the negative is visible, it indicates to us that the time of Christ's return is not yet.

How are we to understand this quandary of two opposing conditions provided for us in scripture?

To help understand what to expect as the coming of Jesus gets ever closer, let us look at a teaching of Jesus to his disciples given in Luke (17:22–36). It is a very interesting part of scripture and provides the conditions at specific time periods which run consecutively up to the rapture of the church and through the Tribulation, concluding at the Second Advent. Along with that, it gives us descriptions of two events in history that explain what will unfold.

Notice the four time periods this passage mentions: the days of the Son of Man (verse 22), of Noah (verse 26), and of Lot (verse 28), and the day when the Son of Man is revealed (verse 30). This last period is singular, meaning it will take place in one day! The two events which are given to describe the end times are the time of Noah and the destruction of Sodom and Gomorrah. Both of these examples provide frightening scenarios of what is to come on the earth in the latter days. No one survived the flood in the days of Noah except those who were in the ark. No one survived the fire and brimstone that fell on Sodom and Gomorrah except Lot and his family. Even then, it was only himself and his two daughters who escaped unharmed. His wife looked back and was turned to a pillar of salt. She failed to heed the Word of God not to look back.

How can we apply the days of Noah to understand the events Jesus spoke about? The story of Noah is found in the book of Genesis. At this time, the sons of God appeared. Jude tells us that they were angels who left their first estate. We read about the sons of God in the book of Job. They are mentioned in the beginning of that book, and they are also mentioned later when they were gathered together as God laid the foundations of the earth (Job 38). They took the daughters of men for wives, producing giants (*Nephilim*) as offspring. The result of this mixing of species contaminated the DNA which man had inherited from Adam. In corrupting man's DNA, the aim was to stop the Word of God being fulfilled, which called for the seed of the woman to bruise the serpent's head. That would put all the plans of Satan, the one who in his original form was the anointed cherub, up in the air. When scripture speaks of Noah being perfect in his generation, it does not mean perfect in the sense of not having sin, but perfect in the sense of being pure, in terms of his DNA being unchanged. In the midst of all that is going on around him, it is recorded that he was a preacher of righteousness.

Before this incident took place, there are no records of how long the giants existed. How long this cohabitation lasted before Noah was born (for it is not the case that all the details are in chronological order), scripture does not say. It could have lasted for an extended period of time, perhaps even for a number of centuries. In the book of Job, we find references to a former age (Job 8:8) when wicked men were cut down and their foundations taken away by a flood (Job 22:15–16). Job describes what happens when such wickedness begins at a young age, so that even the bones of a person are full of sin (Job 20:11). Corruption and violence marked conditions on the earth, and every conceivable imagination of the heart was on display for all to see.

Noah was not the only righteous man living at this time. Scripture tells us of another man who walked closely with the Lord. His name is Enoch. His testimony is perhaps one of the greatest we read of in scripture, for he had such a marvellous relationship with his God that he was taken up to heaven without dying. He walked with God and was not, for God took him. Now we have two witnesses before the flood arrived: Noah and Enoch.

Due to Enoch being caught up to heaven without dying, many people expect that he will be one of the two witnesses whom we find in the book of Revelation, the other of course being Elijah. However, there are three reasons why this will not be the case. Firstly, Enoch is not Jewish; he is a Gentile. In the Tribulation, the two witnesses are Jewish, and both of them come with signs and wonders which they were known for when they lived. Enoch does not fall into this category. Secondly, in scripture we always have 'types' given that represent future events. Enoch is a type of the church being raptured before judgement is poured out on the earth, for the church is not appointed to wrath. Thirdly, there are examples in both the Old Testament and New Testament of people who died and God raised them back to life. There are several exceptions to the rule that people only die once.

The New Testament description is one of perilous times (2 Timothy 3). People will be self-centred lovers of themselves. They will covet after things. They will be blasphemers, unholy and untrustworthy. They will be lacking in natural affections. They will not be the kind of people whom you can trust. For gain, they will betray others. They may put forward a religious veneer and have rituals, but they will have no power. They will resist truth and have their minds corrupted.

In the midst of a world where rebellion against God reaches the heights seen in the days of Noah, God will retain for himself those who will be anointed with the Holy Ghost. They will boldly proclaim the Lordship of Jesus Christ. They will stand before councils and kings. They will be living testimonies to the goodness of God in an evil world, and a testimony to all so that none will be without excuse when they stand before their Maker. Before judgement falls, God will remove his glorious church, for the church is not appointed to the destruction that will cover the world. Like Enoch, their testimony will be they walked with God and were not, for God took them to glory.

When Christ came into the world, the nation of Israel had been conquered by the Romans. The Romans had a multiplicity of gods like the Greeks before them. The environment which Christ operated in was not one of tolerance but opposition from both the secular rulers and the Jewish Sanhedrin. For three and a half years, Jesus faced constant harassment and attempts on his life. However, by the end of his ministry, dedicated disciples and followers, under persecution, were taking the gospel throughout the Roman Empire and beyond. As the gospel took root, temples to Roman gods began to disappear.

The days of Lot follow the days of Noah. It is in the days of Lot that the day of the Son of Man will take place. The designation 'Son of Man' is not connected with the church in New Testament writings. It is a Jewish designation. The apostle Paul, instead of using this designation, always uses the term 'Son of God'. It is in the Old Testament, in the book of Ezekiel, that we find the repeated phrase 'son of man'. The question asked by God of Ezekiel, which is so closely associated with his book, is 'Can these bones live?' It is a reference to the house of Israel.

The book of Jude in the New Testament links the sons of God who left their first estate to the wicked cities of Sodom and Gomorrah in two ways: fornication and going after strange flesh. Fornication deals with the area of immorality and perversion. The word describes sexual relations that are outside the bounds of biblical marriage. This covers premarital relationships, adultery, and a host of other sexual perversions. When something is perverted, it is no longer being used for its true purpose. In scripture, 'fornication' was the term applied to Israel when it turned away from Jehovah to worship idols.

However, Jude goes further than just fornication between human beings. He talks of fornication with strange flesh. 'Strange flesh' can cover the fallen angels who took to themselves the daughters of men, and it can also cover bestiality. When it comes to the *Nephilim* and the degeneration they brought to earth—bestiality that created hybrid beings—it is just a further step of corruption. For all flesh is corrupted, which includes animals. The mythology of the Greeks with their endless array of hybrid beings is easily understood in this context.

When we come to the laws that Moses received from God, bestiality is specifically stated and Israel was told it was forbidden (Leviticus 18). Israel was informed that the land God was giving the Israelites had been defiled by former inhabitants taking part in the act of bestiality. They are given clear commandment not to lie with beasts, for it is sodomy. The punishment for such immorality was death.

Therefore, the days of Lot are associated with the most corrupt sexual perversion imaginable. The Bible unveils a great falling away. The man of sin, the Antichrist, is revealed in this time period. It is also the time period when the DNA of man will once again be interfered with to such an extent as to bring about complete corruption, thereby jeopardising the whole human race. One must never forget that man is Satan's mortal enemy. He hates man and will do everything in his power to eliminate man altogether.

During this time period, God will have a remnant to testify for him. We know about the two witnesses who have power to bring plagues, change weather patterns, and call fire down from heaven. We also know of twelve thousand witnesses from each of the twelve tribes of

Israel, preaching the everlasting gospel. The one hundred and forty-four thousand will proclaim this gospel to the nations of the earth. And just like Lot, who was rescued before the fire and brimstone fell on Sodom and Gomorrah, so there will be a rapture before the Lord Jesus Christ comes with his armies from heaven. The day of the wrath of God is the day that the Son of Man will be revealed!

Immediately before the fire and brimstone wiped out Sodom and Gomorrah from the face of the earth, Lot was delivered. In Luke, we have an account of a rapture taking place before the day of wrath. In one part of the world, people are sleeping. In another part, they are working through the day. Simultaneously, they are all removed from this world. Then follows judgement upon Satan and the remainder of the inhabitants of the earth.

The premillennial system of interpretation has scripture at its foundation to substantiate the sequence of events that we can expect in the latter days. It is not proposed to avoid persecution, for persecution has always been around. It is given to demonstrate that in all things, God is in control. We should never lose our confidence in him. Society can turn from God, immorality can be prevalent, and the spiritual dynamics of evil can be made manifest before our eyes. No matter the type of environment we find ourselves in, we are to be a testimony before men and angels to the love, mercy, and compassion of the living God. That is our calling.

APPENDIX 6

Further Notes on Chapter 15

Subject:
Israel

In the book of Genesis we find the story of Abraham, who was called out of Ur of the Chaldees. God led him to the land that we now call Israel, named after Abraham's son Jacob, whose name was changed after he wrestled with an angel. God made two major covenants found in Genesis 12. The first promise is the land grant. God promised Abraham that his descendants would inhabit the land that stretched from the Nile in Egypt to the River Euphrates, which is found today in Iraq. The second promise is how through Abraham's seed, all the nations of the earth would be blessed.

When we turn to any major work on eschatology, the study of end times, we find that theologians omit Israel. Yet a biblical calendar is rendered ineffective without having Israel at the forefront of end-time theology. In the book of Romans, the apostle Paul provides three chapters explaining Israel's present dilemma and also her restoration. This book lays out how God has punished Israel for her sins but, crucially, kept the promises of bringing the Israelites back to the land of their forefathers. In fact, it is the prophet Jeremiah who gives us revelation of the days to come, when a new covenant will be given to the house of Israel and to the house of Judah (Jeremiah 31). This new covenant will not be comparable to the covenant given to Israel in Egypt, for this time God is going to put his law in them, writing it upon their hearts. All will know the Lord, from the least to the greatest.

When we turn to the book of Hebrews in the New Testament, this covenant is spelled out once more (Hebrews 8). The day is coming when a new covenant will be given to the house of Israel and the house of Judah. It will not be like the covenant given to Israel in Egypt, a covenant that they could not keep. This new covenant will be put in their minds and in their hearts, and all the people of Israel will know God.

Ezekiel in his day gave a similar message to the people, telling them that God would cleanse them from all their idols and make them clean. The people will receive a new heart. A new spirit will be put within them. Their stony hearts will be replaced by hearts of flesh. The outcome of this regeneration can be summed up as follows:

- Israel will be in the land permanently, never more to be removed.
- There will be a covenant relationship with God.
- There will be no more relapses back into idolatry.
- God will supply abundantly every need.
- Israel will humble herself and repent past sins.

Ezekiel sums up by stating Israel should be ashamed and confounded due to the path the nation has walked. The Israelites' restoration will have nothing to do with what they have done—God will restore them for his own sake.

Zechariah prophesied of this time when all will know the Lord (Zechariah 13). He goes on to say that if a person prophesies, they will be stoned to death, for there will be no need of prophets. Zechariah also provides details of God bringing together the house of Israel and the house of Judah to be a blessing to the nations (Zechariah 8). At that day, many people and strong nations will come to Jerusalem to seek the Lord of hosts.

This new covenant is framed in the context of the ordinances set up by God, defined as the sun, moon, and stars for light. The dividing of the sea should depart from him. If the heavens can be measured and the foundation of the earth discovered, then the seed of Israel will cease and be cast away (Jeremiah 31).

Isaiah provides a similar assurance stating that as the new heavens and the new earth will remain before the Lord, so shall the seed of Israel remain along with their name (Isaiah 66). The prophet Amos unveils God's plan for them to be established in the land, never more to be uprooted (Amos 9). Micah details how God will turn again to Israel and have compassion on them, forgiving their iniquities, and casting their sin into the depths of the sea (Micah 7). As Paul stated in Romans, out of Sion will come a deliverer and shall turn away Israel's ungodliness (Romans 11:26).

There is much more that can be written. In Deuteronomy, speaking of God turning the captivity of Israel makes an incredible statement, for it is not only bringing them back from the nations, but it is also bringing them back if they have been driven out unto the outmost parts of heaven (Deuteronomy 30)!

ABOUT THE AUTHOR

Melvyn Lawson is the pastor of Life Centre Livingston, Livingston, Scotland. He originally had a career in finance and administration after graduating from London University with a Bachelor of Science degree with honours in economics. (UK English) In later life, he undertook theological studies, obtaining his qualifications to become an ordained minister of the Assemblies of God. Visit him online at lifecentrelivingston.com.

Printed in the United States
by Baker & Taylor Publisher Services